FROM VALOIS TO BOURBON

Dynasty, State and Society
in Early Modern France

FROM VALOIS TO BOURBON

Dynasty, State and Society
in Early Modern France

Edited by Keith Cameron

EXETER STUDIES IN HISTORY No. 24

First published by the University of Exeter 1989.

EXETER STUDIES IN HISTORY
General Editors   Colin Jones and Jonathan Barry
Editorial Committee

David Braund   Michael Duffy

Robert Higham   Malyn Newitt

Printed and bound by Short Run Press Ltd, Exeter

ISBN 0 85989 310 3
ISSN 0260 8628

..

Contents

LIST OF FIGURES

Acknowledgements

Secretarial Assistance : T. Allaway, V. Cooper, R. Luffman

Introduction

KEITH CAMERON

The transition from the ruling dynasty of the Valois to that of the Bourbons was marked by regicide, civil and bloody war, and religious controversy. Henri III, catholic king of France, was assassinated by a Dominican Friar, Jacques Clément, at Saint Cloud on 1 August 1589. His chosen successor, the Protestant Henri de Navarre, was unacceptable to those who supported the Guises, the Holy League and their chosen successor, the Cardinal de Bourbon, the presumptive Charles X. Even after the early death of Charles de Bourbon, there was fierce fighting throughout the kingdom between the League and the forces of Henri IV. Eventually, peace was restored in 1593, when Henri abjured the Protestant faith, became a catholic and entered Paris to claim his capital and to seek his crown at Saint Denis in 1594.

The distortion of popular history has left us with the images of an effeminate Henri III and a very virile Henri IV. There can be no doubt that they were of different temperament, no doubt that they had different styles of government. In the sixteenth century, in spite and sometimes because of the growth of an administrative structure, the king still had ultimate theoretical control and his temperament was directly linked with his ability to govern. The personality of the dynast mattered. Did the character

of the dynasty? What effect did a transition from Valois to Bourbon have upon the relations between government and society in early modern France? The importance of these questions is highlighted by the fact that France, following generations of crippling internecine strife, emerged as the most powerful state in Europe in the century following the accession of Henri IV.

Like most important questions these problems are difficult to resolve, not least because many of the source materials on which historians draw are incomplete and highly partial. Our appreciation of the 1580-1590s is coloured, in particular, by the tone of the pamphlets and polemical literature which, in spite of Henri IV's attempts to burn all available copies when he gained control of the country, still survive. These reveal propaganda forces at work, first to unseat Henri III and discredit Henri IV, and then to sing the praises of the new Bourbon dynasty. Religious concerns are inextricably mingled with political objectives. Henri III is seen as the enemy both of the true Catholic faith and of the Huguenots. The Huguenots and the reformers are blamed for all the troubles that befell France; the view of the world is that since man has turned his back on God, he has become worse than an animal. The Catholic author of *De l'estat present de ce Royaume...*[1] makes the following claims:

> C'est alors que le pere ne s'est point voulu fier à son filz, et que le filz se deffiant de son pere luy à meschamment preparé des embusches pour le faire mourir. C'est alors que la mere a aymé mieux nourrir des Singes et Chiens en son gyron qu'allaicter et substanter de sa mammelle ses propres enfans, et que le frere a meurtry cruellement son propre frere: et que les Eglises que noz devanciers avoient sainctement consacrees à l'honneur de la divine majesté ont esté bruslees, saccagees, et pillees par ces mal'heureux et detestables ministres de la religion pretendue, lesquels se transfigurent bien souvent (comme leur pere qui est le Diable) en Ange de lumiere. C'est alors que l'honneur de la divine majesté a esté foulé aux pieds, que les Vierges ont esté violees, et qu'un chacun exposant l'escriture saincte à sa fantasie, a delaissé les traditions Apostolicques et Romaines, pour suivre et maintenir sa faulse et mensongere opinion(pp. 5-6).

And yet the Protestant d'Aubigné in his epic poem *Les Tragiques* will make similar charges against the Catholic church and its supporters. It is an age

---

[1] Published in Paris by A. Pinet, in 1583.

in which the devil is seen at every turn. It is an age in which comparisons between the living and the characters of the Bible or of mythology are widespread. And yet, it is also an age which marks the beginning of Modern France, one which shows great cultural awareness and sensitivity. It is an age full of paradox, learning and ignorance, splendour and poverty.

To try and sift fact from propaganda, and to achieve a more balanced appraisal of the issues at stake was the aim of a conference held at the University of Exeter in December 1988, on the theme of 'From Valois to Bourbon'[2]. The present volume is based upon that conference. The date was chosen to coincide with the quatercentenary of the assassination of the Duke of Guise and his brother, the Cardinal of Lorraine, in Blois, on orders given by Henri III, on 23 and 24 December 1588. The collection of papers that follows illustrates the new light that modern scholarship can shed on the complex subject that the transition from the last of the Valois to the first of the Bourbons presents and makes a valuable contribution to our knowledge of early Modern Europe.

---

[2] The Conference was organised with the help of a grant from the Nuffield Foundation.

1. Henri III:
Some Determinants of vituperation

Sydney Anglo

In his study of the satirical iconography of Henri de Valois, Keith Cameron suggested that any attempt to study that enigmatic monarch's life and character had to confront the problem of 'stylised distortion'[1]. Henri's enemies were numerous and vociferous; and they subjected his capacity for kingship, his personal behaviour, and his moral fibre to a systematic attack the themes of which were determined by commonly–held views concerning the qualities of a good — and, conversely, of a bad — prince. There was a rhetorical and intellectual context of kingship which meant that accusations of heresy, murder, degeneracy and tyranny, were inevitably levelled at any ruler of a violently divided nation, by those who disapproved of him.

There were, however, other determinants of vituperation — other contexts within which rancour could spawn and multiply like fungi. Political and personal violence, religious bigotry and persecution, ruthless egoism and place–seeking, all came to be systematised in the latter half of the sixteenth century and, in the course of that systematisation, they all offered further scope for polemic. My purpose here is to suggest a few such contexts

---

[1] Keith Cameron, *Henri III. A Maligned or Malignant King? (Aspects of the Satirical Iconography of Henri de Valois)*, University of Exeter, 1978, p. 11.

which were especially relevant to the evolution of Henri III's unwholesome reputation.

The extent of the atrocities of August 1572 and the question of their premeditation have provided matter for continuing debate among historians; the St Bartholomew massacre has passed into the mythology of European history. It has become the classic instance of political duplicity and religious hypocrisy, and of cold–blooded extremism terminating in unbridled mob psychopathy. The verities of the deed do not concern us here. It suffices that the massacre happened: because its aftermath furnishes the essential context for the political and personal excesses which poisoned the reign of Henri III.

Historians have, in general, been properly shocked by the St Bartholomew. They have expressed moral indignation, and have assumed that contemporary Europe had been similarly affected. But in this they err. Contemporary Protestant Europe was, of course, deeply distressed; and some Catholics, too, regarded both the treachery and the violence with horror. It is nevertheless difficult to escape the conviction that there was a good deal of rejoicing at the elimination of so many Huguenots. This is shown by private letters exchanged at the time and, more important, by the spate of apologetic literature. Such justificatory pamphleteering is customarily dismissed as 'propaganda' by historians who thereby imply that it was not possible for people to write honestly in defence of the massacre. This notion of an army of reluctant conscripts is the result of a failure of imagination. In the first place — given the generally embittered attitudes adopted by both Catholics and Reformers throughout the century, and the frequent persecutions, tortures, civil slayings and open wars, which characterised their relations — it is not difficult to understand why, to many observers, the mass murders of August 1572 would have seemed a just retribution and a healthy purging of dissident and polluted elements from within the body of Christendom. Secondly, the view that apologists had to be coerced is scarcely tenable the moment we take note of the exultant language in which most of this material is couched. It is not very difficult to force writers to produce arguments, however specious, to justify extreme deeds. It is, I suggest, extremely difficult to compel in them a deep sense of joy, satisfaction, and triumph.

The most blatant and infamous paean of joy celebrating the massacre is Camillo Capilupi's *Lo stratagema di Carlo IX re di Francia*: but the arguments deployed therein, and the enthusiasm with which they are expressed, are commonplace[2]. Claude Nouvellet, for example, praises Charles for having erected his crown upon the twin columns of Piety and Justice; and then has God address his readers, urging that the King should finish the work he has only just begun[3]. For the author of the *Allegresse chrestienne*, it is God Himself who has inspired Charles to maintain France in its ancient faith:[4]

> O heureuse victoire: à toy seul est Seigneur
> Non à nous, la trophée insigne de l'honneur.
> D'un coup as arraché le tronc, et la racine,
> Et la terre jonché d'heretique vermine.

Another pamphleteer pungently argued that it was the King's bounden duty to punish the Huguenots. There was no faith to be kept with such heretics: 'Considere, je te prie, peuple François, qu'on ne doit garder la foy, à celuy qui l'a rompu le premier: car comme dit le Seigneur par Isaye, Il n'y a point de paix aux meschans'. You have seen, cries the author, how the rebels have tried to seize the kingdom. They must be punished immediately, openly, and without tarrying for due legal methods. Urgent dangers require urgent remedies; long-winded processes are useless; and it is necessary to make a salutary example of the leaders so that the lesser people will shrink back from their follies like a monkey who imitates what it sees being done. The King was right to have the Admiral and his adherents put to death. Moses was the first of the prophets to take up the knife to kill those who turned the Israelites away from God: and, ever since, his actions have been imitated by Kings. The Church of God cannot be divided[5].

The opinion that the Huguenots had been conspiring against the King, and that this had been merely the culmination of more than a decade of insurrection, was advanced in the greater number of Catholic pamphlets subsequent to the massacre. The Huguenots were regarded as the archetypal hypocrites — as the Jesuits were later to be regarded by their Protestant enemies, and as Henri III came to be regarded by almost everybody. They used religion and other ideals as the conscious instrument of a purely

---

[2] See my article, 'A Rhetoric of Hate', in Keith Cameron, ed., *Montaigne and his Age*, University of Exeter, 1981, especially pp.5–9.

[3] Claude Nouvellet, *Ode trionfale au roy, sus l'equitable iustice que sa maiesté feit des rebelles*, Paris, 1572, sig. A.iv[v].

[4] *Allegresse chrestienne de l'heureux succes des guerres de ce royaume, et de la iustice de Dieu contre les rebelles au Roy*, Paris, 1572, sig. B.ii[v].

[5] *Brieve remonstrance sur la mort de l'Admiral*, Paris, 1572, sigs. C.i, C.iv[r-v], D.iv[v].

temporal policy. It was argued that the Admiral and his rebel adherents
used two principal pretexts, religion and the public weal, to take up arms
against the King; and, while continually asserting that they were the King's
servants, they were in reality seeking to subvert the kingdom[6]. Conspirators always cloak their pernicious intentions with some beautiful garment
— most commonly the shadows of a feigned religion and of a public good
— things which most incline the ears and hearts of men to receive a new
impression. Led by Coligny, the Huguenots have consistently employed this
disguise to conceal their ceaseless attempts to overthrow both the state and
the true faith[7].

These accusations are repeatedly hurled at the Huguenots. The twin
virtues to which they lay claim are degraded into 'mauvais et dangereux pre-
textes'. Their malicious crimes — slaying the elderly, deflowering maidens,
profaning the temples of God — are all committed under these colours: but
's'armeront de finesse et non pas de vertu'. Their use of religion is cynical
and incurs the wrath of God[8]. Even Coligny's adherence to the reformed
religion is itself deemed a fraud adopted merely to surprise the King:[9]

> Ainsi ypochrisant je suis traistre à toute l'heure,
> Ainsi le vieux Regnard, toujours Regnard demeure.

His words are full of dissimulation; he humbles himself while beguiling
his prince with lies and sleights; his mouth speaks marvels, but his heart
conceives unparalleled injuries; he has caused the deaths of a million people;
while, all the time, his poison and ambition have remained hidden beneath
the painted shadow of religion[10]. He is, in truth, a monster of iniquity:
but to modern historians his character, as sketched by the apologists for
the St Bartholomew — along with the catalogue of crimes attributed to the
Huguenots — bears a startling resemblance to everything usually associated

---

[6] *Ibid.*, Sig. D.i[v].

[7] *Sommaire Discours des Causes de tous les troubles de ce royaume, proce-
dentes des impostures et coniurations des heretiques et des rebelles*, Paris and
Poictiers, 1573, fos. 2–5[v].

[8] *Discours sur les causes de l'Execution faicte és personnes de ceux qui avoient
coniuré contre le Roy et son Estat*, Paris, 1572, sigs. A.ii[v], A.iv. See also the *Exhortation au Roy, pour vertueusement poursuivre ce que sagement il a commencé
contre les Huguenots*, Paris, 1572, sig. A.iv.

[9] François de Chantelouve, *La Tragedie de feu Gaspard de Colligny jadis admiral de France*, n.p., 1572, p. 6.

[10] I.S.P., *Discours sur la mort de Gaspart de Coligny, qui fut Admiral de France
et de ses complices*, Paris, 1572, sig. C.i.

with Henri III.

The Huguenots did not remain silent in the face of these accusations; and much of what they wrote was as violent, self–righteous, and hysterical as the productions of their enemies. However, the most elaborate, comprehensive, and by far the most important treatment of the issues arising from the St Bartholomew and its apologists was Innocent Gentillet's *Discours sur les moyens de bien gouverner . . . contre Nicolas Machiavel Florentin*, which was sufficiently well received to warrant a further six French language editions within the first four years after its initial publication in 1576, together with one German and two Latin translations within the same period[11].

The *Contre Machiavel* has come in for much critical abuse. It has been castigated as methodologically naive and unfair; and as being intemperate and unreasonable. It was also, for a long time, regarded as the principal stimulus for the stereotyped Machiavel figure which emerged in the later sixteenth century and, consequently, as the ultimate source for subsequent denigration of the Florentine[12]. Later criticism dealt even more harshly with Gentillet who, while remaining fatuous, was even denied having had any influence at all[13]; and, although this extreme view has been modified, he has been kept firmly in place as a Huguenot of little brain whose sole significance is that he dared write against one of the great men of the Renaissance.

However, debate concerning the *Contre Machiavel* has largely missed the point. Of moderate ability Gentillet may have been — conventional, literal–minded, stolid, unimaginative and, occasionally, stupid — but he set himself an extremely difficult task; and, on the whole, he accomplished it (even when viewed from a modern critical standpoint) moderately well. From a sixteenth–century standpoint, his achievement must have seemed far more imposing, as is evidenced by the wide success of his book and the authoritative status it long retained not only as a convincing exposé of Machiavelli's doctrines but also — and more significantly — as an acute

---

[11] For the bibliographical history of the text, see the introduction to the edition of A. D'Andrea and P.D. Stewart, Florence, 1974.

[12] The most frequently cited exposition of this view is E. Meyer, *Machiavelli and the Elizabethan Drama*, Weimar, 1897.

[13] See I. Ribner, 'The Significance of Gentillet's *Contre-Machiavel*', *Modern Language Quarterly*, X, 1949, who is followed by F. Raab, *The English Face of Machiavelli*, London, 1964.

analysis of the political and social sickness of the French king and his court.

Gentillet's intentions were complex and multiform, and their interdependence was both intellectual and emotional. They are largely set out in the Preface to the first book: though this is by no means a full statement of the author's purposes or of what he actually does in the course of his very long work. On the other hand, there is a greater relationship between what he says that he is going to do and what he does do than was often the case in contemporary historical and political writing. He is not, he stresses, setting out to write a comprehensive treatise on political science[14]:

> Mais mon but est seulement de monstrer que Nicolas Machiavel, jadis secretaire de la republique (maintenant duché) de Florence; n'a rien entendu, ou peu, en ceste science politique dont nous parlons, et qu'il a prins des maximes toutes meschantes, et basty sur icelles non une science politique mais tyrannique.

In this first preface Gentillet also makes the striking assumption which underlies, and indeed provoked, his entire enterprise. He believes that Machiavelli's doctrines are at the root of France's present degradation which has culminated in the St Bartholomew massacres and the glee of its perverted admirers. Doubtless, courtiers who deal with affairs of state will think it strange that he should find fault with their 'grand docteur Machiavel'. Yet, until the death of Henri II, Machiavelli had not even been spoken of in France, and the kingdom had been ruled in the traditional French manner. It was only subsequently that government had been discharged according to the rules of Machiavelli, 'et ses livres tenus chers et precieux par les courtisans italiens et italianisez, comme si c'estoyent livres des sibilles'[15].

Gentillet is not surprised that the old modes of government have been abandoned, because now all principal offices are held by Italians who, doubtless, share their master's contempt for French political customs. This, though bad enough, might have been supported in silence, were it not for

---

[14] Innocent Gentillet, *Discours sur les moyens be bien gouverner, et maintenir en bonne paix un Royaume ou autre Principauté*, Geneva, 1576, p. 3. There have been two modern editions of this text: that by D'Andrea and Stewart (referred to above, n.11), and another by C. Edward Rathé, Geneva, 1968. Both are keyed to the pagination of the first edition (1576) to which I refer in this article.

[15] *Ibid.*, p. 8.

the fact that:

> Machiavel par sa doctrine et enseignemens a fait changer le
> bon et ancien gouvernement de France, en la maniere de gou-
> verner florentine, dont nous voyons à l'oeil que la ruine entiere
> de tout le royaume s'ensuyvra infalliblement, si Dieu par sa
> grace n'y remedie bien tost, il seroit maintenant temps (si
> jamais) de mettre la main à la besongne, pour remettre en
> France le gouvernement de nos ancestres.

France is now governed according to those Machiavellian principles which
it is Gentillet's purpose to lay bare; and if anyone doubts his assertion of
contemporary French corruption, then a consideration of current political
practice will take the doubter straight back to Machiavelli's maxims, so
that 'par toutes les deux voyes, des maximes aux effects, et des effects aux
maximes, l'on peut clairement conoistre que la France est aujourdhuy gou-
vernee par la doctrine de Machiavel'. Are they not Machiavellists, 'italiens
ou italianisez', who handle the seals of France, issue edicts, send despatches
within and without the kingdom, and hold the best and most lucrative offices? Moreover — and this is crucial for Gentillet — it is notorious that
for the last fifteen years, Machiavelli's books have become as familiar and
ordinary in the hands of the courtiers as the breviary in the hands of a
village curate[16].

First Machiavelli; then Machiavellists; and finally corruption. That is
the historical sequence assumed and demonstrated by Gentillet who com-
pletes this as a circular structure by identifying Machiavelli's own purpose
as the establishing of tyranny, and by arguing that the present condition
of France results from the deliberate practice of such tyranny. This, in
turn, demands a further demonstration. If the application of Machiavelli's
principles results in corruption, Gentillet must elucidate the precise nature
of that corruption, the superior conditions which had formerly prevailed in
France, and the reasons for that superiority. In other words, although Gentillet denies that he is writing a political treatise, he is obliged to highlight
the inutility of Machiavelli's doctrines by showing the positive utility of an
alternative set of precepts. The difference, he argues, between the ancient
government of France and modern degradation is manifest. Formerly the
kingdom, free of civil discord had been maintained in peace and prosperity. Now Italian domination has suppressed the ancient laws; civil war has
ensued; the people are destroyed and eaten; and commerce has decayed to

---

[16] *Ibid.*, pp. 9–11.

nothing. All this is held to be obvious. But it remains vital for Gentillet to demonstrate the superiority of the past. He therefore announces his intention that, after every single maxim derived from Machiavelli, he will prove by examples, 'que nos anciens François se sont conduits et gouvernez par bonne raison et sage prudence, tout au rebours que ne porte la doctrine de Machiavel'[17].

These then are Gentillet's explicit aims: to refute Machiavelli's false, tyrannical doctrines; to demonstrate how they have corrupted France; and to show how states should be governed. But, stated thus, these purposes conceal the passionate core of the *Contre Machiavel*. Despite all the positive advice offered by Gentillet, his claim not to be writing a political treatise is largely valid. He is, primarily, a polemicist: and his principal target is not really Machiavelli at all. It is, rather, contemporary depravity; and every citation, and every historical parallel both ancient and modern, contains either explicitly or implicitly a reproof to the French court. It is this which provides much of the latent force and energy of the *Contre Machiavel* and which supports the vast structure of historical exempla. Gentillet believed that, in Machiavelli's writings, he had discovered the theoretical enunciation of the principles upon which tyranny had been built. He attacked the theory and its practice; and he has been remembered more for Machiavelli's sake than for the tyrant he opposed. Yet it was the tyrant who was really the object of disgust, and Machiavelli was simply the stick with which to beat him.

Gentillet was an exiled Huguenot, and his thought was naturally dominated by recent atrocities. The St Bartholomew massacre had been bad enough. But far worse was the wide-spread and heavily–publicised rejoicing after the event: and it was this which provided the true context of the *Contre Machiavel*. Gentillet felt compelled to argue the case for his co-religionists and to show that the accusations levelled against them by the defenders of the St Bartholomew — accusations based upon a show of conventional morality — were themselves nothing but a hypocritical veil hiding the true villains of contemporary France. There are, he says, many perverters of truth and apologists for evil who argue that cruelty for a good end is not reprehensible: but there never has been a murder or iniquity which was not covered with some virtuous pretext by its perpetrators. Some use the need to abbreviate the normal legal processes as their cloak for murder and vengeance; some veil their killings under the guise of the public good — saying that their massacres are committed to avoid a greater evil which

---

[17] *Ibid.*, p. 12.

would have been perpetrated by their victims. Others cover themselves
with a desire for peace and tranquillity, saying that their murders are necessary to bring an end to troubles. Nevertheless, whatever their excuses,
'l'ouvrage monstre tousjours quel est l'ouvrier'; and in the end they will
outsmart themselves with their colours 'comme le fard des putains'. They
might beguile folk for a while, yet in the end they will always be recognised
as foxes. Furthermore, if princes permit men to commit murders under the
colour of good intentions, then they break the order of justice and turn
everything upside down. Murders and massacres never remain long un-
punished: 'et de nostre temps nous en voyons assez d'exemples, et croy que
nous en verrons bien davantage en ceux que la main de Dieu n'a pas encores
attrappez'[18].

This foul web of duplicity and violence is not, in Gentillet's opinion, in-
digenous to France. For him, contemporary corruption is wholly Italianate:
and he misses no opportunity for an attack on these pestilent foreigners.
Degenerate Italian, or Italianised, courtiers appear constantly as the practi-
tioners of Machiavellian principles. They govern by his books and recognise
no other political wisdom[19]. They have usurped authority, contaminate everything, grasp power, and advance only their own countrymen or 'quelques
François bastards et degenereux, qui sont façonnez à leur humeur et à leur
mode, et qui leur servent comme d'esclaves et vils ministres de leurs perfi-
dies, cruautez, rapines, et autres vices'. They nourish the partialities and
divisions which have destroyed France. Diversity of religion might have
been resolved by preaching, disputation and conferences: but it was when
they fell to arms and massacres, and attempted to enforce beliefs, that
the parties became irreconcilable. This was the real aim of the foreigners:
to divide the nation 'pour pouvoir planter en France le gouvernement de
Machiavel'[20].

Italians are steeped in every vice. They are disloyal, perfidious, and
cowardly. They dissemble, flatter, and change sides whenever they deem
it profitable, resembling harlots 'lesquelles ayment chascun et n'ayment
personne, et qui virent ça et là sans arrest, comme girouettes'[21]. It is no
wonder that simple, honest Frenchmen who speak openly and expose their
hearts are easily trapped in the nets of intrigue cast by these Machiavellists
who never let a word fall from their mouths without premeditating its

---

[18] *Ibid.*, p. 396
[19] *Ibid.*, pp. 236, 277.
[20] *Ibid.*, pp.138–9.
[21] *Ibid.*, pp. 131–2, 287–8, 508.

meaning which is usually the opposite of what you think[22]. They are greedy usurers who pillage France with new and arbitrary taxation which does not even find its way to the Crown; while even their nobles handle trade and merchandise more commonly than the arms proper to their rank[23]. But worst of all is their implacable cruelty, lust for revenge, and sheer murderousness[24]:

> De manière que quand ils peuvent avoir leur ennemi à gré
> pour s'en venger, ils le meurtrissent de quelque façon estrange
> et barbare, et en le meurtrissant luy ramentoyvent l'offense
> qu'il leur a faite, luy font des reproches, luy disent des injures,
> pour tourmenter l'ame et le corps tout ensemble, et quelque
> fois lavent leurs mains et leur bouche de son sang, et le con-
> traignent à se donner au diable, afin de faire damner l'ame
> en tuant le corps, s'ils peuvent.

Gentillet hopes that, infected though they are by other Italian vices, the French may yet escape this bloodthirstiness: though elsewhere he accuses the Italianised courtiers of already grounding their advice to slay all such as they hate, upon the saying that the dead man makes no war. And he associates this sentiment with the massacre of Vassy in 1561 and with the St Bartholomew itself. The Italians, he remarks laconically, have always had a strong inclination to massacre Frenchmen[25].

Their classic depravity had been known as the Sicilian Vespers: and it was in imitation of this that they had plotted the horrible general massacre of 1572, 'qui saigne tousjours, et duquel ils ont encores les mains et leurs espees ensanglantees'. Worse still, they have incessantly boasted of this crime, calling it the 'Matines parisiennes' (the very phrase which occurs towards the end of Capilupi's *Lo stratagema*) [26].

---

[22] *Ibid.*, p. 430.

[23] *Ibid.*, pp. 173, 526, 565, 567.

[24] *Ibid.*, p. 311.

[25] *Ibid.*, pp. 125, 467–8.

[26] *Ibid.*, p. 125. Cf. also, *Allegresse chrestienne*, sig. C.ii, for a prior accusation against the Huguenots:

> Puis que les ennemis de la messe chrestienne,
> Pensoient nous dire vespre, à la Sicilienne,
> C'a esté justement, qu'ils ont devant le jour,
> Des matines, senty vn semblable retour..

In short, the Italians have corrupted the French both in mind and body: even venereal disease was imported from Italy at the time of Charles VIII's Neapolitan campaign — though Gentillet tactfully refrains from explaining how his honest countrymen contracted the malady. Of whom, he demands, have the Frenchmen learned 'l'atheisme, la sodomie, la perfidie, la cruauté, les usures, et autres semblables vices, que de Machiavel et de ceux de sa nation?' Thus may the Italians well brag that they have avenged the wars that the French formerly waged in their land[27].

This last brief but pregnant lament may remind the modern reader of the heartfelt cry with which Machiavelli had ended his *Il Principe*: demanding a saviour who would free his land from the barbarians who stank in every Italian's nostrils. The relationship is, I believe, deliberate. Gentillet — though he does not refer specifically to the closing pages of *Il Principe* — does criticise Machiavelli for describing the French as ignorant, barbarous, covetous and disloyal[28]. And he certainly echoes Machiavelli's rousing sentiment in his own appeals to his countrymen and especially to the French nobility who should consider their duty and not stand on one side, coldly watching the foreigners pollute their native land with every filthy vice.

At about the time that Gentillet was diagnosing the causes of corruption at court, another French author was similarly pondering contemporary political morality.

> Je ne voudrois pas conseiller aucun, de se patronner selon les preceptes que plusieurs, qui en cest endroit introduisent une nouvelle espece de Philosophie, nous veulent apprendre. Car ils enflamment les coeurs des hommes d'une convoitise de grandeur, et les moyens qu'ils enseignent d'y parvenir ce, sont flatteries, desloyautez, dissimulations et infidelitez. Bref, il semble que — laissant les grandes et louables actions de ceux qui ont versé anciennement aux gouvernementz des republiques — ils se soyent efforcez de recueillir les plus meschantes pour les proposer à imiter à ceux qui veullent entrer en mesme splendeur de vie: et que ce ne soit autre chose d'estre grand personnage en l'administration du public que par quelque moyen que ce soit, ou à tort ou à droit, si bien faire ses affaires.

---

[27] Gentillet (1576), pp. 308–9.
[28] *Ibid.*, p. 9.

One might imagine that here we have a spirit akin to that of Gentillet, lamenting the passing of old French honesty, and hostile to Italian
guile. But, in fact, these moral sentiments come from the dedication which
prefaces the French translation of Corbinelli's edition of Guicciardini's *Ricordi*[29]. Clearly the translator believes that the ruthless pursuit of worldly
success is current in his own day. He also considers that Guicciardini's
aphorisms offer something very different from the evil precepts followed by
self–seekers. Yet what did readers really find in the *Ricordi* edited by Corbinelli — a man praised by the French translator as one who loved virtue?

They were, in the first place, constantly reminded that self–interest
is a much more common human motivation than conscience. All men are
naturally virtuous, when they derive neither pleasure nor profit from vice;
but worldly corruption — and especially selfishness — inclines them to
evil. Even lofty spirits desire greatness of degree and superiority, because
in nothing else can they more resemble God. Friends must be cultivated
because they may be useful; enemies should not be made 'sans propos et de
gayeté de cœur'. Wealth is to be coveted because, in this iniquitous world,
it is necessary for reputation; while virtuous actions are also advantageous
because they earn a good name and reputation which, in many cases, shall
be 'un proffit incroiable'. Everything should be accomplished so that one
does not end up the loser; and for those who follow court life it is crucial
to keep continually in the sight of the prince so that, when occasion arises,
they may be employed in his business. Even a small beginning may be the
introduction to great things. With regard to colleagues, the politic reader
is advised to count more certainly on somebody who has need of him, or
who has a common interest, than upon somebody whom he has benefited.
Benefits are not remembered. Men act through hope of gain.

In order to operate successfully within this morass of self–interest,
various ruses are recommended. It is, for instance, a good thing to deny
something that you wish secretly to bring about because, even when people
are certain of your involvement, a bold denial will cast doubts in their
minds. Tricks which serve rulers may also serve private individuals. A
prince who wishes to cousen a rival by means of an ambassador should first
deceive the ambassador who will then act and speak more convincingly
than if he knew the truth: and the same trick will serve any man who
wishes to persuade somebody falsely. Especially helpful to the dissimulator
is a reputation for frankness and honesty which enables him to employ

---

[29] *Plusieurs advis et conseils de François Guicciardin, tant pour les affaires
d'estat que privées. Traduits d'Italien en François*, Paris, 1576, fol.2$^{\text{r-v}}$.

deceit in matters of importance with more likelihood of being credited. Personal dissatisfaction is to be dissembled, because manifest displeasure might alienate somebody who could still be useful. It is also profitable not to make difficulties when friends seek assistance: for one gains more by being liberal with hopes and promises, even when nothing is actually done. When one desires a favour from people, it is a sound principle to talk in such a way that they will believe that they first thought of the idea, for vanity will lead them to accept proposals which they might otherwise have rejected. Sycophancy is the shortest route to favour: if a man wishes to be loved by those who are greater than himself, he must show himself full of regard and reverence toward them, and therein be 'plustot prodigue que chiche'. There is nothing more offensive to a superior than a seeming lack of regard, reverence and obedience, which he considers his due. Conversely, with regard to injuries received from those whose lofty position renders revenge impossible, the only course is 'de l'endurer et dissimuler'. Flattery and fair words, the superficials of benevolence, may seem of less avail than deeds: yet it is astonishing to what extent caresses and gentleness of speech may gain approbation, for every man assesses himself higher than his true worth.

The *Ricordi* are essentially private meditations upon public activities: though the care with which Guicciardini revised, pruned and augmented them leaves no doubt as to the seriousness of their content. These observations laid bare the realities of early sixteenth–century political life; and their explicit cynicism was not intended for contemporary scrutiny. In fact, Corbinelli's edition of 1576 was the first appearance of the *Ricordi* in print. This version was immediately issued in the French translation just discussed; and, within the same year, the text was already being cited elsewhere[30]. Soon other versions of Guicciardini's maxims were being published, translated, and adapted throughout Europe. What had once been the personal reflexions of an acute intelligence upon the inner workings of the politics of his own period became the public property of another[31]. And this transition, from the secrecy of a private notebook to the publicity of print and popular acclaim, tells us something about the degree to which overt self-seeking had become socially acceptable in the late sixteenth century — especially when we bear in mind that this collection of hard–boiled cynicisms was being offered by its French translator, in all seriousness, as

---

[30] Pierre de Dampmartin, *Amiable accusation et charitable excuse des maus et evenemens de la France*, Paris, 1576, fol. 50^V–51.

[31] For the history of the *Ricordi* and its diffusion, see V. Lucciani, *Francesco Guicciardini e la fortuna dell'opera sua*, Florence, 1949.

an antidote to the current poisonous standards of courtly behaviour.

This bizarre attempt to cure Machiavellism by Guicciardinism requires no further comment from me: though there are some related nuggets of information which are worth noting. Davila tells us that every day, after dinner, Henri III would withdraw in the company of Baccio del Bene and Jacopo Corbinelli to read Polybius, Tacitus, and especially Machiavelli's *Il Principe* and *Discorsi*, to draw out rules for political designs[32]. Davila, of course, was writing long after the deaths of Henri and his two Italian mentors — both of whom were certainly regarded by their contemporaries as keen students of Machiavelli[33]. But it is surely curious, if there were nothing at all in the story, that something similar should occur buried in one of the vituperative pamphlets written against Henri III after the assassination of the Guises:[34]

> imbu de la Religion de Machiavel, et ayant ouy en son Cabinet les lectures d'un vieillard bazanné conroyé en l'Atheisme: il a creu, comme il y a apparence qu'il croid encores, que les ames meurent avec le corps. Qu'est un heritage qu'il a eu de la maison de Medicis: et des instructions qu'il a voulu choisir.

My last observation — the last, that is, for which space remains — can only be arrived at by a convulsive Montaignesque sideways leap via Montaigne himself. 'Nous allons', he wrote, 'apprendre en Italie à escrimer, et l'exerçons aux depens de nos vies avant le sçavoir'[35]. We move from corrupt courtiers seeking self-advancement to corrupt courtiers seeking self-destruction in the duel: and this vice, like political and courtly cynicism,

---

[32] Enrico Davila, *Historia delle guerre civili di Francia*, London, 1755, I, p. 410.

[33] See Lucien Romier, *Les origines politiques des guerres de religion*, Paris, 1913, I, p. 160 n.4; G. Procacci, *Studi sulla fortuna del Machiavelli*, Rome, 1965, pp. 173–91; Jean Balsamo, 'Note sur Jacopo Corbinelli', *Bulletin de l'Association d'Etude sur l'Humanisme, la Réforme et la Renaissance (France du Centre et du Sud-Est)*, XIX, 1984, pp. 48–54.

[34] *Contre les fausses allegations que les plus qu'Architofels, Conseillers Cabinalistes, proposent pour excuser Henry le meurtrier de l'assassinat par luy perfidement commis en la personne du tresillustre Duc de Guyse*, n.p., 1589, p. 32.

[35] P. Villey and V.-L. Saulnier, eds., *Les Essais de Michel de Montaigne*, Paris, 1965, II, 27, p. 697.

was identified as essentially Italianate in origin. The evolution of rapier fencing in the sixteenth century was primarily the work of Italian schools of arms; the systematisation of the code of honour was due to Italian theorists; and French courtiers learned both their homicidal dexterity and the punctilios of formal duelling from Italian masters or from those influenced by their teaching. Even Henri de Sainct–Didier's *Traicté contenant les secrets du premier livre sur l'espée seule* published in Paris in 1573, and famous as the first French treatise on modern rapier-play, is nothing but an adaptation of earlier Italian manuals[36]. Indeed, Henri III had himself been taught the art of fencing by Italian masters: while, before his accession (if Brantôme is to be credited), he had even challenged Besigny to a duel — and would have fought it, too, had his adversary not taken flight[37].

Henri's implication in the duelling craze, however, was achieved by proxy. On 27 April 1578, six of the King's 'mignons' fought a combat arising from some 'fort légère occasion'. They thrust and hacked at each other in the courtyard of the Louvre to such effect that:

> le beau Maugiron et le jeune Chomberg demeurèrent morts, sur la place. Riberac, des coups qu'il y receust, mourust le lendemain à midi. Livarrot, d'un grand coup qu'il eut sur la teste, fut six sepmaines malade et enfin reschappa. Antraguet s'en alla sain et sauf aveq un petit coup, qui n'estoit qu'une esgratigneure au bras. Quélus, aucteur et agresseur de la noise, de dix–neuf coups qu'il y receust, languist trente–trois jours, et mourust le jeudi vingt–neuvième may.

The King was beside himself with grief and anxiety, and promised a fortune to the surgeons if only they could save his favourite: but, 'nonobstant lesquelles promesses, il passa de ce monde en l'autre, aiant toujours en la bouche ces mots, mesmes entre ses derniers souspirs qu'il jettoit avec grande force et gran regret: "Ah! mon Roy, mon Roy!" sans parler autrement de Dieu ne de sa Mere'. Henri's behaviour toward the dead duellists — kissing them, and cutting off their blonde locks — did not create a favourable impression. 'Telles et semblables façons de faire (indigne à la verité d'un

---

[36] On Sainct-Didier, see Egerton Castle, *Schools and Masters of Fence from the Middle Ages to the Eighteenth Century*, London, 1885 (repr. Arms and Armour Society, 1969), pp. 54–61; G. Letainturier-Fradin, *Les Joueurs d'Epée à travers les siècles*, Paris, n.d., pp. 113–28.

[37] *Oeuvres complètes de Pierre de Bourdeille, Abbé séculier de Brantôme*, ed. J.A.C. Buchon, Paris, 1838, I, pp.567, 778–9.

grand Roy et magnanime comme il estoit) causèrent peu à peu le mespris de
ce Prince'. Nor was Henri's reputation enhanced by the elaborate funerary
monuments erected to the memory of his squad of squalid and murderous
perverts[38].

The point I am trying to make is a simple one. There is a context of unbridled intellectual and verbal violence where public disorders, cruelties and
massacres are justified and exulted over. Associated with this is a cogent
diagnosis of courtly corruption, which — though written by a Huguenot —
came to be widely accepted by all those who, for whatever reason, hated
the King and his Medici mother. Moreover, accusations of Italianate degeneracy, both political and moral, are given plausibility by the court itself
where cynical self–seeking, favouritism and personal violence are shame-
lessly flaunted. And it is this mixture of cynicism and brutality on the one
hand, and their systematic enunciation on the other, which — as inevitably
as the stereotype of evil kingship — threw a lurid light upon Henri's numerous deficiencies and ensured that his portrait was permanently deformed
and distorted.

---

[38] *Mémoires-journaux de Pierre de L'Estoile*, ed. G. Brunet *et al.*, Paris, 1875–
83, I, pp. 243–54.

2. Henri III, The Guises and the Huguenots

N. M. SUTHERLAND

I studied Henri III predominantly through the eyes of those who served him constantly and laboured to preserve him from himself. This material, penetrating if incomplete, mainly related to Henri in his political capacity[1]. With, as I supposed, rehabilitation in the air, I was ready to look again, only to be disconcerted by the damning nature of the evidence. Years ago, I described Henri as a tragic misfit. I still see his reign as a tragedy of Shakespearean dimensions, complete with multiple deaths. In spite of an unbroken record of fecklessness and failure, Henri seems not to have been contemptible. Doubtless I am influenced by Villeroy, secretary and confidant, who distinguished between the monarch and the man[2]. The judgement of fecklessness and failure, however, may not pass unchallenged. Mademoiselle Boucher has said: 'le grand politique qu'il fut a été ignoré'. Had the lack of an heir, she wrote, not provoked a great politico-religious crisis late in his reign, Henri through his work and projects might have been

---

[1] N. M. Sutherland, *The French Secretaries of State in the Age of Catherine de Medici*, London, 1962. (Note : This chapter represents a half-hour paper delivered to a specialist audience and was, inevitably, condensed.)

[2] Nicolas III de Neufville, seigneur de Villeroy, secretary of state, 1567–88, 1594–1617.

successful[3]. As a defence of Henri's political distinction, that is unimpressive. Since he had already procrastinated for so long, there is no reason to suppose that he might have become decisive and effective. Furthermore, the proposition is erroneous. The succession question, which arose in 1584, was not the *cause* of the great politico-religious crisis — which was international — but a subsequent aspect of its development in France.

Obviously Henri's character is of central importance to his destiny. France *needed* a warrior king, whereas Henri was an intellectual. He was not lacking in dignity, presence and eloquence, albeit prone to indulge in irresponsible pranks. He was sensitive and cultivated, but also a wayward and increasingly sick depressive. He was not idle, *when* available, but his habitual reaction to adversity was to escape into cloistered unreality. Hapless and forlorn, Henri in his weakness afflicted himself as well as others. Occasionally, when he paid attention, he would see with awful clarity the deficiencies he was unable to surmount[4]. His self-examination could be candid, if maudlin, but it lacked the essential of true repentance — amendment of life. Fitful and petulant outbursts of authoritarianism were no substitute for persevering effort. If failure has to be forgivable Henri, in spite of his undoubted intelligence, largely evaded his function of monarch, while magnifying his estate.

Henri inherited, and may have been partly responsible for, the accumulated debris of problems which had long defied solution[5]; or perhaps one should say whose solutions had long been defied[6]. Was Henri, upon his accession in 1574, already in a no-win situation?[7] While that is debatable,

---

[3] Jacqueline Boucher, *Société et mentalités autour de Henri III*, 4 vols, Paris, 1984, i, 53, 69.

[4] Sutherland, *The French Secretaries of State*, 248–50.

[5] The massacre of St Bartholomew, 1572, had greatly exacerbated the problems arising from diversity of religion. Contemporaries believed Henri to have been implicated. However, Jean-Louis Bourgeon has recently proposed that the role of Anjou — as he then was — 'doit probablement être entièrement révisé,' suggesting that in appearing in the streets of Paris, Anjou [lieutenant general] was seeking to re-assert the royal authority. 'Une source sur la Saint-Barthélemy: l'Histoire de Monsieur de Thou relue et décryptée', *Bulletin de la société de l'histoire du protestantisme francais*, 134, 1988, 530–1 and n.81.

[6] Five successive edicts of religion had all been defied: January 1562, Amboise, March 1563, Longjumeau, March 1568, Saint-Germain, August 1570, Boulogne (peace of La Rochelle), July 1573.

[7] Lack of time precluded an analysis of this situation, which was critically

Henri of Navarre, robustly pragmatic, would surely have ventured something more positive and vigorous? It is easy to establish what Henri III really wanted: he wanted peace and universal catholicism in France assuming, apparently, that his royalty entitled him to such satisfaction. By 1574, however, peace in France with unity of religion was a mirage. Craving the impossible, Henri vacillated over the inevitable. Whether, initially, he could have enforced an edict comparable to that of Saint-Germain 1570 — the basis of all later edicts — is also debatable[8]. But Henri never considered it. It was later observed by Villeroy that Henri III was equally incapable of making peace or waging war[9]. Indeed, his reign was largely submerged in the anarchy which lay between. Though receiving sound advice as well as frequent warnings, Henri was entirely without prescience. Consequently, each successive crisis caught him totally unprepared, repeatedly entailing humiliating capitulations, concluded under duress. Pliant and fatalistic, Henri allowed himself to be driven into corners. Once at bay, he would yield his assent, vent his fury indiscriminately upon all around him, and stubbornly withhold his co-operation.

Having postulated fecklessness and failure, I want, however sketchily, to identify the major problems and the major crises, in order to consider Henri's role. Between the Guises and the Huguenots, Scylla and Charybdis, Henri was to fix upon no course of his own — not that they were the only terrors in his ocean. Three closely connected circumstantial factors overshadowed Henri's reign. The first of these, on the Huguenot side, was the extensive consequences of the massacres of 1572, which disposed of no problems but created a leadership vacuum. The result was a degree of disintegration, the unleashing of revolutionary elements and the emergence of ephemeral political liaisons. Thereafter the actual nature of the Huguenots

---

dangerous. See N. M. Sutherland, *The Huguenot Struggle for Recognition*, New Haven, London, 1980, chap. 7; Mack P. Holt, *The Duke of Anjou and the Politique Struggle during the Wars of Religion*, Cambridge, 1986, chap. 3.

[8] A. Fontanon, *Les Edits et ordonnances des rois de France*, 4 vols, Paris, 1611, iv, 300–4; Sutherland, *The Huguenot Struggle*, 172–84, 358–60. The comprehensive Edict of Saint-Germain was the first to require the restoration of mass (art. 3) wherever it had been suppressed. Two cult towns per *gouvernement* were named in the edict. It was also the first to embody civil and judicial rights for the protestants, including eligibility for all offices. Four 'places de sûreté' were ceded for security and art. 32 attempted to tackle the problem of enforcement, specifying severe penalties for obstruction.

[9] Paris, Bibliothèque nationale, Mss fr., 15906, fol. 288, 23 March 1581, Villeroy to Bellièvre.

as a party or group and their position in the state was never clear until the Edict of Nantes, 1598. The second factor was the return of the Guise family and faction to dominance at court, after having been in varying degrees eclipsed since about the end of 1561. The third factor was the emergence into public life of Henri's brother and heir apparent, the duc d'Alençon, aged twenty in March 1574. Henri himself was generally believed to have been implicated in the massacre[10], and the Huguenots earnestly hoped that he would disappear in Poland[11]. They were never again to trust the crown — not even Henri IV[12]. The Guises, definitely implicated in the massacre[13], triumphed because they were then unopposed at court by any leading family[14]. Their power, backed or soon to be backed by Spain and the Papacy, rendered an adequate and effective Huguenot settlement virtually impossible[15]. Furthermore, their ostentatious supremacy was directly inimical to the interests of Alençon, who craved recognition as lieutenant general, a position promised him in January 1574[16]. Alençon, by virtue of his rank, briefly assumed the leadership, not of the Huguenots as Calvinists, but of mostly anti-Guisard malcontents. This did nothing to improve relations between the royal brothers whose mutual antipathy was very damaging. The massacre had averted a Huguenot invasion of the Netherlands, whose leaders quickly perceived Alençon's growing significance. Open to flattery and exploitation, Alençon, appeared potentially very useful to the Netherlands' cause, not least because he attracted the support of Queen

---

[10] See note 5 above.

[11] As Henri duc d'Anjou, he was elected king of Poland 9 May /10 September 1573. He entered Cracow on 10 February 1574, departed secretly on 18 June and returned to Lyons on 6 September 1574, dallying by the way.

[12] On the turbulent relations between the Huguenots and Henri IV, see N. M. Sutherland, 'The Crown, the Huguenots and the Edict of Nantes,' in R.M. Golden, ed. *The Huguenot Connection: the Edict of Nantes, its Revocation and Early French Migration to South Carolina*, Dordrecht, 1988.

[13] The responsibility of the Guises is central to the new and important work of Jean-Louis Bourgeon. See note 5 above.

[14] The marshals Montmorency (François duc de) and Cossé (Artus de Cossé, comte de Segondigny, seigneur de Gonnor) were both imprisoned; Coligny and his Châtillon brothers were all dead and the prince de Condé had escaped to Germany after the conspiracy of 1574.

[15] According to Jean-Louis Bourgeon, 'les Guises ont été achetés par Philippe II dès 1568,' *BSHPF*, 134, 1988, 527. The details of their relations with Spain or Spanish agents are not precisely established.

[16] Holt, *The Duke of Anjou*, 34–6.

Elizabeth[17]. Their further objective, achieved in 1582, was to embroil the powers with Spain, to their own advantage. Thus, from the start, Henri's domestic problems had an alarming international dimension, independent of the crown.

Henri's principal problems derived from these three factors. Alençon's Netherlands connection did bring conflict with Spain, and Spain supported the Guises initially, in Henri's reign, to counteract Alençon and the threat to the Netherlands. When Alençon died, in June 1584, his mantle fell upon Navarre, elected 'protector' of the Huguenots. Although the royal succession was neither urgent nor a crisis, lack of a direct, catholic heir certainly compounded Henri's problems. By the same token, the foreign-backed catholic opposition came to be focused, not on the Huguenots, but on the crown; a power struggle which comprised the interests of the Guise clan and one facet of Spanish foreign policy. Implicit in all this is the problem of faction. Abandoned by the nobility, Henri raised up favourites. The offices, power and patronage of Epernon, in particular, became a key factor in the drama of 1585–8[18]. It was Epernon who dislodged Villeroy and these are aspects which merit deeper investigation[19]. Further to Henri's isolation, another major problem was his lack of allies. The Treaty of Blois with England, 1572, which Henri ratified, disturbed Philip II without protecting France. Above all, Henri failed to secure the support of the Papacy. Instead, it went to the Guises and was effectively used against the king, not least in the excommunication of Navarre and Condé in September 1585[20]. At home, Henri lost the support of catholic Paris, a traditional source of revenue[21].

These problems gave rise to a series of crises, the first of which was the flight from court of Alençon in September 1575, precipitated by quarrels with the Guises. The second arose at the Estates General of Blois, 1576–

---

[17] Queen Elizabeth may be found to have supported Anjou whenever he appeared to be in danger because he was the principal opponent of the Guises who threatened her.

[18] Jean-Louis de Nogaret, duc d'Epernon, 1554–1642.

[19] Epernon blamed Villeroy for Henri's policy of seeking to bribe and detach Guise, his principal rival for power. Sutherland, *The French Secretaries of State*, 278–9.

[20] E. Haag, *La France protestante*, 10 vols, Paris, 1846–59, x, 187–91, 9 September 1585.

[21] On the role of Paris see, most recently, Jean-Pierre Babelon, *Nouvelle histoire de Paris: Paris au XVIᵉ siècle*, Paris, 1986.

7, and the third, greatest and fatal crisis came with the Guise rebellion of 1584–5, from which stemmed three subsidiary crises. These were the foreign invasion of 1587; the barricades in Paris in May 1588 and Henri's submission to the Edict of Union in July. The Union led straight to the second Estates of Blois and the bloody dénouement of Henri's reign.

Henri, who had only been in Poland for some four months before his accession in May 1574, and departed barely three weeks later, must have been aware of the danger of the unresolved Huguenot problem following the partial Peace of La Rochelle, 1573[22]. Since their Edict of Saint-Germain had never been rescinded, the Huguenots were bound to demand a comparably favourable resolution to the current juridical confusion. When Henri returned to Lyons in September 1574, Huguenot deputies presented their petition of August 1573, which defined their basic needs and objectives[23]. Ignoring their organised strength, Henri dismissively offered them pardon if they abjured in peace, and threatened to purge the realm of all who refused. He never learnt the folly of expressing his authority in vain fulmination. The significance of this blundering début is that Henri evaded — then and for ever — the fundamental necessity of formulating a clear, practicable Huguenot policy. Constant only in his infirmity of purpose, Henri oscillated between one extreme and the other, only to be universally distrusted. Consequently it was he alone who disarmed. By 1575, the Huguenots had completed their 'state within the state'[24]; resistance theories were openly propounded, and they were seeking foreign support, which shortly materialised[25].

Alençon's flight and declaration in September 1575 reveal not only his resentment and covetous ambition, but also the extent to which resistance was focused on the Guises; and Henri failed to realise that they would isolate him[26]. In order to avert the foreign invasion and, predominantly,

---

[22] See note 11 above. The Peace of La Rochelle (Edict of Boulogne), [2] July 1573, was concluded only with La Rochelle, Montauban and Nîmes, allowing virtually no religious freedom elsewhere. The real purpose of the Peace was to extricate Anjou from La Rochelle. Haag, *La France protestante*, x, 110–14; Sutherland, *The Huguenot Struggle*, 212–13, 360–1.

[23] Haag, *La France protestante*, x, 114–21, requête de l'assemblée de Montauban.

[24] On the Huguenot 'state', see Sutherland, *The Huguenot Struggle*, chaps. 7 and 9, *passim*.

[25] The prince de Condé entered Burgundy in January 1576. B.N., Mss Italien, 1729, fol. 455, 25 January 1576.

[26] B.N., Mss fr., 3342, fos 4–5, 17 September 1575, Alençon's declaration;

to detach and reconcile Alençon, Henri accepted his first humiliating capitulation under duress. Alençon, who became Anjou, received enormous benefits, while Henri agreed to pay the invading forces and to disband his own, commanded by Guise[27]. What did Henri expect to happen? The story of the unenforceably liberal Peace of Monsieur, May 1576, is fairly well known; so much for the king who would purge his realm of those who declined to abjure. If Henri had faced certain defeat in war, he simultaneously neglected an unique opportunity. This failure is not received opinion, although the consequences are clearly apparent. Navarre, like Alençon, had been detained at court, following a conspiracy in March 1574; and he was still there. Able and flexible, Navarre was no fanatical Calvinist and he was too young to have held any Huguenot position[28]. Roughly saved from the massacre in 1572 and forced to abjure, his enemies were not catholics in general, but the Guises; hence some community of interest with Alençon. In 1575, Navarre's historic role as leader of the Huguenots was not inevitable; nor was it in his own best interests. To judge from his later conduct he might, if freed, have been conciliated, for instance with the vacant office of constable. The support of Navarre in 1575 must surely have altered the sequence of Henri's reign. If there are possible objections to this point, it has undeniable validity because Henri *did* seek to conciliate Navarre, as soon as it was too late; and thereafter he continued to do so at intervals until the conclusion of the *traité de la trève* of April 1589[29]. In the event, Navarre's escape was only a matter of time — February 1576[30]. He then had no alternative to the Huguenot camp, which could not wantonly be abandoned. Nor could Navarre avoid the second change of religion, which proved so costly to himself and so disastrous to the king. Relations between

---

Sutherland, *The Huguenot Struggle*, 226–7.

[27] The six months truce of Champigny, November 1575–May 1576, B.N., Mss Italien, 1729, fol. 376, 30 November 1575; fol. 455, 25 January 1576. The Peace of Monsieur (Edict of Beaulieu), 6 May 1576, Haag, *La France protestante*, x, 127–41; Sutherland, *The Huguenot Struggle*, 226–31, 361–2. By separate letters patent, Alençon's appanage was increased by the duchies of Anjou, Touraine and Berry, plus a pension of 100,000 écus per annum. Holt, *The Duke of Anjou*, 66–7.

[28] Navarre was twenty-two on 14 December 1575.

[29] Dr. Mark Greengrass has suggested that had Navarre rallied to the king in 1575, he might have risked losing support in his own power base of Navarre and Béarn. Yet, given freedom and time, he also *might* have overcome such problems. The point stands, however, that Henri should have at least attempted to conciliate Navarre sooner, while he was a prisoner, rather than later, when he was at liberty and heavily committed.

[30] Sutherland, *The Huguenot Struggle*, 227.

Henri and Navarre also merit further research.

The Peace of Monsieur provoked immediate catholic resistance, apparently spontaneous catholic leagues and, on their side also, highly subversive propositions; even deposition was in the air, and Henri became alarmed. Against this background, he made an effort to seize the initiative at the Estates of Blois[31]. If the catholics insisted upon one religion, Henri intended to pre-empt the credit, shelter behind the demands of the Estates — which he manipulated — and make them shoulder the responsibility for any adverse outcome, as well as the cost. The deputies, however, had no financial mandate. Evidence suggests that, had Henri been more perceptive, he just might have succeeded in using the Estates to resist the catholic *ligueurs*, whose threats were thinly veiled. However, on 3 Januari 1577, Henry performed a startling volte-face, abrogated the Peace of Monsieur, with no substitution, and threatened that if anyone took up arms, he would oppose them to the end, without any hope that he might incline to peace; more vain fulmination. Thereafter, he issued numerous instructions for peace, which were ignored[32]. This second crisis illustrates Henri's volatility, his escapism and his utopian desire for both peace and catholicism. War or peace was beyond his control: the Huguenots forced the issue and won a sensible agreement in the treaty of Bergerac, which included forty-eight secret clauses with Navarre[33]. But they knew that Henri could not protect them, and that something similar could recur. Difficulties arose, and they never completely disarmed.

After the Peace of Bergerac and the dissolution of the leagues that Henri had so recently promoted — a double volte-face — the attention of the Guises turned outwards, to the Netherlands. They shared with the governor, Don John of Austria, theatrical projects, involving England[34]. The Guise/Anjou conflict continued, mainly in that context, rapidly involving Spain on the one hand, and England on the other. Thus Anjou is the key to the years between 1577 and the Guise rebellion of 1584.

---

[31] Sutherland, *The Huguenot Struggle*, chap. 8.

[32] Michel François, *Lettres de Henri III*, 4 vols, Paris, 1959...in progress, iii, 129, 3 January 1577, Henri to Navarre; Sutherland, *The Huguenot Struggle*, 257–8.

[33] The Peace of Bergerac (Edict of Poitiers), 17 September 1577, Fontanon, *Les ordonnances*, iv, 318–26; Sutherland, *The Huguenot Struggle*, 270–5, 362–3.

[34] N. M. Sutherland, *Princes, Politics and Religion*, 1547–1589, London, 1984, chap. 12, 'William of Orange and the Revolt of the Netherlands: A Missing Dimension'.

There was, however, a period of relative calm, during which Catherine and Villeroy strove to enforce the Huguenot edict of Poitiers, to which Henri was apparently resigned. During this period, he could, and should have executed various projects to stabilize and secure the realm against impending dangers. But Catherine and Villeroy battled in vain to induce him to act. In January 1579, with Anjou back in France from the Netherlands, Villeroy warned the king of the seriousness of his frequent absences. Amidst mounting perils, in December 1580 Henri quit the court for four months, declining to be disturbed and refusing to issue instructions. In 1582–4, as the implications of Anjou's Netherlands connections frightened everyone, Henri spent some two thirds of his time in seclusion. In 1582, Navarre submitted the first of several warnings of Guise complicity with Spain[35]; by September Villeroy was frantic. In January next he warned Henri of the danger of rebellion against the ascendancy of Epernon and Joyeuse, and implored the king to assemble forces[36]. In October 1582 Henri attended to affairs of state for the first time for five months, calling an assembly of notables. But he was absent again in 1584 as Anjou's approaching death threatened civil war[37]. Catherine and Villeroy had both collapsed and were seriously ill for many months. In December 1584, when the Guises were planning to strike in Paris, Henri was furiously ineffective, helpless as an infant in the snow. Guise had even engrossed every available horse.

The problem of Anjou, which darkened these years, may be thought to have been insoluble, given his character and the circumstances which unfolded. Arguably, Henri faced insuperable odds[38]. Only by the most skilful handling of his hated brother could he have averted serious trouble; such was the opinion of Villeroy[39]. Nevertheless, in this, as in other things, Henri oscillated, capitulated, and resisted; no one could fathom his policy. He did not want Anjou to embrace the uncertain Netherlands cause, still less to support him. But he was pressurised by Anjou and the Dutch and outmanoeuvred by Queen Elizabeth; they trapped him. Anjou's first *essai*

---

[35] Abel Desjardins, *Négociations diplomatiques de la France avec la Toscane*, 5 vols, Paris, 1859–75, iv, 449, 16 November 1582.

[36] B.N., Mss fr., 6629, fol. 3, 20 January 1583, Villeroy to the king; Sutherland, *The French Secretaries of State*, 239–40.

[37] On Henri's absences, see Sutherland, *The French Secretaries of State*, 210, 217–24 *passim* and chap. 15 *passim*.

[38] On the whole subject of Anjou's career, see Mack P. Holt, *The Duke of Anjou...*

[39] B.N., Mss fr., 15906, fol. 371, 16 April 1581, Villeroy to Bellièvre. Anne d'Arques, duc de Joyeuse; killed at the battle of Coutras, 1587.

was a limited agreement with Hainaut in 1578, from which he erupted into France in January 1579. The English marriage negotiations, renewed that summer, were a forlorn and ill-defined attempt to divert and accommodate Anjou; forlorn because Elizabeth was far too clever to promote the interests of France.

During 1579, the success of the duke of Parma in the Netherlands rendered the United Provinces desperate for foreign help. Thus by the summer of 1580, Anjou was universally courted: by Parma himself, by Elizabeth and the Dutch and, in France, by the Huguenots who were stirring[40]. Everyone hoped to pre-empt Anjou's alliance elsewhere. Consequently, he was able to blackmail the king, extorting the title of lieutenant general — which signalled recognition — in return for mediation with the Huguenots. He also extorted a vague promise of royal support, upon which his agreement with the Netherlands depended. The Dutch objective was to obtain material help and force the king into war with Spain. Their requirements were incorporated into articles XV and XVI of Anjou's agreement of 19 September 1580[41]. Henri, who had no intention of obliging, cavilled over technicalities. He was uncontainably angry and disclaimed any commitment. Nonetheless, France had been irreversibly compromised. When Henri returned from one of his retreats, in April 1581, he protested that he would obstruct Anjou in every way. Yet by August, when Anjou departed for Cambrai, Henri conceded that he would have to be helped; and so it went on[42]. Henri again turned to England, where Anjou himself spent several months from October[43]. Then, in February 1582, he embarked for Flushing, imposingly escorted — which surely must illuminate his flirtation with Elizabeth. At Antwerp, on 19 February, in the presence of the earl of Leicester and the prince dauphin, among other noblemen, Anjou was solemnly invested with Philip's title, duke of Brabant, amidst elaborate ceremonies[44]. His new function was to oppose the prince of Parma, with French and English support. The Dutch triumph did not consist in winning Anjou, who had never played hard to catch, but in the nature of the ceremony through which England and France were ostentatiously committed to the Netherlands,

---

[40] Holt, *The Duke of Anjou*, 127–8.

[41] Holt, *The Duke of Anjou*, 139; text in P.L. Muller and I.L.A. Diegerick, *Documents concernant les relations entre le duc d'Anjou et les Pays-Bas, 1576–1584*, 5 vols, Amsterdam, The Hague, 1889–99, iii, 469–79.

[42] Holt, *The Duke of Anjou*, 155–6.

[43] He landed at Rye on 31 October 1581, accompanied by the protestant, Philippe de Marnix. Holt, *The Duke of Anjou*, 160.

[44] Holt, *The Duke of Anjou*, 166–9.

just when the dispersal of Spanish energies was essential to the survival of the United Provinces. Thereafter, both countries were the immediate objects of Spanish anger and revenge. Hitherto Henri had disavowed Anjou seeking to ruin him by lack of support. But from 1582, Henri was inextricably ensnared and subsequently expended large sums on the vain cause of Anjou's sovereignty in the Netherlands[45]. To the world, if not to Henri, the lieutenant general of France represented the crown. Even after his *débâcle* at Antwerp and his flight in January 1583, the Netherlands pursued a further agreement, clearly engaging the King of France. Henri consented in February 1584 and the treaty was signed on 25 April[46]. Anjou was plainly dying and the Dutch sought to bind the king to their cause and Anjou's commitments after his death. Anjou's condition already threatened a major catholic/Huguenot confrontation, focused on the succession. Since Henri had no intention of intervening in the Netherlands, *why* did he consent to a treaty which guaranteed Spanish intervention in France?

France was sliding towards disaster in which Henri only half believed, and never for long at a time. Childlike, he seems to have trusted that Catherine, Villeroy, and possibly God, would make everything all right; never mind that his mother and minister were gravely ill. But Henri, who had unwillingly offended the King of Spain, had little hope of mastering the duc de Guise when, by the treaty of Joinville, in December 1584, he was formally appointed the instrument of Spain's revenge[47]. It is not now possible to examine Philip's exploitation of French faction and related conflicts including, fortuitously, the succession. Instead, I want to redirect attention and to shift the usual emphasis.

It was Anjou's investiture in February 1582 which crystallized the dramatic power struggles of the later sixteenth century, forcing England and France into more than matrimony. That crucial event in Antwerp was a turning point in the history of western Europe. From 1582, there were steady signs of Spanish hostility to both countries, and Guise became a Spanish pensioner not later than September. Anjou's death, in June 1584, following the Netherlands agreement in April, was not causal, though it affected the form of the conflict in France, as did that of William the Silent in

---

[45] The sums spent on Anjou by Henri III and queen Elizabeth have been established by Holt for the first time. Henri's role was, hitherto, very uncertain. *The Duke of Anjou*, 196.

[46] Holt, *The Duke of Anjou*, 207; text in Muller and Diegerick, *Documents*, v, 686–700, 25 April 1584.

[47] B.N., Mss fr., 3363, fol. 9, 31 December 1584.

the Netherlands, albeit to a lesser extent. Spain's supreme offensive against both powers came in 1588: with the invincible Armada and, in France, the imperfectly synchronised Guise rebellion in Paris which, nonetheless, indirectly effected Henri's perdition.

Navarre had informed the king of the Guise conspiracy — *and* a possible Spanish invasion — well before Anjou died[48]. His death was a godsend to the Guises, assisting them to make religion their pretext, whereby to exclude Navarre from the succession and enhance their own prospects. Henri unwisely disclosed his hand by sending Epernon, with an imposing entourage, to seek Navarre's abjuration. In 1585, Henri's predominant concern was peace. He finally accepted the treaty of Nemours, 7 July, as the price of averting hostilities with Guise, lamentably justifying the Huguenots' lasting distrust[49]. Guise extorted the revocation of the Edicts of Pacification. Henri's sole advantage was that the treaty contained no undertaking to fight[50]. The Guise purpose was proclaimed by the excommunication, in September 1585, of Navarre and Condé — an elliptical threat to Henri himself. Consequently, Navarre declared war on the pope and the *ligueurs*, without mention of the king[51].

Henri's reaction was emotional. He continued to shun the court, wasting money as well as time. He became increasingly angry, trusted no one, and adopted an attitude of resigned hopelessness, punctuated by fits of fury and defiance[52]. He blamed those who failed to save him, without opposing those who sought his ruin. He did consider arresting Guise, but merely made some effort to diminish his power, and to defend Picardy[53]. In general, however, he appears to have hoped, either that Guise could be bribed and detached — a policy which aroused the dangerous fury of Epernon, who stood to lose — or else that Navarre would intervene.

---

[48] B.N., Mss fr., 16911, fol. 144, 18 February 1584, Villeroy to Revol.

[49] Sutherland, *The French Secretaries of State*, 262–4; Haag, *La France protestante*, x, 184–7, 7 July 1585.

[50] The Edicts of Pacification were those of Poitiers, 17 September 1577, Nérac, 28 February 1579 and Fleix, 26 November 1580. Haag, *La France protestante*, x, 142–56, 159–67, 171–8.

[51] Haag, *La France protestante*, x, 194–5, 30 November 1585, déclaration du roi de Navarre.

[52] Sutherland, *The French Secretaries of State*, 286.

[53] Sutherland, *The French Secretaries of State*, 274. Villeroy advised the king against arresting Guise because Henri was too vulnerable. B.N., Mss nouvelles acquisitions françaises, 7260, fol. 7, 1 August 1584, letter to Du Vair.

Two uneasy years passed before the inevitable crisis arose, in the summer of 1587, when Henri placed his hopes in Navarre's approaching mercenaries. When, however, Guise was twice victorious against them, Henri openly assisted the foreigners with money and protection. Henri could be forced to capitulate but not to co-operate. Guise was publicly mocked and that was the turning point. Thereafter the powerful catholic movement swung overtly against the fanatically catholic king. In March 1588, Guise reverted to his original plan, a rising focused on Paris. The story of the barricades in May 1588 is well-known, if ill-explained. The Guise challenge to Henri's authority was now undisguised, the confrontation public and personal[54]. Henry indulged in more vain fulmination and, as ever, appealed to Navarre. Guise, significantly, appealed to Parma[55]. Henri's flight to Chartres and later to Rouen, was probably not unwise, but why did he *do* nothing but negotiate — throwing Catherine and Villeroy once more into the fray — thereby handing Guise the advantage?

The duc's ultimatum in Paris was pursued in an insolent petition of 24 May. Guise demanded the immediate disgrace of his rival, Epernon, who controlled areas sensitive to Spain. He wanted an Estates General, supreme command, the exclusion of Navarre from the succession and Henri's return to Paris, unarmed. To all but the latter, Henri agreed[56]. Apparently under the influence of Mendoza, in June 1588, before the Armada arrived, Guise called for a rupture with England. Guise was rewarded with a hybrid commission of constable and lieutenant general[57] — viceregal powers — and achieved in the Edict of Union, 12 July, the triumph which had eluded him in 1577[58]. This final, and most abject of Henri's capitulations bound him to the League, renewed his uncompromising coronation oath against heretics and excluded Navarre, for whose help he longed. Henri's only remaining hope lay in the second Estates General of Blois; and that hope was dashed. When they endorsed the Edict of Union and demanded the

---

[54] Henri, for his part, clearly saw Guise as his enemy. B.N., Mss fr., 15909, fol. 70, 24 April 1588, Henri to Bellièvre.

[55] J. de Croze, *Les Guises, les Valois et Philippe II*, 2 vols, Paris, 1866, ii, 86, 88–9.

[56] J. de Croze, *Les Guises*, ii, 68, 94–5.

[57] Sutherland, *The French Secretaries of State*, 290–2; C.B. Petitot, *Collection complète des mémoires relatifs à l'histoire de France*, sér. i, 52 vols, Paris, 1819–26, xliv, *Mémoires d'estat de Villeroy*, 69, 74. Villeroy recounted that Henri signed that commission with regret and determined to disgrace those who had advised it — a typical trait of character.

[58] Haag, *La France protestante*, x, 201–3.

resumption of the edicts of religious persecution which obtained in the reign of Henri II, Henry had only one recourse: the murder of Guise had long been expected. The Sorbonne declared the king deposed, and excommunication was to follow for the murder of cardinal Guise[59]. The way was now open for Navarre to champion authority and redeem his own inheritance[60]. But for Henri III, it was probably too late. Had he prospered in arms by Navarre's success, instead of perishing by the assassin's knife[61], could Henri have retained — or regained — his throne? If not, there was no choice of exit for a deposed king; probably it was all one.

---

[59] Louis II de Lorraine, cardinal de Guise, archbishop of Rheims, 1583, president of the first estate at Blois 1588; murdered on 24 December 1588, the day after his brother, the duc de Guise.

[60] Henri and Navarre agreed to the *traité de la trève*, 3 April 1589. Philippe Duplessis-Mornay, *Mémoires et correspondance*, 12 vols, Paris, 1824-5, iv, 351-5; declarations of Navarre and Henri on the traité de la trève, 24, 26 April 1589, Haag, *La France protestante*, x, 203-5, 205-8; Sutherland, *The Huguenot Struggle*, 366-7.

[61] Henri was knifed by the Dominican, Jacques Clément at Saint-Cloud on 1 August 1589.

3. The Politiques and the Politique Party: A Reappraisal

The civil wars in France have often been seen as 'tidily stowed behind the Edict of Nantes, 1598' or at most as the first phase of a whole century of crisis from which the monarchy emerged triumphant under the personal rule of Louis XIV[1]. It used also to be commonly held by French scholars that the 'wars of religion' represent an embarrassing hiccup between a period of internal peace and increasing national consolidation under the first two Valois kings and the resumption of this process under the creative leadership of the first Bourbon whose work was continued by Richelieu and then Mazarin. Anglo-Saxon scholars have been more ready to tackle the complexities of sixteenth-century France as a number of important studies by Sutherland, Knecht, Bonney and Greengrass, among others, reveals[2].

---

[1] See N. M. Sutherland, Princes, *Politics and Religion, 1547–1589*, The Hambleton Press, 1984, pp. 31ff.

[2] e.g. N. M. Sutherland, *The French Secretaries of State in the Age of Catherine de Medici* (1962), *The Massacre of St Bartholomew and the European Conflict, 1559–1572* (1973), *The Huguenot Struggle for Recognition* (1980); R.J. Knecht, *Francis I* (1982); R. Bonney, *The King's Debts: finance and politics in France* (1981); M. Greengrass, *France in the age of Henry IV: the struggle for stability* (1984).

In particular, the traditional view of the French civil wars was challenged by J.H.M. Salmon in his very useful text-book *Society in Crisis. France in the Sixteenth Century* (1975). According to Salmon the civil wars, far from being an element of discontinuity 'are the crucible in which some of the competing forces from an earlier age were consumed in the fire and others blended and transmuted into new compounds. It is the matrix for all that came after'[3]. Briefly summarized, Salmon's interpretation highlights not only the continuity of old battles involving royal power, aristocratic independence and local particularism but also the emergence of a new historicist vision involving liberation from outdated models and old habits of thought. In identifying this new *Weltanschauung* (which owes a little, incidentally, to Henri Hauser's *La Modernité du XVIe siècle* (1930) and much to Franco Simone's interpretation of the French renaissance[4]) Salmon defines the key social group in which it was forged — the *noblesse de robe*, the high *robins* and professional bureaucrats who emerged in the course of the century as a new governing elite, witness their predominance in Henri IV's *conseil des affaires* as well as, a little later, in the *conseil des finances*[5]. We may note the continuity here, in terms of personalities and family connexions, with the secretaries of state and *conseil d'état* under Henri III and indeed further back to the group of lawyer-humanists assembled by Michel de L'Hospital and Catherine of Medici in the 1560s which merged with the career bureaucrats in the royal councils of Francis I, Henri II and Francis II.

The hallmarks of this developing royal bureaucracy are loyalty to the Crown, group solidarity, shared social and cultural values. An additional ideological factor has to be brought into play to explain the eventual *ralliement* to Henri IV. For, the Valois kings were beset with four main sets of problems: economic processes (inflation, price-revolution) and their impact on the traditional aristocracy; the institutional reforms undertaken and their associated acute financial problems; the development of factions as feudal ties of obligation changed into a system of clientage; the advent of religious dissent interwoven with political, economic, social and institutional factors. In simple terms, first a Protestant, then a Catholic faction became the opponents of royal authority and as a result a loyalist Catholic group merged with a loyalist Protestant group to rally to the Bourbon monarchy in the name of national unity and a need for strong monarchical authority.

---

[3] *Op. cit.*, p. 13.

[4] F. Simone, *Il rinascimento francese: studi e ricerche* (1961).

[5] Salmon, pp. 316 ff.

This composite group is called by Salmon the *Politique* party and its identity is based on the undoubted existence. of a flood of what he calls *Politique* political theory, in the period following the death of Anjou and the emergence of Navarre as heir presumptive, as a reaction to the resurgence of the League and the constitutional excesses of its pamphleteers. *Politique* theory is defined as an amalgam of many elements of Renaissance political thought. Old style absolutism (Budé, Grassaille) and other traditional views of kingship (Seyssel and L'Hospital) combine, with Gallican imperatives and elements of *raison d'état* from Stoic and Machiavellian sources, to produce powerful arguments for monarchical absolutism and the divine right of Kings. In effect a *fin-de-siècle* world view is posited which represents the mature reflection of the French renaissance in the fields of moral and political philosophy and whose main architects are Montaigne, Charron, Justus-Lipsius, Machiavelli, Bodin, de Belloy and Pierre Pithou.

A number of interesting issues arise from Salmon's impressive and thought-provoking synthesis. This study will restrict itself to those surrounding the use of the term *Politique* party to designate a definable group of actors and thinkers during the period of the French civil wars. In the first place the scholarly origins of this interpretation are clear and are to be found in Anglo-Saxon histories of political thought. J.W. Allen in his *History of Political Thought in the Sixteenth Century* (1928) calls *politique* a style of royalist thinking after the massacre of St Bartholomew. '*Politiques*', he says, 'may be defined as a group of Catholics who advocated toleration of the heretics for the sake of peace and national unity' (p.370). The movement is said to grow out of the failure of the royal army at the siege of La Rochelle and the formation of Huguenot leagues in the South and led to the view that only a negotiated peace was possible. Basing himself on his knowledge of post-1572 pamphlet literature, he claims that 'the word *Politique* was first applied to the Party by its enemies, derisively, as signifying men who set their own ease before their duty to God and peace and quiet above religion' (p.370). The next 130 pages of Allen link the divine right of kings, *Politique* political theory, Bodin, Montaigne and Machiavelli. The interpretation is fleshed out by two earlier assertions in relation to Michel de L'Hospital, firstly that 'L'Hospital was the real founder of the party of the *Politiques*' and also that 'the *Politiques* were the founders of the "modern state"' (p.292).

Allen's own intellectual masters in this view of the *Politiques* and their central significance in the French civil wars can also be identified. His definition of the party of the *Politiques* as a group of Catholic nobles in the early 1570s loosely grouped around Alençon/Anjou derives from the work by F. Decrue de Stoutz, *Le parti des politiques au lendemain de la Saint-Barthelémy* (1892). This work is also responsible for identifying the L'Hospital circle in the early 1560s as well as the anti-Guise faction centred on the Montmorency family as the earlier manifestation of the *politique* party. At the same time, Allen's typology of much of the pamphlet literature of the period draws heavily on G. Weill, *Les théories sur le pouvoir royal en France* (1888). Finally, his use of *Politique* to describe a particular emerging style of political thought owes much to J.N. Figgis's *The divine right of Kings* (1914) but, more particularly, to a chapter in his earlier *Studies of political thought from Gerson to Grotius, 1414-1625*, published in 1909.

These comments on the possible sources of Salmon's view of the *Politique* party and *politique* thinking do not arise from a desire to challenge his overall interpretation of the intellectual trends of the civil war period. What is at issue is the contention that a definable group called *Politiques* existed in the early 1560s and in particular that a *Politique* party in the 1570s took up these ideas and initiated a growing movement of moderate Catholics and moderate Protestants thus facilitating the accession of Henri IV. While this describes in very broad terms the general drift of ideas, it is a gross oversimplification in historical terms and the use of the word *Politique* somewhat imprecise. It influences Baumgartner in the introduction to his *Radical Reactionaries: the political thought of the French catholic League* (1975), where he echoes Allen as well as Salmon, and gives a good demonstration of this crude tendency:

> *Politique* works urging religious toleration appeared shortly after 1559 but the *Politique* platform gained supporters as the wars dragged on and especially after the St Bartholomew's Day Massacre of 1572. The *Politiques* combined religious toleration for the Calvinists with a programme for a strong effective monarchy (p.16).

This particular view has been examined in a recent thesis by Robert C. Clay[6]. What emerges is firstly the extreme difficulty in defining the nature of *Politique* thought and secondly the near impossibility of clearly linking *Politiques*, commitment to religious toleration and the secularisation of the

---

[6] *The Political Vocabulary of the Politiques*, Oxford, (D.Phil. thesis, examined Michaelmas 1987).

State[7].

It does not follow of course that the predecessors of what Salmon calls *Politique* attitudes are not to be found in and around the Council of Catherine de Medici in the early 1560s in the minds of policy-makers, professional civil servants and humanist diplomats. Most of the elements of the *Politique* ideology of the 1580s are already present in the years following the death of Henri II: a sense of impending anarchy and the workings of powerful factions; fear of civil war and the collapse of the Valois dynasty; the need to rally to the authority of the legitimate monarch; the attachment to the reform of the judiciary and administration as well as to royally granted legal toleration to Huguenots[8]. Similar ideological strands are detectable in what has sometimes been seen as the Gallican tendencies of Catherine's toleration policy, particularly in the search at the Colloquy of Poissy for an interim national settlement of religious disputes, inspired by the colloquy policies of the 1540s and 1550s and imitating other 'national' solutions, such as the Interim of Augsburg of Charles V or the contemporary attempts by Ferdinand II, to obtain concessions from the Council of Trent. Furthermore, not without significance in the situation is the currency of anti-war notions, culled from Erasmian and neo-platonic sources as well as stoical and even Machiavellian elements, pointing to the desire of the French crown to resist outside 'interference' and take political decisions dictated by the circumstances and the law of necessity[9].

The problem of historical interpretation arises not from our awareness of the similarities between these two ideological moments but rather in attempts by historians to construct links between the early period of the 1560s and the later period of *ralliement* to Henri IV. This problem is not unrelated to attempts to explain the significance of the whole civil war period in the light of institutional processes begun under the early Valois and continued under the early Bourbons. The very complexities of the pe-

---

[7] See the report of this thesis in *The French Historian*, Vol. III, 2, December 1988, pp. 8–10.

[8] On this see C.D. Bettinson, *The Intellectual Background and Development of the Toleration Policy of Catherine de Medici*, (unpub. Ph.D. thesis, Reading), 1973, chapters 6 and 7; N. M. Sutherland, *The Huguenot Struggle for Recognition*, pp. 101–136.

[9] See C.D. Bettinson, '*La plume ensemble avec la lance*. The Humanist contribution to the toleration policy of Catherine de Medici and Michel de L'Hospital', *The French Experience. Essays in Honour of Richard Griffiths*, Cardiff, 1988, pp. 9–17.

riod of the civil wars, its relative neglect by historians and the difficulties with sources (or their paucity), has led to a tendency to look for factors and principles of continuity and point to a number of horizontal developments which connect Francis I and Henri II with Bourbon moves towards absolutism.

There have been many lines of approach. There is the notion of an emerging 'national' consciousness sharpened by the continuing threat of Spain and represented by Condé/Coligny and the attempts at a 'Protestant' foreign policy involving England, the Netherlands and German Protestant princes. This line is clearly pro-Bourbon and anti-Guise and leads to the Gallican/national consciousness of the 1580s and 1590s providing for the *ralliement* to Henri IV[10].

There is also the thesis of the two reformations whereby a moderate, home-grown French movement of *réforme* grouped and regrouped at different times from the 1520s onwards and stood constantly in opposition to the more intransigent Catholicism of the Sorbonne and Parlements on the one hand and to the ultramontane views of the Guises and others culminating in the extremism of the preachers of the League which provoked a French national reaction[11]. And because it is often a question of looking for the persistence of moderate views this reformist Catholic movement has been linked to the influence of Erasmus and Erasmianism in France and elsewhere in Europe, seen as a moderate, conciliatory tendency which had considerable impact in the 1540s and 1550s and then only sporadically until it was integrated into a more purposefully stoic setting at the end of the century[12].

Loyalty to the French monarchy and its traditions is a theme leading not only, somewhat tendentiously, to a focus on Condé's actions in the

---

[10] See among others C. Vivanti, *Lotta politica e pace religiosa in Francia fra Cinque e Seicento* (1963).

[11] On the theory of the two reformations see, for example, H.A. Enno van Gelder, *Two Reformations in the Sixteenth Century* (1964). Such notions are prevalent in many Protestant studies.

[12] Renaudet's work on Erasmus was influential in this respect, especially *Etudes érasmiennes* (1939), *Erasme et l'Italie* (1954), *Humanisme et Renaissance...* (1958). Other works are M. Bataillon, *Erasme et l'Espagne* (1937) and on England, J. McConica, *English Humanists and Reformation Politics under Henry VIII and Edward VI* (1965); also J. Lecler, *Toleration and Reformation*, 2 vols (1960).

conspiracy of Amboise, but to a consideration of Montmorency the loyal servant of Francis I and Henri II whose true heirs were François de Montmorency and other 'moderate' Catholic or Protestant nobles who remained loyal to Catherine de Medici's desire to work for peaceful solutions[13]. For the thirty-year political career of Catherine de Medici is clearly an important link between the relatively settled reigns of Henri II and Henri IV and her main aim was to protect the Valois dynasty thus permitting 'a regeneration of the monarchy which in the following century was to scale the heights of its power and achievement'[14].

Her attempts to counter the collapse of authority in the state and the policies she developed with Michel de L'Hospital in the early 1560s are seen, therefore, as the most significant element of continuity and the edicts of toleration or pacification themselves as a spinal cord running from the edicts of amnesty, granted at the end of the Conspiracy of Amboise, to the issue of the Edict of Nantes in 1598. According to this developing argument, the Edict of Nantes was at best a triumph, at worst a political necessity. It also represents the kind of settlement that Catherine would have imposed from the start but for her inability to control the Parlements as well as the Catholic nobility. By means of a post-hoc rationalization, all the stages on the way to the Edict of Nantes are high points and those responsible for them are on the side of the angels. More specifically, all who contributed ideologically, or politically, tend to be grouped generically as advocates of what emerged as the final solution to the French civil wars.

What is more, when one considers that the Peace of Monsieur of 1576 was the high point in the recognition of the Huguenots in the period, going well beyond the Edict of Nantes itself, the reasons for attaching moral significance to the political and military instruments of this edict — Alençon and his supporters — become apparent. And by connecting the pro-Bourbon, anti-Guise line, first with the fight to establish the edicts of toleration and, secondly, with the view of the pusillanimity, even tyranny, of Henri III, we have a formula which explains the need to create a party called *le parti des politiques* in the period 1572–1576.

After the Massacre of St Bartholomew leading figures, like Navarre,

---

[13] Seen as a model of wisdom and moderation by Ronsard and the Humanists, he is a key figure in F. Decrue de Stoutz, *Le parti des politiques au lendemain de la Saint Barthélemy* (1892).

[14] N. M. Sutherland 'Catherine de Medici and the Ancien Régime', *Princes, Politics and Religion, 1547–1589* (1984), p. 48.

Condé, Montmorency and Danville, were confined to court and each, in turn, conspired to leave, resulting in a series of dramatic escapes. There is also the conspiracy surrounding Alençon in 1574, organized by La Molle and Coconat. The issue is whether these various factional moves were coordinated and part of a national movement. Decrue de Stoutz certainly seeks to identify a community of interests and sees the Montmorency clan (including Damville), Alençon, a number of 'moderate' Catholic *nobles d'épée* like Cossé, as well as Condé and Navarre, forming a solid anti-Guise faction. They created, it seems, a kind of Valois-Bourbon axis, devoted to national interests and those of the legitimate monarchy. This contention is re-echoed, as we have seen, by many later scholars, notably Anglo-Saxon scholars, following Figgis and Allen. Salmon uses the term *Politiques* constantly and accepts the existence of the *Politique* party in the 1570s in order to clarify the complexities produced by the increased factional strife and the highly volatile political situation between 1572 and the death of Alençon in 1584.

Not so N. M. Sutherland who is particularly forceful on the point. Salmon uses the term *Politique* to describe all those (including Damville, the Alençon group) who, having fought in 1575–76, were persuaded to stop as a result of the Peace of Monsieur in 1576[15]. Sutherland, on the other hand, does not see any evidence for seeing these various moves and conspiracies as a clearly coordinated national movement. In fact, 'Alencon's treachery was ...the first instance of a new form of opposition, arising from within the royal family itself, and backed by a medley of greedy aspirants and one of a long series of shockingly cynical *malcontent* movements'[16]. She also points out the complexities of the strange coalition of Condé, Navarre, Damville, Montmorency and Alençon — not to mention the prince of Orange and Jean-Casimir of the Palatinate — that nearly brought down the monarchy in the summer of 1576 and forced on Catherine and Henri III a peace that was politically disastrous for the last Valois King, in that it provoked a massive Catholic reaction[17].

What emerges from this analysis are doubts about the usefulness of the term '*Politique* party' to describe a set of very loosely interconnected initiatives in the period between 1572 and 1584 taken by assorted professional malcontents from both religious persuasions who unscrupulously exploited the break-down of royal authority. There was no party and even

---

[15] Salmon, pp. 96–201.
[16] *Princes, Politics and Religion, 1547–1589*, p. 50.
[17] *The Huguenot Struggle for Recognition*, pp. 211–31.

to describe them as *Politiques* seems inappropriate except in the pejorative sense as used by pamphleteers of the League to designate all those who proposed to withdraw politics from subjection to the religious demand for purity[18]. Those who, like Decrue de Stoutz and scholars who follow him, see Alençon and others in the 1570s as the vital link between attempts at pacification in the 1560s and those leading up to the Edict of Nantes are imposing a pattern of continuity where none exists and systematizing at a level of generality not rooted in historical reality. In other words, what might seem to be part of a pattern in the shift of ideas and attitudes cannot easily be justified in the context of a more descriptive or *événementiel* kind of historical analysis.

The *Politique* party, then, does not as such exist. What, then, of the use of the word *politique* itself, used conventionally to describe the Alençon coalition as well as the group of politicians and thinkers in favour of a negotiated settlement to the civil wars and *ralliement* to Henri IV? From an examination of the currency of this word in sixteenth-century French it is possible to identify its meaning and ideological significance.

There are four main stages in what will perforce be a perfunctory analysis of the situation. The middle French word most commonly used is *police* meaning sound administration, especially of justice, and it is used in this way right through the Renaissance period by Commynes, Seyssel, La Boétie, Gentillet and Montaigne[19]. The appearance of the words *politica* and *politique* in Latin and medieval French is closely connected with the thirteenth-century translations of Aristotle's *Politics*[20]. These words imply the existence of an art or science of politics. All the writers of the *De regimine principum* tradition, including Budé, acknowledge this but insist that *la politique* is inseparable from *la morale*. Alongside this the adjective *politic* or *politique*, dating from the same period, soon comes to define the temporal and secular sphere as distinct from the spiritual sphere with echoes of the Church/State controversies of the Fourteenth Century. In this way

---

[18] Many of these pamphlets were studied by Weill, *Les théories sur le pouvoir royal ...*, esp. pp. 208–10, 215, 293–94. For another analysis see Bettinson, *The Intellectual Background and Development of the Toleration Policy of Catherine de Medici*, (unpub. Ph.D., Reading), 1973, chapter 9, esp. pp. 390–400.

[19] E. Huguet, *Dictionnaire de la langue française du seizième siècle*, 7 vols., 1925–27, vol. VI, pp. 61–2.

[20] E. Littré, *Dictionnaire de la langue française*, 4 vols., 1889, vol. III, p. 1201; W. von Wartburg, *Französisches etymologisches Wörterbuch*, 17 Bände, 1928–66, 9. Band, pp. 130–1.

the word has certain Gallican associations.

In the work of Calvin, however, there is a very clear distinction between the spiritual and 'politic' or civil spheres. This links with his trenchant attack on the faint-hearted occupants of the middle-ground in his *Excuse à Messieurs les Nicodémites* (1544) as well as the attack on *The Adultero-German Interim* (1548). For Calvin, 'specious Pacification' and moderation involved treachery and falsehood.

This distinction between *Politiques* and *religieux* was made by the Crown itself in respect of those who were involved in the Conspiracy of Amboise. By attempting to distinguish heretics from political malcontents and deal separately with each, the Crown felt safe in attacking all the leaders of armed protest as men with political ambitions, acting under cover of their avowed religious principles[21]. This basic approach underlay all royal legislation between the edicts of amnesty of 1560 and the edict of January 1562[22].

During the months leading up to the Colloquy of Poissy, Catherine de Medici and Charles IX were under great pressure from Philip II and the Pope because of an ambiguous attitude towards Calvinists. They complained that the Crown was meddling in spiritual matters, 'temporising' and abandoning its religious duty. Catherine defended her position by pointing to such political considerations as the youth of the King and the civil disorders of the realm. Accused by Guise of trying to 'boire à deux fontaines' and by Chantonnay and Philip II of wishing to swim 'entre deux eaux', Catherine and Charles IX point to the law of necessity, claiming that the toleration policy 'est pur politique'[23]. Thus, at a time when opinion in the Parlements, among many of the leading Catholic magnates, in Rome and in Madrid, is stiffening towards the religious concessions given to Huguenots and against the background of the final sessions of the Council of Trent, *politique* is firmly applied to those Catholics who refuse to commit themselves fully to the eradication of heresy. In particular, the targets are those in the royal Council and other supporters of the royal edicts.

In 1564 Granvelle, chief minister of Margaret of Parma in the Nether-

---

[21] Cf. Regnier de la Planche who distinguished between *les huguenots de religion* and *les huguenots d'Etat*.

[22] See N. M. Sutherland, *The Huguenot Struggle for Recognition*, pp.347–56.

[23] *Lettres de Catherine de Médicis*, vols. I-V, 1880–95, vols. VI-XI, 1897–1909, vol. I, pp. xciii, cxii, cxv, 188, 264–5, 223.

lands, applied it to the Châtillon brothers, when both Coligny and d'Andelot were strong in their support of the Crown after the Peace of Amboise in 1563, which had ended the first civil war[24].

> L'on est en opinion que l'amiral Châtillon et le sieur d'Andelot son frère, ou se rangeront à être Catholiques, ou faindront de l'être, pour s'entre-tenir au crédit et se pouvoir soutenir contre leurs adversaires. Je ne sais ce que j'en dois croire, mais bien suis-je pour moi en opinion que spécialement l'amiral se soit plus servi de la religion pour prétexte, et pour faire ses affaires et parvenir à ses desseins, que non pas pour y avoir fort assurément les opinions qu'il a démontrées et le tiens plus pour politique, *comme ils appellent en France*, que pour dévot.

Clearly a fairly new usage is being signalled, imposed by current religious controversies. It is reasonable to suppose that Granvelle is here echoing the official Spanish view originating with his son Chantonnay in the period of the Colloquy of Poissy.

By 1568 the noun form *les politiques* had fully emerged to designate luke-warm or suspect Catholics or those who deviate from the view represented by the Cardinal of Lorraine. The evidence for this may be found in the attacks by the Guisard Sorbonne professor, Jacques Charpentier, on Ramus, Lambin, Turnèbe and Forcadel: all scholars in the orbit of L'Hospital and the Pléiade. They had taken the oath of religious uniformity decreed in June 1568 and were accused of hypocrisy[25]. In particular, Lambin was censured in a series of polemics for his Protestant sympathies. Ramus had already fled to Condé's camp at St Germain. Ramus and his friends were accused of enthusiastically supporting 'cette loi d'amnestie, appelée vulgairement l'édit de pacification' and of praising 'les politiques, c'est à dire, ceux qui donnent plus aux hommes qu'à Dieu'[26].

It is not clear when this particular term first had currency, but it is likely that it was in the period 1567–68 during the controversy in the Sor-

---

[24] Letter to Bolwiller, 5.6.64. *Papiers d'Etat du Cardinal de Granvelle*, pub. Ch. Weiss, 9 vols, 1841–52, vol. XIII, p. 118.

[25] A. Fontanon, *Les édits et ordonnances des roys de France depuis S. Loys jusques à présent . . .*, Paris, 1585, B.L. 503. K. 4–6.

[26] Ch. Waddington, *Ramus. Sa vie, ses écrits et ses opinions*, 1855, p. 236; W.J. Ong, *Ramus, Method and the Decay of Dialogue*, 1958, pp. 17–35.

bonne over Jesuit affiliation at the latest, and at the earliest, in the course of the clash between Lorraine and the Court over the publication of the decrees of Trent from 1564 onwards. It is fairly clear to whom Charpentier was referring, for Ramus and Lambin had strong court connections with leading humanist diplomats, like Du Ferrier and Paul de Foix, and enjoyed the protection of Catherine de Medici, L'Hospital, Monluc and the Coligny brothers. Ramus and Lambin had also criticized the Sorbonne's opposition to the edict of January 1562. The name *les politiques* is used as a term of censure, therefore, to describe the architects of the religious policy and its professional supporters in the royal administration, although not, it seems, all those who express agreement with the policy.

From 1568 onwards the term is more current and becomes associated with a generalized attack on self-seeking, hypocrisy, untrustworthy behaviour and cameleon-like transformations. This connects with the growing attacks on courtiers and dissimulation generally seen, for example, in Buchanan's satire against William Lethington and in Etienne Jodelle's vicious tirade against Michel de L'Hospital describing him as *hérétique, pipeur, menteur, trompeur, athée* and *Protée*[27].

Thus, by 1572 at the latest, *les politiques* were identified as a group of politicians and administrators committed to a negotiated settlement with the Huguenots. Furthermore, measured against demands for the state to reflect the rule of God, they were a notorious and assorted band of courtiers and loyal servants of the Crown taxed for their insincerity and moral corruption. They were unsafe men.

The effect of the St Bartholomew massacre was to magnify these attacks on the Italianate court and its treacherous ways. Dissimulators, religious hypocrites, base flatterers, atheists, fickle slaves to fashion and circumstance, Machiavellians, *Politiques* — these were the names applied to the court and its supporters. To the fundamental antipathy to compromise in religious matters, seen in Calvin in the 1540s and 1550s and in ultramontane Catholics in the 1560s, must be added the growing wave of italophobia, in evidence since the middle of the reign of Francis I, and the culmination of this in the anti-tyrannical tracts of the Huguenots after 1572.

The butt of these attacks is always the same — the court of Catherine

---

[27] G. Buchanan, *The works of Mr. George Buchanan in the Scottish Language containing The Chamaeleon ...* (1823). E. Jodelle, *Oeuvres complètes*, 2 vols., 1965, vol. I, pp.229–301.

de Medici and her sons. One of them, Alençon, raised the banner in the name of his *cause publique* and organized a loose coalition in 1575–76, only to be dubbed by Leaguers a *Politique*. And when Henri III and Catherine vacillated between the League and the military power of these malcontents and appeared to yield to their demands in the far-reaching Peace of Monsieur, the Court was, once again, to be the focus of attacks on *les Politiques* in League pamphlets. J. Richer denigrated 'ces politiques et gens d'Estat' who wish to 'gouverner les Estats par leur sens et jugement naturel et par une prudence humaine'[28]. The author of *Le Karesme et moeurs du politique* exposed the shortcomings of *Politique* morality[29]:

> Politique est celui qui est immédiatement délibéré pour la commodité et aise de sa ville afin que l'utilité en redonde en sa maison.

Finally, in *La foi et religion des politiques de ce temps*, the *Politique* heresy was catalogued, and in a later poem the heresiarch was identified as none other than Michel de L'Hospital[30].

> L'auteur et le patron de l'erreur politique,
> Ce fut un grand vieillard, maigre, aride et étique,
> Portant l'œuil enfoncé et le grave sourcil,
> Chargé d'ans et de poil, d'horreur et de souci.

By 1586, Louis D'Orléans, in his *Avertissement des Catholiques anglais aux Catholiques français*, ascribed the decline of France to the corruption of morals, the toleration policy of the Crown, the subversive activities of Huguenot magnates and the inertia of Catholics. He trembled at the thought that the heir apparent, Henri of Navarre, was a Calvinist, and a relapsed heretic to boot, and considered that his only support would come from 'hérétiques', 'Catholiques unis', 'machiavélistes' and 'politiques'[31]. And Bichon's insistence in 1588 that the name 'politique' was 'souillé de mille vices'[32] was taken up in a sonnet entitled *Le Politique* in which all of the common criticisms were combined. The emphasis is on various forms of hypocrisy and 'feinte sainteté' and a preference for 'L'Etat'

---

[28] *Remonstrance au clergé de France*, quoted in Vivanti, *op. cit.*, p. 86.

[29] B.N. Lb^{34} 715 in Weill, *op. cit.*, pp.293–4.

[30] Quoted in Weill, *op. cit.*, pp. 215, note 2, 134.

[31] Weill, *op. cit.*, pp. 207–210.

[32] See Vivanti, *op. cit.*, pp. 145–6. Note also *La vie des traistres politicques navarrois*, Paris, R. Le Fizelier, and Lyons, L. Tantillon, 1589 (B.N. 8° Y^e 3474 Pièce). I am grateful to my colleague Richard Cooper for details of this pamphlet.

over 'la piété', for peace over a just war, for following the precepts of Machiavelli and not those of the Church. All these things 'sont les couleurs du masque Politique'[33].

This identification of *politique* behaviour in Leaguer pamphlets with support of Huguenots by luke-warm Catholics and attempts by the Crown to implement negotiated settlements rather than launch a holy war against heretics gives rise to some final thoughts about the issues raised in this study of the *Politiques*. The evidence presented suggests, at first sight, that the Salmon hypothesis (derived from Allen, Figgis, Decrue de Stoutz and Weill, as well as Vivanti) is correct. The issues and arguments struggling for dominance in the period of transition from Valois to Bourbon do bear a close similarity to those clustering round the pacification policy developed by Catherine de Medici and Michel de L'Hospital. All of the strands of what Allen calls the *Politique* ideology are explicit or heavily implicit in the statements and political behaviour of Catherine and her chancellor. The Gallican aspects, the traditional views of the French monarchy with absolutist overtones, the clear assertion that the dynasty must take whatever measures are *necessary* for its survival and that of the commonwealth, the need for judicial reform and a loyal bureaucracy: all these are present. There are even Erasmian, Stoic and Machiavellian prescriptions for prudence, the need to sometimes trim the sails and obey the law of necessity. Finally, that historicism which Salmon sees as emerging in the 1580s is very much present in the humanist circles of the 1560s. In the collaboration between the world of scholarship and the practical world of the royal council one is tempted to see the meeting of theory and practice.

However, is it useful to use the term *Politique* both for the *conjoncture* of the 1560s and that of the 1580s? We have already eliminated the Alençon coalition as the connecting link between these two ideological and political initiatives. Even so, given the close connection between the term *Politique* and the pacification policy and its apparent challenge to solutions based on religious absolutism, it is tempting to adopt the term to describe the shift of ideas from 1559 to 1589, even though it stems from the overactive imagination of Leaguer pamphleteers.

If the term is to be used, it must always be borne in mind that the relevant set of ideas is extremely difficult to pin down and, what is more, representative figures not easy to identify. There was in the 1560s a vision

---

[33] In P. Matthieu, *Histoire des derniers troubles de France*, Paris, 1600, quoted in Vivanti, *op. cit.*, p. 86.

of the state which separated politics from religion, implicitly at least, but it was the vision of a very small number and it was supported in the 1560s and the 1580s by many who remained firmly attached to the notion of religious uniformity and who were prepared for the sake of the survival of the state to lend their provisional support.

What is certain is that to represent the toleration policy and its advocates as heralding a major change in the nature of French society and a secularisation of the state cannot be justified any more than Allen's and Salmon's use of the word *Politique* to suggest that such a process took place in France during the transfer of power from Valois to Bourbon. Even if the ideological excesses of the League provoked some to grope towards the notion of a secular absolutism in the 1580s and 1590s, the reality, as the development of royal absolutism in the seventeenth century shows, was a gradual return to the dominant notion of 'une foi, une loi, un roi'.

4. The Blois Assassinations:
Sources in the Vatican

RICHARD COOPER

The fourth centenary of this fateful preemptive strike seems an appropriate occasion to seek new light on the events in contemporary documents. The collections of correspondence belonging to this period in the Vatican Archives are remarkably rich, as was noted by L'Epinois in the study he published just before the tercentenary[1]: he made some use of the volumes of dispatches from the legate in France, Cardinal Morosini, and drew upon other documents sent to Sixtus V during 1588–89, some of which had also been published by Tempesti over a century before[2]. There is however more material than he or Pastor noticed, scattered in various *fondi* in both the Secret Archives and the Library. The Nuncial archives, now called *Segretario di Stato, Francia,* include, besides the regular dispatches, many original letters from Henri III, from the Duc de Guise and his family, as well as a number of *avvisi*. The miscellanies of documents in the former Castel Sant'Angelo Archives contain translations of letters, submissions from pressure-groups in France, collections of pamphlets — mostly in Italian

---

[1] P. de L'Epinois, *La Ligue et les Papes*, Paris, 1886; cf. F. Rocquain, *La France et Rome pendant les guerres de religion*, Paris, 1924, pp. 331–84.

[2] C. Tempesti, *Storia della vita e geste di Sisto Quinto*, Rome, 1754, II, pp. 109–14.

translation, and various briefing documents collected by the commission of Cardinals preparing the *Monitorium* of May 1589, including opinions of canon lawyers and testimonies to the character of the King. Two further important volumes of documents are in the Library rather than the Archives[3].

Attention will be focussed here on the Vatican material which sheds light on the events of the 23–24 December 1588, on the factors which may have motivated the assassinations, and on the position of the Legate, who is an important and highly controversial witness. A second study will concentrate on the aftermath and on the war of words between the Royal and the Guise parties, each seeking to convince the Pope of the justice of its cause[4].

The letters of Cardinal Morosini confirm how, throughout 1588, Sixtus V had been working through the Nuncio for accommodation between the Duc de Guise and the King[5]. They are borne out by a number of letters from the Duke to the Pope and to Cardinal Montalto: one of 23 July expresses delight at the return of peace and reconciliation, defining the King's declaration as 'expresse' and 'trescrestienne' and observing that the Pope should be overjoyed that his conciliatory policies have borne fruit[6]. A letter of Cardinal Lenoncourt to Montalto of 1 August affirms that the King himself is seeking peace and concord and places great hopes in the imminent meeting at Chartres, at which the Cardinal de Bourbon and the Duc de Guise will pledge allegiance to the King and cement peace with him[7]. A further letter of the Duke of 5 August congratulates Sixtus on the beneficial influence he has exerted on the King and on promoting Morosoni to cardinal, whose advice he promises to follow[8].

Following the *pacte d'union*, the Pope continued to urge upon the Duke concord and loyalty. He charged Gondi to press this with him, and the Cardinal reports to the Pope on 8 September on their interview: in reponse

---

[3]   B(ibliotheca) A(postolica) V(aticana) *Urb.Lat.*, 868 and 1113.

[4]   'The aftermath of the Blois assassinations: documents in the Vatican', forthcoming in *French History*.

[5]   See for instance those of May 1588 in A(rchivio) S(egreto) V(aticano) *Segr. di Stato: Francia*, 28.

[6]   *Segr. di Stato: Francia*, 26, fol. 157.

[7]   *Ibid.* 23, fol. 15.

[8]   *Ibid.* 26, fol. 163.

to strenuous urgings to cooperate with Henri, especially in the stamping out of heresy, and to be a 'buono et leale suggetto', Guise has promised absolute fidelity[9]. Indeed he had already written as much to Sixtus on 18 August, asserting not only that 'mon but n'est que de bien faire, que de servir fidelement mon Roy, employant ma vie pour son estat', but also that the King is not unaware of this, 'estant fort bien informée et monstrant en avoir beaucoup de satisfaction'[10]. Such protestations are reiterated in his letters of 13 September and 15 October[11].

Henri III himself responds by publishing a highly flattering testimonial in favour of the Duke's brother, Cardinal Louis de Lorraine. His letter to Sixtus of 15 November 1588, published here (Document 1) and bearing his autograph signature, makes formal request for the Legation of Avignon, resigned by the Cardinal de Bourbon in favour of the Cardinal de Guise, arguing that for this strategic post[12] he needs a man of absolute loyalty to himself[13]. This testimonial contrasts eloquently with the official Royal justification of the Cardinal's assassination five weeks later on grounds of disloyalty and *lèse-majesté*.

The Savoyard occupation, in the autumn, of Saluzzo and other French-held outposts in Piedmont gave a new twist to events[14]. Sixtus wrote an autograph letter to Henri de Guise defending this enterprise of Charles Emmanuel and suggesting that these places were better in the hands of the Catholic Piedmontese than prey to heretic Frenchmen. The last traced letter of the Duke is his four-page autograph reply to the Pope of 10 December, published below (Document 2)[15], in which, far from showing disloyalty to Henri III, he argues against the Pope on behalf of the French cause. Fearing that this invasion of French territory will distract French arms from the purpose of the Estates General in Blois, namely the uniting of France behind the King in waging war on heretics, a cause which Savoy should be supporting not subverting, Guise asserts in proudly patriotic language that

---

[9] *Ibid.* 23, fos. 40–42.

[10] *Ibid.* 26, fol. 167.

[11] *Ibid.* 26, fos. 170, 179ᵛ–180.

[12] Threatened with Huguenot infestation, see Tempesti, *op.cit.*, II, p. 189.

[13] *Ibid.* 24, fol. 197, Blois, 15 Nov. 1588.

[14] Tempesti, *op.cit.*, II, pp. 87–88, 99–105.

[15] This confirms Morosini's report of 24 Dec., *Segr. di Stato*, 27, fol. 325 and the later testimony of the Duke's secretary Péricard. See: *Revue retrospective*, IV, 1834, pp.214–15; *Archives curieuses de l'histoire de France*, Paris, 1836, XII, 198; Valois, *op.cit.*, pp. 275–76.

the defence of French soil is a higher priority for him and his family than the interests of the Church; he consequently urges Sixtus to intervene and snuff out this diversionary spark before it ignites[16]. This appeal contrasts with Morosini's report in cipher of 8 December[17], according to which Guise had asserted in Council that even if the Duke of Savoy returned the occupied territory promptly, this would not be sufficient to purge the offence, and had called for a punitive campaign against Savoy. Whilst the majority of the Council preferred an accommodation so that they might press on with the war against heresy, the King's position was reportedly close to that of Guise and won the day, opting for retaliation: 'Hora pare che con questa rissolutione della guerra Sua Maestà si trova molto ristretto con Mons. de Guisa'[18]. Morosini sees as further evidence of rapprochement between Guise and Henri III the fact that some close Royal counsellors, including the physician Miron and his brother, had been dismissed because the Duke did not like them.

Two dispatches by Morosini of 19 December give first-hand evidence of relations between the King and the Duke in the few days before the assassination[19]. In the first deciphered letter we learn that Guise had been complaining that Henri did not take him into his confidence, and had been dragging his feet on putting into practice what had been agreed in Council. So the Legate went to see Henri, and urged him to find ways to satisfy the Duke. When the King asked him for suggestions, Morosini replied by encouraging him not to believe the evil spoken against the Duke, and by suggesting that he win the Duke's allegiance by helping him to meet his massive debts and by giving him responsibilities, especially military commands, in which he could exercise his authority. The King reportedly welcomed this advice and asked the Legate to pass it on to the Queen Mother, who in turn gave her support when he called on her the following day[20]. By contrast the second dispatch speaks openly of the 'mali sodisfattioni che tuttavia si nutriscono fra Sua Maestà et Mons^or di Guisa'[21], although on the question of war against Savoy they were in agreement. Indeed, Guise was even more ardent for war than the King, leaving himself open to suspicion that he was

[16] *Segr. di Stato*, 26, fol. 192.

[17] *Segr. di Stato*, 27, fol. 307.

[18] *Ibid.* fol. 310.

[19] *Ibid.* 27, fos. 311^v–12^v, 321–23^v.

[20] *Ibid.* 27, fos. 311^v–312^v.

[21] Confirmed by the Savoy ambassador who wrote on 23 Dec. that 'le Roi et Guise sont en plus grande defiance que jamais', *Arch. Stato*, Turin, Lettere ministri, m^o9, lett.100.

seeking thereby to curry favour with nobles and people alike. He was even reported as threatening that unless the King declared war to punish this princeling, he would quit the court 'per non essere partecipe della vergogna che riceverà Sua Maestà quando comportasse questo affronto'[22]. Not only was the Duke seeking to upstage the King in his defence of national honour, but he was also reportedly planning to use his authority with the Estates to make political changes:

'Sua Eccellenza, che conosce il suo vantaggio per il gran potere che ha con essi stati, vorria con l'autorità loro vedere di necessitare il Re a fare un consiglio segreto per trattare tutte le cose del Regno, nel quale non ci fosse alcuno contrario al suo partito, in che non so quello che potrà fare, non essendo possibile che il Re di buona voglia sia per acconsentire; et l'usare violenza [fol. 323ᵛ], come hanno fatto in diverse altre cose [...], potria essere pericoloso di fare rompere; et però io non manco di fare ogni sorte d'officio affine che si conservi la unione et la pace'[23].

This fear that the Ligue was plotting against the King and might use violence was reinforced by the reported words of the Duke to the King on 22 December, asserting in threatening terms that but for the meeting of the Estates General he (Guise) would have killed many of the people around the King who were working against Guise; hearing this Henri is alleged to have decided secretly to strike first[24].

A second factor in the King's decision is alleged to have been the intervention of the Duke's brother Mayenne who, according to Morosini, had sent Alfonso Ornano from Lyons, arriving at Blois on 18 December, warning Henri to beware of Guise who was plotting against him[25]. After the murder the King made much of this, and tried to place some of the responsibility on Mayenne: 'scrivendo a Sua Eccellenza [=Mayenne] che mossa principalmente da l'avvertimento che lei li haveva mandato per il soddetto Signor Alfonso, conforme a molti che da diverse parti haveva havuta del medesimo tenore, si era resoluta a fare quella essecutione contra il Duca di Guisa'[26]. There is however no firm evidence that Mayenne dished his

---

[22] *Ibid.* 27, fol. 322ᵛ; cf.Miron's report of Guise's threatened resignation as commander of the Royal armies, *Archives curieuses, op.cit.*, XII, 125–26.

[23] *Segr. di Stato*, 27, fos. 323–323ᵛ.

[24] Morosini dispatch of 23 Dec., *Segr. di Stato*, 27, fol. 314ᵛ, pub. Tempesti, *op.cit.*, II, p. 109.

[25] *Ibid.* fos. 314ʳ–ᵛ.

[26] Morosini — Montalto, 23 Dec., *Segr.di Stato*, 27, fol. 318.

brother, and it would seem that the King has distorted Mayenne's words for propaganda reasons[27]. An alternative rumour circulating in Blois was that the King had been moved to kill the Guises because he had heard that Mayenne had been killed in Lyons and that Aumale had been arrested in Paris[28], or, according to another rumour, that Mayenne had been captured in Lyons and that the King had ordered him to be executed also[29]. This might suggest that Henri saw an opportunity to neutralize the whole Guise family.

Vatican sources confirm that rumours of the King's intentions had leaked out and that Guise had been warned, even as much as four or five days before (the date of 18 December would coincide with the arrival of Ornano). The warnings became more urgent on the night of 22 December, telling him not to go to the Council early or unaccompanied; but he replied to the pleadings of his mother Madame de Nemours that he could not believe that the King, after all his promises, could have an *animo così diabolico* as to use treacherous violence[30]. The question of the Duke's gullibility was to become an important topic of debate in a long pamphlet published after the assassination[31].

Such momentous events could not pass without signs and portents. The Capuchin provincial Bernardo Osimo reported that a week before the murder a novice had had a vision of the murder, and that on the day of the Cardinal's death another novice had been sent a vision from St Francis of the death of two great men and of tribulations in store for France[32].

It is clear from the varying accounts of L'Estoile, of Miron, of Valois, of Patte, of Matthieu, of Cavriana, from the various depositions before the Parlement de Paris, not to mention from *Ligue* pamphlets like Boucher's *La vie et faits notables de Henry de Valois*, that there is no such thing as a true version of the events of 23–24 December. Even Pierre Matthieu admits that 'il y a merveilleuse incertitude aux circonstances de ceste histoire à

---

[27] Valois, *op.cit.*, pp. 253–56.

[28] Document 3, fol. 194[v].

[29] A. S. V. *Misc. Arm.* I, 21, fol. 204.

[30] Document 3, fol. 192[v]; B. A. V. *Urb. Lat.* 868, fol. 169[v].

[31] *Considerations sur le meurtre commis en la personne de feu M. le Duc de Guise*, s.l.n.d., B. N. Lb[34] 555, and Italian transl. in B. A. V. *Urb. Lat.* 868 fos. 236–49.

[32] A. S. V. *Misc. Arm.* I, 21, fol. 394.

laquelle chacun donne tel visage et telle couleur qu'il luy plaist'[33]. What light is shed by the accounts preserved in the Vatican? The documents in question are: two copies of an important undated *avviso*, apparently two different translations of an unidentified French original hostile to the King and critical of the Legate (Document 3); another *avviso* of 24 December which is not hostile to the assassinations (Document 4); the testimony of Bernardo Osimo, provincial of the Capuchins[34], and Morosini's deciphered dispatches of 23 & 24 December[35].

On the night of 22 December the King ordered his coach to come early and summoned three captains and a dozen or more of his guard of 45 to attend on him early the following morning, pretending that he planned to go hunting or to make a journey[36], and intimating to the captains that he intended to punish some disobedient soldiers. These sources do not mention the subterfuge whereby the castle keys were obtained from Guise by a ruse and the assassins spirited in during the night[37]. When the guards arrived at 5 a.m. he told them that either he or Guise must die that morning, and they in their turn offered to kill the Duke[38]; the King then hid them in his antechamber and withdrew with Lognac, two other captains and Alfonso Ornano into his study, from where he gave orders for the arrest of the Cardinals de Guise and Bourbon[39].

One hour later at 6 a.m., Guise went to chapel to hear mass, and finding it locked, said his prayers outside instead[40]. He then went to the Council chamber where he paced around alone for half an hour 'assai di mala voglia', according to one version, or 'molto malinconico', according to another[41].

---

[33] P. Matthieu, *Histoire des derniers troubles*, Paris, 1613, IV, 157.

[34] B. A. V. *Barberini* 5655, fos. 102–5, published in Valois, *op.cit.*, pp. 299–302.

[35] *Segr. di Stato*, 27, fos. 314–19 & 324–25, pub. in part by Tempesti, *op.cit.*, II, pp. 109–12.

[36] Document 4, fol. 204^v; document 3, fol. 192. French sources mention other excuses, such as going to Notre Dame de Cléry for Christmas, *Archives curieuses*, *op.cit.*, XII, 124, 144, 200; Valois, *op.cit.*, p. 260.

[37] Valois, *op.cit.*, pp. 259–60.

[38] Document 3, fol. 194.

[39] *Ibid.* fol. 194^{r-v}; document 4 fol. 204^v; Morosini's letter of 23 Dec., *Segr. di Stato*, 27, fos. 314^v–315, Tempesti, *op.cit.*, pp. 109–10.

[40] No other sources give this, although Valois, p. 262, speaks of his stopping to pray at an oratory.

[41] Document 3, fol. 192 (and in the other translation, *Urb. Lat.* 868, fol. 168^v).

These sources describe the arrival of other members of the Council, but do not mention the warnings and portents, nor that the Council had begun its deliberations when the Royal secretary Revol summoned Guise to see the King[42]. On the threshold of the King's study the Duke was attacked by sixteen guards[43], some of whom immobilized him, while two stabbed him in the throat, thinking he might be in armour, one in his right breast, one with a hauberk in his kidneys, four others in his navel[44]; he put up stout resistance but was unable to draw his sword[45]. Mortally wounded he was dragged out of study by his feet, watched by the King who called out, 'Finitelo, finitelo d'amazzare'[46]. Another man, not one of killers, urged the dying Duke to commend his soul to God: Guise raised hands and eyes to heaven, crossed his hands on his breast and died 'con un profondissimo sospiro'[47]. Henri ordered the body to be left on a trestle in the antechamber where it was covered in a 'panno di rasa' and where it remained until after Christmas[48].

In the Council chamber the Cardinal de Guise heard the commotion and tried to flee, but soldiers barred the exits and he and the Archbishop of Lyons were arrested by the Captain of the Guard, Larchan, whilst other prominent members and supporters of the family were similarly imprisoned[49]. A false rumour was spread that someone had tried to attack the King[50]: the castle gates were locked, troops occupied the town and the Prevost went to the hall where the Third Estate was in session and broke down the doors, summoning the leaders to accompany him to answer charges of

---

[42] Some sources say there was no formal meeting of the Council.

[43] Other sources say between 6 and 12, see *Archives curieuses, op.cit.*, XII, 83, 133, 145; *Bull. Soc. Hist. France* I, 1834, p. 81.

[44] Document 3, fol. 192; document 4, fol. 205.

[45] Morosini, 23 Dec., *Segr. di Stato*, 27, fol. 315, Tempesti, *op.cit.*, II, pp. 109–10. The Duc d'Aumale claimed that Guise was unarmed, A. S. V. *Arch. Arc. Arm.* I XVIII 6548, fol. 63, 31 Dec.

[46] No mention is made of the King having kicked the body, as reported in Ligue pamphlets.

[47] Document 3, fol. 192[v]; cf. *Archives curieuses*, XII, 136

[48] Document 3, fol. 193[v]; yet document 4, fol. 205 says it was placed in 'un vecchio gabinetto'; French depositions say it was covered with a Turkish carpet, *Revue retrospective*, IV, 1834, pp. 222, 225; *Archives curieuses, op.cit.*, XII, 206.

[49] Document 3, fos. 192[v]–193; document 4, fol. 205; Morosini, 23 Dec., *Segr. di Stato*, 27, fol. 315[v], in Tempesti, II, pp. 109–10.

[50] Document 3, fol. 193; Morosini, *lett.cit.*, of 23 Dec., fol. 316; *Archives curieuses, op. cit.*, XII, 210.

complicity in the attempt on the King's life and threatening them with death if they did not comply. Among those arrested was the Duke's secretary Péricard, who managed, according to French sources, to destroy most of the Duke's papers[51]; but one *avviso* reports what looks like Royalist propaganda, namely that the papers incriminated the Duke, revealing that he had been receiving 150, 000 *écus* a year from the King of Spain and that he had been plotting to capture the King's person[52].

Accounts are given of the important interview of the King with the Queen Mother immediately after the murder. Morosini reports simply that he claimed to have acted in self-defence and to suppress a potential tyrant[53]. The *avvisi* report him as saying 'che già era Re di Francia per haver morto il Duca di Ghisa', and as apologizing for not having told her anything about it beforehand, claiming to have been inspired by God to act thus. Morosini says she was dumbfounded and could not say a word in reply; but the *avvisi* show her more eloquent, replying either 'piaccia a Dio che'l successo sia secondo il vostro desiderio' or 'che più tosto havea messo il Regno in perditione, almeno l'havesse conferito col Cardinale Legato'. Henri's mood is clear from his reported rejoinder: 'Avvenga quello che può venire, ch'io sto vendicato!'[54].

After seeing his mother, the King made a show of maintaining business as usual, going to public mass with Cardinal Vendôme and dining publicly in the usual room with the same Cardinal waiting on him, 'senza mostrare alteratione alcuna in viso', other than asserting that the Duke had behaved in such a way that he could no longer tolerate him[55]. He refused the Legate an audience but sent Cardinal Gondi to him, explaining the motives for the killing and assuring him that the other prisoners would not be harmed![56]

All sources agree on the time and place of the Cardinal de Guise's death, although they are unclear about the manner and about who carried

---

[51] *Archives curieuses, op. cit.*, XII, 194–95; *Revue retrospective*, IV, 211; Valois, *op.cit.*, pp. 266–67.

[52] Document 4, fol. 205ᵛ; cf. a Huguenot report in *Archives curieuses, op. cit.*, XII, 151 and Miron's evidence, *ibid.*, p. 136.

[53] Morosini, 23 Dec., *Segr. di Stato*, 27, fol. 315, Tempesti, II, pp. 109–10.

[54] Document 3, fol. 194; document 4, fol. 205ᵛ; cf.other reports in Valois, pp. 270–71.

[55] Document 3, fol. 194; document 4, fol. 205ᵛ; Morosini, 23 Dec., *Segr. di Stato*, 27, fos. 316ᵛ–317, Tempesti, II, pp. 109–10.

[56] Morosini, 23 Dec., *Segr. di Stato*, 27, fol. 316ᵛ.

out the deed[57]. There was evidently some resistance to the prospect of killing a man of the Church, and indeed this murder caused the Legate even more consternation than that of the Duke, although little surprise, given the open hostility between the Cardinal and the King[58]. L'Estoile, as we know, rather approved of the death of the Cardinal[59].

The Duke's mother sent Bernardo Osimo to Catherine asking for the return of the Duke's body and for protection for her children; Catherine replied that she no longer had any influence over her son, who had not listened to her for twelve years, but she promised to ask for the body; her request met with the retort that the King needed the body, thereby arousing suspicions about his intentions[60]. Osimo's own report of Catherine's words to him is most revealing and prophetic: 'Eh misero, che ha fatto'! Reflecting that it was wrong to kill a man of the Church, she added, 'Et che diranno i principi del mondo? Pregate per lui, che n'ha più bisogno che mai; che lo vedo incaminato ad una gran rovina, et temo che perderà il corpo, l'anima et il regno'. Seeking someone to blame, she continued: 'Dio perdoni al papa, che lui ha gran parte in questo male! Che il re mi disse che il papa gl'haveva scritto molte volte che si levasse dinanzi tutti i seditiosi et turbatori del suo regno, se voleva vivere pacificamente, et che i tumultuosi non potevano castigarsi altramente che con la morte, et che imparava da lui che, oltre che gli lo scriveva, anco gli ne dava essempio con l'opere; et che perciò havea fatto tutto questo'[61]. The argument that Sixtus bore some responsibility for the murders is one which the King was himself to use in his note to the Legate and in his letter to the Pope written straight after the murder[62].

Following the King's refusal to return the bodies, rumours circulated as to what had been done with them. Catherine told Osimo that according to Henri they had been buried, a report confirmed in an *avviso*[63]; the

---

[57] Document 3, fos. 193[V] & 194[V]–95; Morosini, 24 Dec., *Segr. di Stato*, 27, fol. 324; Tempesti, II, pp. 111–12; cf. *Archives curieuses, op.cit.*, XII, 91–95.

[58] Morosini, 23 Dec., *Segr.di Stato*, 27, fol. 317[V]; Morosini, 24 Dec., *ibid.*, fol. 324; cf. *Revue retrospective*, III, 1834, p. 448.

[59] P. de L'Estoile, *Journal du règne de Henri III*, Paris, 1943, ed. L-R. Lefèvre, 1943, p. 582.

[60] Document 3, fol. 193[V].

[61] Valois, *op.cit.*, p. 300.

[62] *Segr. di Stato*, 27, fol. 325[V] (also in Tempesti, II, pp. 112–13) and *ibid.*, 24, fol. 143.

[63] Valois, *op.cit.*, p. 301; document 4, fol. 206.

Legate himself believed this until Osimo opened his eyes to the truth[64]. During the night of 25 December, the King had ordered the heads to be cut off the bodies and kept, and the trunks to be burned, a deed of which L'Estoile approved — 'supplice digne de leur ambition'[65] — but which fired the imagination of *Ligue* pampleteers[66]; depositions at the Paris enquiry affirm that the bloodstained room still stank a month later[67].

If the King had intended, by this coup, to reassert his authority, there is evidence of short-term success: Morosini reported that although some members had sought safety in flight, the Estates were apparently coming to heel. Already on 24 December the King ordered them to press on with their deliberations[68]. Two days later we read: 'Insomma tutte le cose hanno mutata faccia, e hora si vide in tutti grandissimo ossequio et massime nelli stati che dicono di voler dare ogni satisfattione a Sua Maestà'[69]. To head off criticism Henri also gave orders for the war against the Huguenots to be stepped up, lest people thought he had only been carrying it on to please the Duke of Guise and not out of his own inclination[70]. He devoted most of 23 and 24 December to the feverish composition of over forty self-justifying dispatches which he sent off to his ambassadors abroad, to the *parlements* and major cities of France, and to the Pope[71].

The attitude of the Pope and the position of the Legate are highly significant here. Both Henri and Catherine indicate that Sixtus had incited the King to suppress troublesome rivals; and there was suspicion that Morosini had connived at the assassinations. There is evidence that the news of the murders provoked an anti-Italian reaction, and that the houses of

[64] Valois, *op.cit.*, p. 303.

[65] L'Estoile, *Journal...*, *op.cit.*, p. 582.

[66] *Histoire au vray du meurtre et assassinement proditoirement commis en la personne de Mons. le Duc de Guise*, s.l., 1589, pp. 44–54 (B. N. Lb[34] 546A); *Archives curieuses*, *op.cit.*, XII, 96–97; K. C. Cameron, *Henri III, a maligned or a malignant King?*, Exeter, 1978, p. 168.

[67] *Archives curieuses*, *op.cit.*, XII, 213.

[68] Morosini — Montalto, 24 Dec., *Segr. di Stato*, 22, fol. 312.

[69] *Ibid.*, 22, fol. 317[v], 26 Dec.

[70] Morosini, 23 Dec., *Segr. di Stato*, 27, fos. 317[v]–318, Tempesti, II, pp. 109–10.

[71] See the follow-up study mentioned in note 3; also B. N. Ms. Dupuy 245 and *Revue retrospective*, III, 1834, pp. 432–55.

three prominent Italians were ransacked[72]. An *avviso* of 27 January claims that four days before the murders the Legate had been seen with his secretary going to the house of Cardinal Gondi, and that this had caused great scandal and suspicion that Morosini was in cahoots with Henri III[73]. The Legate himself claims to have known nothing about the murder until the visit from Gondi; his servants just saw the castle gates being locked, and heard the false rumour of the attempt on the King's life; but the King refused to grant him an audience until 25 December[74]. Morosini's letters express total bewilderment, especially at the second killing, and Osimo says he found him speechless with shock[75]. He was in a difficult position, having been promoting Sixtus' policy of reconciliation, and yet remaining in close rapport with Florentine bankers in Paris, including Orazio Rucellai who supported the assassination of Guise. Osimo told Morosini bluntly of the rumours 'che habbia havuta prescienza del caso assai prima, et — quello che è peggio — che vi habbia havuto parte et assenso', and an open row broke out between them[76]. Osimo reproached him furiously for not having openly condemned the deeds, declared him totally compromised and urged him to leave the Court without delay, as he himself was shortly to do. The difference between their reactions is seen in the fact that Osimo ordered his Capuchins to refuse henceforth to say mass for the King, whilst Morosini could not see that this ban was necessary. When the King turned up to mass there on Christmas day, Osimo prepared to carry out his threat, but the Legate managed to avert a diplomatic incident by detaining the King outside in the park until mass was over[77].

One *avviso* casts grave doubts on the Legate's conduct, reporting that at first he had avoided talking to the King, but then had had audience on 26 December in the park, and although no one could hear what they said, they appeared to be laughing and joking[78]. Morosini's own version is that King had summoned him on that date, and that during their protracted interview in the gardens he had defended his actions, citing the Cardinal de Guise's threat to give him a Capuchin tonsure, the high-handed conduct of

---

[72] *Segr. di Stato*, 21, fol. 197.

[73] A. S. V. *Misc. Arm.* I, 21, fol. 210.

[74] Morosini, 23 Dec., *Segr. di Stato*, 27, fol. 316^{r-v}, Tempesti, II, pp. 109–10; cf. the note from Henri III of 24 Dec., *ibid.*, fol. 325^{v}, Tempesti, II, pp. 112–13.

[75] Valois, *op.cit.*, p. 296.

[76] *Ibidem*, pp. 297–299.

[77] *Ibidem*, pp. 298–99.

[78] Document 3, fol. 195; confirmed in the Huguenot report in *Archives curieuses*, *op.cit.*, p. 153.

the Guises towards him, the warnings received from Mayenne and Aumale, and the way Guise had been opposing him in the Estates General, turning the people against him and undermining his authority. He stated that 'per sei giorni continui era stato risolutissimo di non lo voler fare, temendo di non offendere Dio, ma che considerando che Sua Divina Maestà l'haveva fatto nascere Re et che ogni ragione voleva che egli per tale si facesse ubedire', and remembering the Pope's advice 'che bisogna farsi ubedire et castigare quelli che l'offendono, era venuto in risolutione di farli più tosto morire loro che aspettare che loro facessero morire lui'; their influence in the Kingdom made it impossible to put them on trial, and so he had no alternative but to assassinate them. The Legate made a tactical reply, defining the murders as a 'gravissimo errore', but arguing pragmatically that, since nothing could change the past, the King must repent, seek absolution and try to win back his reputation by fighting heresy[79].

It is clear that Morosini chose throughout not to react openly or to express public condemnation, but that he stalled for time, sent all the news to Rome and waited for guidance. This policy was widely interpreted as evidence of his own (and probably papal) connivance: the *avviso* of 27 January reports that the Legate had no hesitation about talking to the King and even appeared to be finding excuses for his actions[80], and the Duc d'Aumale openly challenged the Pope to deny that he had assented to the Blois assassinations[81]. The propaganda campaigns were only just beginning.

1

Henri III — Sixtus V, Blois, 15 November 1588. [A. S. V. *Segretario di Stato: Francia*, 24,

Tressainct pere,

Nostre trescher et tresamé oncle le Cardinal de Bourbon auroit cyde-vant resigné la legation d'Avignon en faveur de nostre trescher et bien amé

---

[79] *Segr. di Stato*, 27, fol. 326, 31 Dec.; some in Tempesti, II, pp. 113–14.
[80] A. S. V. *Misc. Arm.* I, 21, fol. 210.
[81] A. S. V. *Arch. Arc.* I–XVIII 6548, fol. 63, 31 Dec.1588.

cousin le Cardinal de Guyse, dont neantmoings il n'avoit encores obtenu l'expedition de vostre Saincteté, et d'aultant que nous desirons en cela le contentement de nostredict cousin, non seullement pour la bonne volonté que nous luy portons, mais aussy pour nous estre de grande importance es affaires de noz pays de Languedoc et Provence que ladicte charge soit en main de personne qui nous soit confidente et affectionnee au bien de nostre service comme est nostredict cousin, de la devotion duquel en nostre endroict nous avons toute fiance; à ceste cause nous avons ordonné à nostre amé et feal cousin et ambassadeur pres vostre Saincteté, le Marquis de Pisany, et à nostre aussy amé et feal le sr. de Gondy que nous envoyons presentement devers elle, de la supplier de nostre part, comme nous faisons pareillement par la presente, que le bon plaisir d'icelle soit pour l'amour de nous et en nostre contemplation accorder et commander l'expedition de ladicte legation en faveur de nostredict cousin, selon qu'il en sera faict plus particuliere instance et requeste à vostre Saincteté en nostre nom par lesdicts srs. Marquis et de Gondy, lesquelz elle croira, s'il luy plaist, de ce qu'ilz luy diront sur ce de nostre part, comme nous mesmes. Et en cest endroict nous prierons Dieu, Tressainct pere, qu'il vueille icelle vostre Saincteté longuement preserver, maintenir et garder au bon regime, gouvernement et administration de sa saincte Eglise. Escrit à Bloys le xvme jour de Novembre 1588.

Vostre bon et devot filz,

Henry.

2

Henri, Duc de Guise — Sixtus V, Blois, 10 December 1588. [A. S. V. *Segretario di Stato: Francia*, 26 fos. 192–193^v; autograph].

Tressaint pere,

Ie tiens à tresgrant honneur et speciale faveur qu'il ayt pleu à vostre Sainteté par ses lettres escrites le xiiiie du moys passé m'envoier ses intentions et son tresclair et exquis iugement sur le fait de Piemont, ayant fort pesé les graves et importantes considerations qu'elle met en avant, quy ne peuvent partir que d'un amour vrayement paternel, sogneux du bien et repos universel des princes crestiens, ne montrant autre affection ny interest que de maintenir l'estroite lyaison de tous. Mais son bon plaisir sera de m'excuser sy, avecq la reverence et submission de tresfidel serviteur et filz d'obedience que ie luy suis, ie la supplie treshumblement de vouloir balancer egalement les raisons du Roy mon souverain seigneur, les iustes resentymens d'un puissant estat, la valeur et courage de l'une des premieres nations du monde, plus nourrye et acoustumee aux conquestes et à l'acroissement des lymites de la monarchye qu'à la dyminution, n'estymant la pouvoir souffrir de quy que ce soit sans encourir un tresgrant blasme et dechoir de l'ancyenne reputation et generosité françoise.

Vostre Sainteté se representera pareillement les causes et ocasions quy ont meu le Roy mon seigneur de convocquer cette generale assemblee d'estatz, [fol. 192ᵛ] et à quel but tous les gens de bien tendent, quy n'est que de restaurer l'eglize et extirper toutes erreurs. Et ce saint desir meryte d'estre conforté des vœux de tous les Roys et potentatz quy font mesme profession de foy que nous, tant pour la charyté crestyenne que pour un commun benefice qui en redonde à eux et au salut et tranquilyté de leurs peuples. C'est pourquoy, tressaint pere, deslors que le remuement de Saluces fut aryvé, ie feiz entendre à vostre Sainteté le regret que i'en avois, avecq beaucoup de doute et d'aprehension que ce nouvel et subit accydent avenu sur la tenue des estatz et à la face de toute la France ne fust un suiet trop plusque suffizant de traverser les saintes resolutions que l'on prenoit de faire la guerre irreconcyliable aux heretiques pour traiter une treve aveq eux et convertir les armes allieurs, dont s'ensuivroit la desertion et ruyne de nostre sainte religion; estant une maxime d'estat que, les frontieres gardees, le dedans se peut tousiours remetre. Estant ce que ie suis tresvoué et affectionné à la manutention du service de dieu et du saint siege iusques au dernier soupir de ma vye, ie tiendray la main à la continuation et poursuite de cette sainte entreprize, mais aussy, estant né françois, je reconnois par le droit de ma naissance, par la [fol. 193] fidelité de mes progeniteurs et la myenne particuliere, par les bienfais des Roys mes souverains et par l'amour de ma patrie, estre tresobligé à la defence de mon prince et de la couronne. Et, pour tous les respetz du monde, ie n'y voudrois manquer. Parmy ces difficultez tresimportantes et quy attirent de tresdangereux evenemens, le repos et le remede gist et repoze en la prudence et autoryté de vostre Sainteté, laquelle y peut apporter un tel acommodement que le Roy mon seigneur soit satisfait par la restitution de ses places, quy soient mizes entre les mains de sy bons catoliques et gens d'honneur que, ny pour la religion ny pour le devoir d'obeissance, on n'en puisse douter. Monsieur le duc de Savoye demeure son bon parent et la guerre contre les heretiques soit avancee avec toute ferveur, dont la grace sera deue à vostre Sainteté, et son nom à iamais beny et glorifié par tous les catoliques. Ie l'en supplie treshumblement et de vouloir esteindre et amortir cette estincelle de feu, la quelle negligee embraseroit en peu de tens les plus paisibles contrees de sa crestienté. [fol. 193^v]

Apres avoir en toute humilité et reverence baisé les piez sacrez de vostre Sainteté, ie supplie le createur, Tressaint pere, luy donner en parfaite santé treslongue et tresheureuse vye. De Blois le xe decembre 1588.

De vostre Sainteté treshumble, tresobeissant et tresfidel servyteur,

Henry de Lorraine.

3

Relatione di quel che successo in Bles dalli xxiii di Dicembre del MDLXXXVIII fin alli xxv del detto. [A. S. V. *Misc. Arm.* I, 21, fos. 192–95 and B. A. V. *Urb. Lat.* 868, fos. 168–76; contemporary copy].

Il Re Christianissimo mandò alli xxiii di Dicembre, alle cinque hore della mattina, che le facessero venire le carrozze per andare a caccia. Et il Duca di Guisa, che era alloggiato nel Castello, levandosi la matina a buon hora come era solito, uscì alle sei hore dalle sue stantie et andò alla Capella per sentir messa et, trovandola serrata, fece oratione dalla Porta[82]; et li ne andò a la sala dove si fa il consiglio e li si tratenne passegiando più di meza hora molto malinconico.

Arrivati che furono alcuni del consiglio, il secretario Revol fece una ambasciata al Duca che il Re lo chiamava et, intrando per la porta del Cabineto del Re, erano li sedici gentilhuomini delli 45 della guardia, otto da una banda et otto dall'altra, li quali tutti insieme assaltorno il Duca dale spalle: et doi dinanzi tirandoli il primo una pugnalata a la gola dubitando che venisse armato, et una altra al petto dritto, et un altro con una alabarda dale spalle gli passò li rognoni; altri diedero quattro ferite sotto l'ombellico,

---

[82] *Urb.*: 'in ginocchioni'

con le quali tutte cascò in terra. Et cavandolo dal Cabineto stracciandolo per li piedi, dicono che ancora haveva spirito et che il Re era in una altra stantia guardando la [fol. 192ᵛ] tragedia per un altro buggio, disse alli altri 'Finitelo, finitelo!'[83]. Et essendo fuora s'approssimò un gentilhuomo al Duca quasi morto et li disse che non era di quelli che gli havevano messo le mani a dosso et che, perché haveva ancor vita, raccommandase a Iddio l'anima sua; et il Duca, levando le mani al Cielo, rese l'anima con un profondissimo suspiro.

Dicono che quattro o sei giorni prima era stato avisato il Duca di Guisa che lo volevano tradire, et che quella notte gli havevano dato polize con l'aviso, et che un gentilhuomo di quelli che lo seguitavano gli haveva detto che il giorno seguente sarìa amazato, che si guardasse, aggiongendo che non pensava quella mattina accompagnarlo tanto a buon hora perché non gli succedesse qualche cosa[84]. La propria notte avisò Madama di Nemours sua madre con grandissime lacrime, affirmandogli che sapeva di certo che lo volevano amazar nel Cabinetto del Re il giorno seguente; et il Duca le rispose[85], 'Madre io non posso credere dal Re tal cosa, havendomi promesso che mi ha promesso, ne che una cosa tanto bruta possa essere in un cuore regio[86]; non videte quanto macularia questo caso la sincera et buona intentione con che ho vissuto et vivo'.

Questa morte non si fece con tanto poco rumore che non fusse sentita nel consiglio, et il Cardinale di Guisa se volse levar per uscire, però Monsr de Laccian, Capitan della guardia del Re, lo trattenne fin [fol. 193] tanto che vennero a pigliar lui et l'Arcivescovo di Lione, li quali furno menati verso le galerie del Palazo, dove il Re fabrica un quarto per li Capuccini nel medesimo Castello.

Al hora che il Duca di Guisa haveva da andar a consiglio, il gran Priore mandò a chiamar il Prencipe di Giambille per andar a jocar al palamaglio; et a Monsr de Termes fu ordinato che trattenesse a Monsr di Nemours, et altri fecero la spia al Duca del Buf che era nel suo allogiamento, liquali furono subito prigioni.

Morto il Duca di Guisa, furono serrate le porte del Castello et quelle de la Terra furono pigliati da soldati dissimulati, tocando al'arme nel Castello,

---

[83] Urb.: 'Finitelo, finitelo d'ammazzare'.
[84] Urb.: 'che però si dovesse guardare, offrendosi accompagnarlo'.
[85] Urb.: 'rispose teneramente'.
[86] Urb.: 'et che nel suo cuore ci possa alloggiare un'animo così diabolico'.

con laqual cosa vennero le guardie del Re che erano a punto apresso le muraglie, et entrorono nella Terra.

Fatto questo, il gran Prevoste scese del Castello con 50 arcieri alla Camera dove si congregava il Terzo Stato delle ville, et rompendo le porte, chiamò il Prevoste di Merchanti di Parigi et il Presidente de Nulli suo suocero et a Compen scabino di detta villa et altri; alli quali disce che il Re li chiamava perché vi era uno che lo havea voluto amazare et gli haveva accusato; et volendo loro fermarsi, li replicò il gran Prevoste che li amazzarebbe se non andavano subito, et così andorno. Al medesimo tempo furno mandati a pigliar al stato della Nobiltà il conte Brisac, Monsr di Beaudaulfin[87] et il secretario del Duca, Pelican [fol. 193ᵛ].

Il corpo del Duca di Guisa mandò il Re che si stesse nella sua ante-camera, dove si trovava ancora alli xxv alla sera sopra certe tavole con li medesimi vestiti et coperto con un panno di rasa. Et mandando Madama de Nemours a pregare la Regina Madre che per amor de Dio si ricordasse de suoi figlioli, li rispose che lei non poteva niente con il suo [figlio], però che li mandava a domandar il corpo. Il Re alla richiesta della Madre fece rispondere che luy haveva il corpo ma che ne haveva di besogno, che è signo di voler far qualche altra demostratione.

Al Cardinale de Guisa s'intende che lo amazò la guardia del Re con le proprie alebarde alle xxiiii alla mattina, ala hora che fu amazato il fratello il giorno inanti, et il Principe di Giambille fu alli ...[88] menato al Castello di Amboise.

Il Duca del Buf fece resistentia nella camera sua, però al fine fu preso. Quel di Nemours sta con guardie nella camera sua et il medesimo la madre, alla quale la Regina madre mandò con Monsr di Lansac a darla nuova della morte del suo figliolo. Tutti l'altri pregioni che fecero al hora et poi stanno nel Castello et se fa giuditio, per tenere il corpo del Duca di Guisa senza sepelirlo, che si processa contro di lui et che al tempo di far demostratione si executeranno ancora nell'altri pregioni examinandoli fra tanto; che fin ad esso solo dicono esser' concessa la vita al Conte Brisac [fol. 194] che si passegia in Bles, perché il Re l'haveva guadagnato prima delle fattione.

Il Cardinale di Borbone, che si truovava in letto della podagra, sta

---

[87] *Urb.*: 'Modofin'.
[88] Lacuna.

preso in casa sua, facendoli guardia quella di Scozzesi[89], et si dice nella camera del Re che sia morto[90].

Il Re, subbito che fu amazzato il Duca di Guisa, andò a vedere la Regina Madre et li disse che già era Re di Francia per haver morto il Duca di Guisa. Et che lei li respose che anzi haveva messo il Regno in perditione, che al manco l'havesse detto prima al Cardinale Legato. Et il Re li replicò, 'Avvenga quello che può venire, ch'io sto vendicato![91]'

Il Re uscì quel giorno alla messa in publico come acostumava, accompagnato dal Cardinale di Vandome, et poi desinò in publico nella sala ordinaria et il Cardinale Vandome li servì la tovaglia.

L'ordine che il Re diede per far questa esecutione fu questo; e nella mattina medesima, a buonissima hora, mandò a chiamare li sedici gentilhuomini delle 45 della guardia et li disse che tutti erano creature de lui, et sotto questa confidenza gli voleva significare che o haveva da morire lui proprio o il Duca di Guisa in questa mattina. Et loro si offerirno di amazzare il Duca; et il Re li diede l'ordine come havevano da stare, et retirandosi al Cabineto con Lognac, scrisse due polize a Monsr di Larceran [fol. 194ᵛ] et Chasteauvieulx, accioché prendessero li Cardinali di Borbone et Guisa.

Fece subito bandire il Re, a pena della vita, che nessuno pigliasse l'arme et si continuasse li stati; però la maggior parte sonno fuggiti. Et il Re il giorno seguente, che furno li 24, li mandò a dire che fra otto giorni resolutamente dessero li memoriali che stavano ordinando.

In Orleans havea fatto il Re entrare secretamente soldati nella Citadela, che non è niente forte, et quelli della Terra, al proprio punto che hanno sentito la cosa de Bles, pigliorno le arme attrincienandosi contra la Citadella, che si sente di qua battere[92].

Subito che fu amazato il Duca di Guisa, publiorno in Bles che il Re lo haveva fatto havendo havuto nuova che in Lione havevano amazato il Duca di Menne suo fratello[93] et fatto prigione in Parigi al Duca di Aumale[94],

---

[89] *Urb.*: 'guardia degli Arcieri scozzesi'.
[90] *Urb.*: 'ma non si crede'.
[91] *Urb.*: 'Venga quello che può venire, almeno io mi sono vendicato'.
[92] *Urb.*: 'et cominciorno a battere la Cittadella'.
[93] *Urb.*: 'il che non stato vero'.
[94] *Urb.*: 'ne meno in Parigi il Duca d'Umala'.

di che non si ha certezza; né di quello che ha fatto Monsr de L'Abardin,
al qual dicono havere mandato il Re al Campo di Monsr di Nevers per
amazar Monsr di La Chatre et doi Colonelli di Monsr di Guisa che erano li
con gente.

Il Re volse che li 45 che amazarono il Duca andassaro a amazare il
Cardinale di Guisa; et loro risposero che non lo mandasse, ché il Duca era
huomo di spada et l'altro Prete. Alcuni [fol. 195] vogliono che lo amazzero
soldati della guardia, altri che alabardieri, altri che li Archieri del gran
Prevoste.

Madama di Guisa era partita pochi giorni prima a Parigi, et Madama di
Mompensier sorella di Guisa ancora per metersi in ordine per accompaignar
la Principessa di Lorena, di maniera che figli, mogli et fratelli tutti erano
venuti al Castello de Blois.

Al Arcivescovo di Lion ha dato la vita il Re a istanza di un suo nepote
governator della Citadella di Chialon.

Li corpi del Duca di Guisa et Cardinale suo fratello mandò il Re alli
xxv alla notte che fossero tagliate le teste, le quali si conservano, et il busto
di tutti doi furono mandati abbrusciare, et così si fece.

Li Padri Cappuchini non hanno voluto dire messa al Re doppo la morte
del Cardinale. Il legato ancora si dice che dubitò al principio di parlar col
Re, però alli xxvi hebbe audientia et stette col Re passegiando gran pezzo
nel parco ragionando senza potersi intendere parola, senon che erano in
grande allegrezza et ridendo fortemente.

4

Avviso **from Blois of 24th December 1588.** [A. S. V. *Misc. Arm.* I,
21, fos. 204^v^–206; original].

A 22 la sera di notte il Re commandò a tre Capitani delle sue guardie che
la mattina a buon hora andassero per tempo a parlargli con l'armi loro,
perché voleva che andassero a tagliar a pezzi certi soldati che tenevano
compagnia senza sua saputa, et nell'andar'a letto fece intendere alli suoi
gentilhomini della guardia della sua persona che sono 45, acioché 12 o 15

di loro fussero la matina li instivalati, perché voleva andar'a due leghe di qui. La mattina ogn'uno fu all'ordine, et il Re ritenne apresso di se nel suo Gabinetto li tre Capitani et il signor Alfonso Corso che mandò a chiamare, i quali intratteneva di parole, havendo, prima che detti Capitani et il signor Alfonso fussero arrivati, ordinato che detti gentilhomini della sua guardia stessero nelle camere [fol. 205] vicine al Gabinetto, che nell'andar'il Duca di Guisa al Gabinetto l'amazzassero di pugnalate, il quale era in Consiglio; et fu chiamato da parte del Re da Monsr di Revol, Segretario di Stato, et giunto alle stanze fu amazzato senza poter defendersi, perché tutti a un tratto se gli avventaron adosso, pigliandolo chi per le braccia, chi per le gambe, mentre che altri gli davano, et gridando esso, il re uscì fuori a punto quando egli spirava. Il Cardinale suo fratello et l'Arcivescovo di Lione, che pur sentirono il grido, volsero fugir della stantia, ma un gentil'huomo guadagnando la porta, sfodrata la spada, gli fermò. Venne in questo mezzo Monsr de Larchiam, capitano della guardia, con degli arcieri, et fece condurgli in una stanza di sopra che'l Re ha fatto accommodare a questi giorni con buone ferrate alle finestre, facendo dire volervi mettere de' frati fogliami. Il corpo del Duca fu messo in un vecchio Gabinetto. Fur poi fatte dar subito le guardie alli Duchi di Nemours et d'Albeuf, al Cardinale di Borbone, a Madama di Nemours nelle camere loro, levandogli tutti i servitori da due o tre in poi. Il Principe di Gianville, quando fu amazzato il padre, era in camera del Gran Priore, et scendendo senza sapere niente, fu costretto da gli arcieri a tornare in camera, se ben mise mano alla spada, et ivi ancora sta guardato; il Palazzo stette serrato un pezzo senza sapersi le cose, et furono anco serrate le porte della villa, essendosene prima fuggiti la maggior parte de gli adherenti del Duca, e ritenuti alcuni, et questi furono Monsr de Beudefin, il conte di Brisac, Monsr de Brosses et Monsr di Rambuno, con alcuni altri di più bassa mano, a chi il Re ha perdonato sotto promessa di fedeltà.

Morto il Duca, il Re mandò il Gran Prevosto all'Assamblea del 3° Stato, et fece pigliare il Prevosto de'Mercanti di Parigi co' li due Cravigni chiamati l'uno Compan et l'altro Cotteblanche, et il Presidente di Nugli et il Luogotenente di giustizia d'Amiens, tutti seditiosissimi, et guardati benissimo in una stanza del Palazzo. Il Cardinale di Guisa alle cinque hore la notte passata di oggi sabbato, che erano a 24, è stato morto di pugnalate. Il Barone di Luc, nipote dell'Arcivescovo di Lione, ch'è stato sempre divoto al Re, ha impetrato gratia della vita per il zio, credendosi che lo terrà in prigione perpetua. Il Re andò [fol. 205ᵛ], fatte tutte queste essecutioni, a darne conto alla madre, scusandosi se non le ne haveva detto niente, dicendo che così era stato inspirato da Dio; la quale rispose, 'Piaccia a Dio che'l successo sia secondo il vostro desiderio'. Partendo il Re andò a messa et poi a desinare non più alterato che l'altre volte, se non che disse in publico che il Duca di Guisa gli n'haveva fatte tante che non era più possibile di comportarlo.

Monsr d'Entraghes, governatore d'Orliens, ch'era qui fu subito mandato la, dove la maggior parte de'seguaci del Duca si sono ritirati per dar'animo al popolo di stare alla medesima lega: un poco di Cittadella, che vi è, sta a divotione del Re, laquale saluta alle volte con cannonate la detta terra.

Questa mattina de 24, otto compagnie della fanteria delle guardie del Re sono andate a quella volta per unirsi con altre genti che'l governatore ha da ragunare all'intorno, sperandosi col favore della parte che'l Re ha dentro la Città ritorni a ubbedientia.

Il Re fece pigliare il segretario del Duca et hebbe tutte le lettere et scritture, per lequali et per la confessione s'intendono bellissime cose; et la mano è che il Duca haveva l'anno 150m scudi dal Re di Spagna pagatigli di quattro in quattro mesi, et si chiarirà ancora il disegno ch'egli haveva d'impadronirsi della persona del Re. [...][95].

Openione universale è che tutti questi signori che sono prigioni si mandaranno nel Castel d'Ambuoes che è tra qui e Tours. Il Re scrisse subito al Duca di Nivers, che è in guarnigione di Beauvos, che seguiti la guerra contra gli Ugonotti et che faccia prigione Monsr della Chatra aciò ché restituisca Bourges et la Torre, che si tenevano per quei della Lega, ne sin qui si è inteso che quella terra faccia motivo alcuno; potrebbe essere che il Re qualche giorno inanzi al caso del Duca di Guisa havesse ordinato che fusse ritenuto in Lione il Duca di Humena. Ha scritto poi a tutti l'altre terre che stiano all'ubbidienza della Corona, scacciando i seguaci et capi della lega. Non sappiamo ancora quel che harà fatto Parigi, ma si spera bene, poi che quelli che sono per il Re che in tutte le terre sono più in numero, saranno stati anticipatamente avvertiti. Li corpi del Duca et del fratello Cardinale sono stati sepelliti in sacrato, ma ancora non si saputo dove.

---

[95] Short section on reinforcements sent to Orleans.

5. Henri IV, King of Reason?*

DENIS CROUZET

The religious pacification of France brought about by Henri IV, was the result of a veritable revolution in political ideology. The end of the Wars of Religion was the product of a rethinking or rationalisation of the concept of monarchy. The main argument of the analysis that follows is that at many stages in its development, the monarchy of the Classical Age, the order of triumphant Reason, can be explained by the decisive policy moves that were developed between 1589 and 1610. For Henri of Navarre was also a king of Reason.

Firstly it will be determined on what basis and in what terms the new political ideology was elaborated, representing as it did a radical rethinking both of the significance of the monarchy and of the relationship between the king and his subjects. Secondly, it will be shown how the system of representation which was developed by royalist propaganda and which defined and governed Henri of Navarre's pacification of the kingdom, makes the king a king of Reason. Finally, it will be suggested that this model, paradoxically perhaps, contained within it the regicide of 1610.

---

* Translated from the French by Judith K. Proud, University of Exeter.

In order to understand the clear development in the political representations which occur throughout Henri of Navarre's reign, it is first of all important to redefine the Catholic League and the determining factors behind it.

The League is essentially a religious phenomenon. It must, in effect, be seen within the mental climate of a second strong wave of eschatological angst. There are many sources which testify to the spread of acute anxiety concerning the end of the world at this time, and of increasingly alarmist proclamations of God's wrath during this period which sees the toughening of hard-line Catholicism in the vision developed by the League, in a spirituality of Sacrifice.

There are first of all the irregular publications which appear in increasing numbers throughout the reign of Henri III, and which, whilst both recounting and describing the wonders of the world, explain that they are the harbingers of the great Tribulation. All these texts end with exhortations to repent and with calls for the moral reformation of the masses; never had humanity reached such a stage of moral depravity, of atheism and of abomination, foretelling, 'either a renewal and a transformation of all things, or the coming of that great God in his glory, to destroy this round machine'[1]. It is interesting to note that these works emanate more often than not from ultra-Catholic printers, or that, when the author's name is given, it is that of a person known for his commitment to the Catholic League. This has given rise to the belief that the League's struggle was conceptualised in a context of eschatological imminence and that the movement used the resulting angst to unite Catholics into the holy League.

A second instrument in the diffusion and exacerbation of this anxiety were astrological almanacs, which saw 1583 as the beginning of an astrological sequence that would propel the world towards its end, because of the planetary conjunction identical to that which occurred before the birth of Christ, and which could only occur again at the end of the world. Such prophesies created anxiety. Catholic France is clearly waiting for God, as demonstrated by the White Processions which occurred throughout the North of France after signs of the impending Day of Judgment were seen in the skies over the Ardennes. These processions consisted of the Catholic congregation in towns and villages carrying the *Corpus Christi* covered with

---

[1]   See D. Crouzet, 'La représentation du temps à l'époque de la Ligue — 'Le clouaque et esgout des immondices des autres [siècles] passez', in *Revue historique*, t. 270, 1984, pp. 297–388.

a white alb. They would progress in a spirit of great penitence to the shrines of the Virgin Mary in a mournful *imitatio Christi* ritual[2], a clear indication that the participants were haunted by the belief that the world was to end. Simultaneous processions in Burgundy, the Dauphiné, the Rhône valley and in Languedoc show clearly that it was in the context of a great wave of spiritual panic that the League emerged. In addition the years 1588–89 are seen as dangerous years, years which witness many strange happenings, and in which signs of divine intervention were to become increasingly numerous; years of war, of the murder of princes, of famines, of plagues, and also of the end of the French monarchy. These almanacs are thus another form of guilt-inducement through literature, sparing no efforts in telling their readers that they must go ever forward in their worship of God and in their repentance.

The third instrument is the League's own polemics: often redolent of prophesy, these works also spread the theme of the end of the world, for example in the pamphlets of the theorist Jean de Caumont, and in other unfortunately anonymous texts[3].

In its own apologia, the Union of Catholics presents itself as a means of collective fulfilment in God, in a liminal period which demands a collective reformation. Far from responding simply to social frustrations, as E. Barnavi suggests[4], or, as R. Descimon has argued, to the myth of civic unity[5], the Union of Catholics uses eschatological anxiety as the main source of its strength: Jean de Caumont affirms that the Union is union with God 'with his substance and with his own flesh, union of conjunction and of most fraternal society with Jesus Christ', identified with the union of the faithful with the Redeemer in the eucharistic communion[6]. This Union is the

---

[2] *Id.*, 'Recherches sur les processions blanches — 1583–1584', in *Histoire, économie et société*, 1982, n° 4, pp. 511–563.

[3] Jean de Caumont, *Advertissement des advertissemens au peuple tres-crestien*, 1587.

[4] E. Barnavi, *Le parti de Dieu. Etude sociale et politique de la Ligue parisienne 1585–1594*, Louvain, 1980; *id.*, 'Réponse à Robert Descimon', in *Annales-économies-sociétés-civilisations*, t. 37, n° 1, 1982, pp. 112–120.

[5] R. Descimon, *Qui étaient les Seize? Mythes et réalités de la Ligue parisienne (1585–1594)*, [Mémoires publiés par la Fédération des sociétés historiques et archéologiques de Paris et de l'Ile-de-France, t. 34], Paris, 1983; *id.*, 'La Ligue: des divergences fondamentales', in *A. E. S. C.*, t. 37, n° 1, 1982, pp. 122–128.

[6] J. de Caumont, *De l'Union des Catholiques avec Dieu et entre eux mesmes*, Paris, Robert Nivelle, 1587, p. 14.

ultimate recourse of man so that the earth's inhabitants, in the urgency
of the end of the world, can reconstitute themselves in a mystical body
and triumph over the forces of eternal death which draw it towards divine
punishment. The League is first of all a collective taking of the Cross, in
order that, as the oath of the Union states 'we may follow our captain Jesus Christ'[7]. The Union represents penitential attachment to the Passion,
which unites in the principle of absolute unity, takes man out of man and
makes him as one with God. A tract of 1589 wrote that the Union:[8]

> ... assemble
> mille et mille cœurs ensemble,
> les conserve et n'en fait qu'Un...

But above all, the League is thought of and historically legitimised as a
creation mystically desired by God, who communicated the need for it to
those of the elected who had at last been brought to an awareness that
on the eve of the day of Judgment the Catholic faithful must unite in the
most intense adoration of God. One must return to a literal reading of the
texts, which, falling within the context of current events one must suppose
contained a certain logic for contemporary readers, a logic that responded
to their anxiety. In the *Dialogue d'entre le Maheustre et le Manant*, but
also as early as a pamphlet of 1590[9], it is recounted that the League was
founded through the intervention of divine providence, 'by extraordinary
means'. In the same way as in the past God created an inspired leader
aided by many helpers to save his people from Pharaoh, so he 'used in
the founding and the commencement of the line of Catholics in Paris, M.
Charles Hotman, now deceased, one of the bourgeois of this town, a very
virtuous man of noble, well-established and honest family, who considering
the poverty of the time, and the insolence of the people, and above all the
loss of the Catholic and Apostolic Religion, was moved by the spirit of God,
to speak to several good doctors...'. Amongst the principal of these we
find the *maître des Comptes*, Pierre Acarie, who is, not uncoincidentally,

---

[7] In, for example, *Declaration des Consuls, eschevins, manans et habitans de
la ville de Lyon, sur l'occasion de la prise des armes par eux faicte, le vingt
quatriesme Fevrier 1589. Avec les articles de la resolution par eux prinse sur les
occasions des presents troubles*, Paris, Guillaume Chaudiere, 1589, p. 23.

[8] *Commentaire et Remarques chrestiennes sur l'edict d'Union de l'An 1588.
Où est escrit le devoir d'un vray Catholique contre les Polytiques de nostre temps*,
Paris, Rolin Thierry, 1590, pp. 5–7 and pp. 49–50.

[9] *Harangue au Reverendissime et illustrissime Legat Henry Cajetan, faicte par
aucun Bourgeois de Paris, au moys de Febvrier, 1590*, Paris, Didier Millot, 1590,
pp. 6–7.

the husband of the famous mystic, the lawyer Loys Dorleans who took inspiration from the Bible to denounce corruption in the kingdom, and the theorist of eschatological urgency, Jean de Caumont[10]. Can we not infer from this that the League, from an initial group of inspired prophets and in a time of great spiritual panic, was able to convince a section (which may for a short while have been the majority) of the Catholic population of a prophetic awareness of the need for the mystical fusion of all in Christ?

In other words, are not social, economical and political explanations of the League somewhat secondary, if not anachronistic, in such a time of panic and foreboding of the Day of Judgment, in which a doctrine of salvation through penitential union with God plays a major role? What is more, the way in which the members of the League identify themselves demonstrates their commitment to a mystical tension signifying an intense eschatological anxiety: they call themselves 'les zélés'(the zealous), not only to signify the primacy of God over all things temporal, but above all because they advocate union with God. The leaguer's zeal is rhetorically said to be a distancing of 'man's innate nature', a 'sudden blaze', and the zealot is led by God, possessed by God to the point of being pure spirit, of being the fulfilment of Christ within himself, 'those who experience these sacred and divine flames are as if eaten and devoured from within, from their entrails to their very bone marrow, and are so preoccupied within their souls that they are oblivious to what human reason suggests or dictates'[11].

An analysis of the Paris processions of the winter of 1589[12], in a town which identifies itself with Jerusalem threatened with divine destruction for its sins, shows how the crisis of contrition was a collective experience. A whole town unites in spirit with Christ in the combat against the king antichrist; in the mortification inflicted on everybody, in an internal crusade. Paris, the new Jerusalem, places itself prophetically under the reign of Christ the King, to such an extent that one can wonder whether the

---

[10] [François Morin?], *Dialogue d'entre le maheustre et le manant*. Original text with the variants of the royalist version, established and annotated by P.M. Ascoli, Geneva, 1977, pp. 93–95.

[11] *Discours Apologétique tres veritable, des causes qui ont contrainct les habitans de S. Malo, de s'emparer du Chasteau de leur ville: avec une bresve histoire de la prise d'iceluy, advenüe le 12 de Mars*, 1590, pp. 1–2.

[12] See the fine analysis of D. Richet, 'Politique et religion: les processions à Paris en 1589', in *Mélanges Pierre Goubert*, Paris, 1985, pp. 623–632. And *id.*, 'Aspects socio-culturels des conflits religieux à Paris dans la seconde moitié du XVIe siècle in *A. E. S. C.*, t. 32, n° 4, 1977, pp. 764–789.

assassination of the temporal king does not fall into its logical place in the development of a great movement of collective spiritualisation.

The collective violence is concentrated on 'an earthly and mortal king, unfaithful to God and to his people', a king who is responsible for God's anger with his people, a king whose true nature is at last revealing itself. Looked at in this perspective, the regicide cannot be reduced to the individual act committed by Clément. It is clearly rooted in the mystical piety of Paris, in the processions, and above all in the mourning ceremonies that last for two whole months after the death of the Guise brothers. The mystical itinerary of Clément, filled by the 'power' of God[13], hides a millenarian soteriology, to 'be one in God our master'[14], a paroxysmal experience of the fusion of all in the Passion of Christ, and with Him who is to come.

Following on from this line of analysis, it seems to me that the questions concerning the political restabilisation achieved by Henri of Navarre should be posed in different terms. It is within this context of panic-stricken expectation of a messianic reign that the temporal reign and the relationship between the temporal king and his subjects were re-evaluated after the death of Henri III. The political vision of the reign of Henri of Navarre, on the other hand, acts as a means of dissipating anxiety and thus as a rejection of the desire to see the world moving as close as possible to the spiritual reign of the end of time.

The struggle embarked on against the League by royalist intellectuals, for the most part Catholic members of the Parlement, is rapidly constructed on the fundamental precepts of the [neo-]Stoic philosophy, the ideology of which is the reconstruction of society, shaken by the regicide, and which can be seen as a coherent system of de-dramatisation of eschatalogical angst. It is perhaps Loys Le Caron who first laid the foundations of political renewal in 1588.

The premisses of Le Caron's analysis in *De la tranquillité d'esprit* are borrowed directly from Stoic thinking: namely that, up against a world that encircles him on all sides, man must not allow himself to be submerged and

---

[13] *Histoire des choses les plus remarquables et admirables, advenues en ce royaume de France, és années dernieres, 1587. 88. et 89. reputées estre vraies miracles de Dieu. Dediées A tres-haute, tres-excellente, et vertueuse Princesse, Madame Catherine de Lorraine, Duchesse douairiere de Montpensier*, 1590, pp. 58.

[14] *Commentaire et Remarques...*, op. cit., pp. 5–7.

distressed by the things of which he becomes aware. He must maintain at all times an inner peace by holding to the thought that there is a reason to all things and all events: 'one must not therefore complain about what happens in this world, for (as Seneca says) the things which seem to frustrate and trouble man belong to the conservation of the universe, and are part of that which makes the world turn perfectly. But (...) that which we call and think to be evils are sent to us for our own good, not as evils, but as necessary benefits both to the universal cause or for the public good of the state where they fall or to the individual who is touched by them[15].

---

[15] Louis [Charondas] Le Caron, *De la tranquilité d'esprit, livre singulier. Plus un discours sur le proces criminel faict à une sorciere... Traictez grandement necessaires pour le temps present*, Paris, Arnould Sittard, 1588, p. 11. Stoicism marks an evolution in Le Caron's system of thought. In 1556, he had published *Les Dialogues*, inspired by Platonism, developing within this perspective the notion of tranquillity of the spirit (*Dialogues*, J. A. Buhlmann and D. Gilman ed., Geneva, 1986). A similar point of view is put forward in the same year, 1588, in *Exhortation pour la paix et reunion des Catholiques François*, Paris, Pour la veuve Nicolas Rosset, 1588, (the same text as *Exhortation aux Catholiques François* printed in Paris, 1588), which defines the neo-Stoic vision which the Gallican Catholics are already beginning to advocate even before the rupture of the end of 1588 (perhaps the author is Estienne Pasquier?). The eschatology is secularised, because the danger is the change in the laws, in the mutation of the State, the 'perturbation and confusion of all order, a marvellous and monstrous thing to think of and even more terrible to foretell and foresee' (pp. 21–22). War is absolute evil, cutting short the natural life of man, destroying his civil life and delivering his spiritual life into eternal death. Peace is, on the contrary, desired by God, creator and demiurge of a world which both in heaven and on earth is a theatre of peace and of harmony : 'He has given us here below a fragile and infirm life in order that there should be no one person, even of the highest, that can presume to have no need of others, but that by aiding and helping each other they should retain happiness and unity amongst them: And thus he has made man a domestic and sociable Animal, who likes to live in company and not alone. And in as much as society is necessary to live in contentment and happiness, he is obliged to love peace and patience, without which every group would break apart: God has put man in the world as a Spectator in a huge Theatre, so that in seeing this great Machine of Heaven, and the earth, in such good order and peace, he should be ashamed not to copy this beautiful peaceful order which he sees before his eyes as a lesson and an example, where he can see that all the elements, all the stars, all the spheres have their role: content to remain within their limits without challenging each other'. Absolutist conservatism or immobility is a vision of cosmic order, relying on the permanency and accomplishment of each element

For Le Caron a certain distancing is necessary in order to dissipate human anguish when faced with the future: man must realise that in effect all things in the universe are subject to corruption and destruction, whether they are natural like trees or animals, or artificial like states, but he must also be aware that it is not possible for his finite faculties of understanding to speculate on how long they may survive. God alone possesses the knowledge of the 'period of their decline'[16]. Stoicism offers Le Caron a coherent system of negation or of sublimation of eschatological anxiety. In an indirect but fundamental way, he is setting out a theory of absolutism, to the extent that human evil is born of passions which in the political arena, give rise to discord and sedition[17]. Man's intervention in current political life can only cause him trouble, for the contradictory passions that govern political life make it a strong cause of disunity and violent excess. Political power, on the contrary, is to be aimed at the prevention of the unleashing of instability and of passions. Its aim is to force men to live in a harmony that is the concrete embodiment of a universal affinity. The monarch must be a 'hard master' who lays down the law to his subjects and never allows himself to be dictated to, for the contrary would be 'to make himself a party to their passions, hates and disputes'[18]. He is above his subjects, and even if he is unjust, he must be obeyed. The Magistrate has complete authority, and whoever rises against that authority is courting a certain 'sad end'.

This way of thinking that legitimises absolutism is distilled into a number of printed texts after the death of Henri III. In royalist pamphlets, accusations against enemies return constantly to accusations of 'frenzy' and abandon, to 'the unbridled passions and affections of your souls' and of loss of 'judgment'[19]. Obedience to the rightful king is defined according to a distinction inspired by the Stoic philosophy which counters the passions with reason. It is said to be a natural means of accession to divine order through each subject taking up the 'torch of reason'[20]. It is characterised by the person who experiences within himself the full ethical richness of living

---

of the cosmos in its predetermined position.

[16] *Ibid.*, p. 20.

[17] See G. Oestreich, *Neostoicism and the Early Modern State*, Cambridge, 1982.

[18] L. Charondas Le Caron, *op. cit.*, p. 78.

[19] *Lettre missive aux Parisiens d'un Gentilhomme serviteur du Roy, n'agueres sorti de prison, representant le danger et peril qui menace leur ville, s'ils ne recognoissent promptement leurs fautes, et ne reçoivent sa Majesté, comme ils sont obligez par le commandement de Dieu*, 1591, pp. 4–5.

[20] *De l'obeissance deue au Prince. Pour faire cesser les armes, et restablir la Paix en ce Royaume. Au Roy*, Caen, Jacques le Bas, 1590, p. 4.

in conformity with the will of God: 'our actions are well-intentioned when the reasonable part of us directs, governs and moderates our passions...'[21]. Obeying the king is the same as achieving individual liberty, which is to obey God naturally, rejecting the enslavement of vice, of impiety and of parricide in which, latter-day Epicureans, the members of the Catholic League delight[22]. To obey is to partake fully of the rationality of an authority desired by God, and which is rational because God is Reason. Obedience is the 'Christian virtue'[23], through which the Christian is sure of individually encountering the will of God, unlike the 'foolish and slow people of the world'[24].

Obedience governs the universe: to obey is to act according to God, according to the order that He has given to the Cosmos, to put oneself in harmony with and participate in the Universal, which is based on obedience. The order of 'le grand Tout' (the Universe) implies the legitimacy of the absolute monarchy, for nature indicates in many ways that monarchic government is divine, that it is the only authority compatible with Reason: 'It is a law that was published at every crossroads of the earthly world since the world began, the Sun in the sky was made King of all the Stars, which recognize him as their Prince, take all their light from him, honour him, and as it has been said, precede him and salute him (...) and help him with their advice like his officers and assessors...'[25]. Royalty is thus decreed a 'general rule', it is 'reasonable' because it complies with the reason that God has given the world that he created. To live under a king whose

---

[21] *Tres-prudent et salutaire conseil donné par un Suisse Catholique, pour la pacification des troubles de ce Royaume*, 1590, pp. 69–70.

[22] *Le Labyrinthe de la Ligue et les moyens de s'en retirer par A. D. L. P. A. S.* , 1590, p. 229.

[23] [Pierre Charron], *Discours chrestien, Qu'il n'est permis ny loisible à un sujet, pour quelque cause et raison que ce soit, de se liguer, bander et rebeller contre son Roy. Par P. C. P. Chantre et Chanoine Theologal de Condom*, Paris, David Le Clerc, 1594, pp. 19–20 (text that Charron claims to have written in 1589 having been temporarily seduced by the League). On Pierre Charron, see the analysis of J. F. Sabrié, *De l'humanisme au rationalisme: Pierre Charron: l'homme, l'oeuvre, l'influence*, Paris, 1913. For a more recent study, see J. D. Charron, *Wisdom of Pierre Charron: An Original and Orthodox Code of Morality*, Chapel Hill, 1960, and R. Kogel, *Pierre Charron*, Geneva, 1972.

[24] *De l'obeissance deue au Prince...*, *op. cit.*, p. 4.

[25] *Ibid.*, pp. 14–20. On the idea of eternal reason 'incorporated in the great all', see Seneca *Lettres à Lucilius*, F. Prechac and H. Noblot ed., Paris, 1969, pp. 436–437.

position is naturally God-given, is to participate in the divine harmony of the world, in the solidarity that exists between the Whole and its parts, a universal concord desired by God.

To intervene directly in the political life of the modern City as far as the royalist theorists are concerned is to usurp the domain reserved for God, who, even when he allows a transfer to occur in the monarchy, forbids it from happening as a result of 'disloyalty, perfidiousness and treason of the subjects to their Prince'. The modernity of the sixteenth century is clear here, modernity in the sense that the foundations of classical absolutism are established. The liberty of the individual must not manifest itself in active participation in political life, which could not be impassive. It consists rather in accepting as a fact the system of domination, in wanting things to happen 'not as one would wish, but as they happen' in knowing how to resign oneself in peace or in universal harmony to a course of events which is natural.

In 1594–1595, a printed work provides a clear synthesis of the ideological structure behind the new policy. The work in question is that which Guillaume Du Vair, translator in 1591 of the *Manuel d'Epictète*[26], is supposed to have written during the siege of Paris, entitled *La constance et consolation ès calamitez publiques*. Linus, one of the protagonists in the conversation which is said to take place in the capital besieged by the royalist army rabble, attacks that which is at the source of the Parisians' energetic resistance, the anxiety caused by political transformation and eschatalogical destruction. He underlines that the anxiety caused by this vision of the future is indeed the original force behind the creation of the League, in the sense that his whole discourse is aimed at de-dramatising this anxiety. This reduction of anxiety seems to be the main prerequisite of political reconstruction. Linus makes use of a Stoic argument that can be found, for example, in the thirteenth letter to Lucilius, and which asserts that men's anxieties are out of all proportion to their causes, sometimes anticipating the effects of the cause, sometimes being totally without cause: 'It is a well known maxim in medicine that with acute illness, the outcome is never certain (. . .) It is difficult to promise the well-being of our state, but

---

[26] Guillaume du Vair, *Le Manuel d'Epictète*, Paris, 1591, (*Le manuel d'Epictète suivi des réponses à l'empereur Hadrien et translaté en langue française*, Paris, 1921). On du Vair, see R. Radouant, *Guillaume du Vair, l'homme et l'orateur, jusqu'à la fin des troubles de la Ligue (1556–1596)*, Paris, 1907, and P. Mesnard, 'Du Vair et le néostoïcisme', in *Revue d'histoire de la philosophie*, 1928, pp. 142–166.

it is equally difficult to predict its ruin. How many towns have there been, how many states and empires have been knocked down and overturned by awful accidents, such that onlookers believed their end to be imminent, but which, nevertheless, have taken strength from their disturbances and have returned stronger and more flourishing than ever before...'[27]. There are many examples of states which seemed certain to disappear, but which have nevertheless survived. As a result, no good end can be served by allowing oneself to become overwhelmed by anxiety concerning the future. Anxiety creates obstinacy and only hastens the natural end of the kingdom, for it is the same for states as it is for human bodies and all other things: they are perishable, have a natural start and a natural end; no-one can oppose nature without the risk of hastening that very slide towards death. Man must adopt a Stoical attitude of patience, for no one can pretend to know at what stage in the aging or in the decline of the state one is at[28]. What seems formidable should not be feared 'what we call troubles and calamities, are God's gifts'[29], or rather a restabilising action by God, 'a divine readjustment' aimed at correcting man's natural leaning towards evil.

According to Du Vair's text, all the misfortunes of the current situation can be explained by man's inability or refusal to achieve the serene realisation that it is his own obstinacy in wanting to influence a providential history that creates misfortune, and thus his anxiety. Nothing happens on the world's stage save by the justice of God, which must be accepted without hesitation, reticence or fear[30].

---

[27] *Id., La constance et consolation ès calamitez publiques, deuxiesme edition,* Paris, Abel Langelier, 1595, pp. 20. This theme is present in Seneca, *Lettres...,op. cit.,* pp. 43–44: 'Let us carefully interrogate reality. Is it likely that a disaster will occur? Likelihood does not however necessarily mean truth. How many happenings have there been that were not expected! How many expected happenings that never appeared! Even if it does happen, what do we gain from suffering it in advance? You will suffer only too soon once it really happens (...) Create a balance therefore between the hope and the fear; every time that there is complete incertitude, lean in your favour: believe that which suits you. Even if fear gets more votes, still lean towards hope: stop troubling your heart and always tell yourself that the majority of mortals, without being affected, without being seriously threatened with any evil, live in a frenzy and in complete disorder...'.

[28] *Ibid.,* p. 55.

[29] *Ibid.,* pp. 97–98.

[30] Theme developed in Seneca, *Lettres...,* *op. cit.,* letter 71, pp. 276–277: Stoic physics are explained in this letter, according to the principle that fixed periods regulate the evolution of the universe: 'everything must be born, grow

A single solution is put forward in the form of wisdom, the virtue of which is to be in conformity with nature, to 'acquiesce' in all the potentiality of the future, or rather not to seek to know about it. Wisdom is detachment, realism, and constancy when confronted with all the problems of the world, the very opposite of the passions which stir the members of the Catholic League, which lead them into irrational and unnatural impulses and which encourage them daily into overturning order, the law and the forces of civil order, and into continually worsening the already desperate state of the kingdom. The League can be logically identified with evil, for it was born of man's wholly unreasonable rebellion against divine law and his refusal to live in harmony with nature.

In a time that saw the increasing influence of Justus Lipsius[31], this is how a political ideology of withdrawal from political life and a complete reversal of perspective was codified, and it is interesting to note the similarities with the way the Huguenots looked at things. Could one not suggest that a philosophico-ethical union was at the root of the union between the Huguenots and the politicians for the defence of the state?

The link between Calvinism and Stoicism is not a new idea. As early as 1532, Calvin himself assures a privileged link between the reformation of man and Stoicism by preparing an edition of Seneca's *Libri duo de clementia*. In 1558, Jean de Coras published his *Altercation en forme de dialogue, de l'empereur Adrian et du philosophe Epictete...*[32], whilst in 1567, André de Rivaudeau translated *La doctrine d'Epictete stoïcien, comme l'homme se peut rendre vertueux, libre, heureux et sans passion*[33]. The insistence of

---

and die. Those stars that you see circling over our heads, these elements which support us and carry us and appear so solid, they will waste away and die. There is nothing that does not experience old age. By irregular intervals, nature guides everything towards the same point of disintegration. That which ceases to be does not vanish utterly, but decomposes. We call this decomposition annihilation. This is because we only perceive the superficial aspects (...) A great soul must obey God, and whatever the demands of the univeral law, submit to them without hesitation'.

[31] L. Zanta, *La Renaissance du stoïcisme au XVIe siècle*, Paris, 1914, and M. Fumaroli, *L'âge de l'éloquence. Rhétorique et 'res literaria' de la Renaissance au seuil de l'époque classique*, Geneva, 1980.

[32] Jean de Coras, *Altercation en forme de dialogue, de l'empereur Adrian et du philosophe Epictete, contenant soixante et treize questions et autant de responses. Rendu de latin en françois...*' Toulouse, 1558.

[33] André de Rivaudeau, *La doctrine d'Epictete stoïcien, comme l'homme se*

François de la Noue, of Pierre de La Primaudaye or of Agrippa d'Aubigné on the corruption through passion of their contemporaries can be seen to fall into a cultural tradition deeply impregnated by Stoicism. References to Seneca are also frequent in the *Excellent discours de la vie et de la mort* which Plessis Mornay published in Geneva in 1576[34]. It is interesting to note also that the historian Simon Goulart was the translator of *Les oeuvres morales et meslées de Seneque*[35].

Stoicism is perhaps the explanation behind the fact that an alliance was possible between the Protestant camp and those Catholics whose principal aim was to preserve the unity of the temporal State, and who, faced with the members of the Catholic League whom they considered worse than Turks, Saracens and Cannibals, were ready to 'use every sort of friend'[36].

The reserved or openly hostile attitude of many members of the Parlement to the League seems to me to bear a parallel and fundamental relationship to an adoption of the Stoic ethic, allowing them to transcend the eschatalogical crisis that their contemporaries were experiencing, and which forced them to re-evaluate the relationship between society and political authority as one of absolute obedience and individual non-intervention.

This ideological system is no mere theoretical fiction. The fact that it became a reality results from both the political image and the *Politique* policies which the king of Navarre imposed during his progress towards

---

peut rendre vertueux, libre, heureux et sans passion. Traduitte du grec en françois par A. R., Poitiers, 1567.

[34] Ph. de Mornay, *Excellent discours de la vie et de la mort*, [Geneva], 1576, commented on in Julien Eymard d'Angers, *Recherches sur le Stoïcisme aux XVIe et XVIIe siècles*, L. Antoine ed., [Studien und Materialen zur Geschichte der Philosophie 19, 1979], Hildesheim, p. 16–17. See also the analyses of A. Levi, *French Moralists: The Theory of the Passion 1585 to 1649*, Oxford, 1964, pp. 55–63, and E. F. Rice, *The Renaissance Idea of Wisdom*, Cambridge, 1958.

[35] S. Goulart, *Les oeuvres morales et meslées de Seneque*, Paris, 1595, 3 t.

[36] On the importance of Stoic and neo-Stoic texts in the libraries of *parlementaires*, see G. Abel, *Stoïzmus und frühe Neuzeit. Zur Enstehungsgeschichte modernen Denkens im Felde von Ethik und Politik*, Berlin-New-York, 1978, pp. 72–92, 208–227 and 281–294. On the necessity of the alliance between *Politiques* and Huguenots, *Discours brief, mais tres solide, monstrant clairement qu'il est loisible, honneste, utile et necessaire au Roi de s'allier avec le Roy de Navarre, et s'ayder de ses Armes et moyens contre les rebelles et usurpateurs de son Estat*, printed in London by Richard Fiels, 1589, p. 13.

power. Henri of Navarre is a king of Reason and it was by the imposition of a political order based on reason, that he succeeded in legitimizing a resacralisation of the monarchy.

The first sign of Henri of Navarre's adoption of Stoicism as the objective basis of a process of personal sacralisation is evident at an early stage. It was in 1585 that a Protestant ideologue in the king of Navarre's entourage, perhaps Philippe du Plessis-Mornay, composed a *Declaration du Roy de Navarre sur les calomnies publiées contre luy es Protestations de ceux de la Ligue qui se sont eslevez en ce Royaume*. This text can be seen as one of the starting points of the very particular kind of sacral identification which was to lead the man from the Béarn to the throne. In this work, Henri III is beseeched to give his permission for a duel to take place, which would save the country from the sufferings of civil war, 'an offer which he [Henri of Navarre] is making to Monsieur de Guyse, because they have taken him to task in their Pretexte and because the said Sieur de Guyse is one of their military commanders: that, without further suffering to the Orders and Estates of this Kingdom, and without involving a domestic or foreign army, which could only lead to the ruin of the common people, this quarrel should be sorted out between the two combatants, man to man, or two by two, ten by ten or twenty by twenty, as many as the said Sieur de Guise requests, with the normal arms used by knights'. The combatants were to meet on a field of honour to be chosen outside the kingdom.

But this was not only a question of reviving a tradition of chivalrous combat and of God's judgment. The imagined combat is designed to do away with the image of the king of Navarre as the leader of a particular group. The Béarnais claims to be ready to sacrifice himself for the public good, he makes a gift of his person to the kingdom because he cannot countenance a new war which would be highly destructive to the France he serves. The conflict between the League and his supporters causes him nothing but 'sighs and tears' because it can only lead to the spilling of noble blood, and to the suffering and desolation of the people, to disorder and above all to divine punishment which will soon rain on the country as a result of all the blasphemies that accompany war, and the 'rise of uncontrollable vice' which the 'lax usage of arms' will encourage. The image of a pure and Stoical man comes into being with this project for man-to-man combat with Guise; Henri of Navarre admits that he may die in the struggle, but immediately confides that he does not fear death, and that on the contrary he is prepared to meet his death calmly in order that reason may triumph over violence.

If Henri opposes the League by putting his life in jeopardy, it is to show that he is not motivated by personal ambition or hatred. He is claiming to be the man who has his passions under control: rather than living for himself alone, he is offering himself to the nation, to the king and to God. In order to prevent France from sinking like a 'shipwreck' and in order to cut short a business that seems only likely to end when there are no Frenchmen left in France, he is giving himself like Christ gave himself to all men: he sets out his desire to 'buy back' the kingdom 'with his own blood', moved by his sole desire to see God revered, the State pacified and the people at peace[37].

The imagined duel is the starting point for the achievement of a sacral position, for it is, according to the definition of F. Billacois, 'an individual move, at the same time both superior to the monarchy and a means of approach to it'[38]. Henceforth, Henri of Navarre, by facing up to death in such a serene and Stoic manner, has placed himself firmly under the scrutiny of God alone. The only real witness to his struggle for the good of the French people will be God, just as God was the only real witness to the redemptive offering made by His Son.

Without it ever being made explicit, Henri of Navarre is abandoning the conception of heroism that Condé and even Guise adhere to. In the suggested duel, he is proposing to abandon his social rank, his identity, to set himself before God naked and full of humility[39]. And it is in response to this unprecedented and total humanisation of a life when faced with death, this identification of man with Christ, as a result of this Christian Stoicism, that proof of God's existence will be revealed, in a divine judgment that will

---

[37] [Philippe Du Plessis-Mornay?], *Declaration du Roy de Navarre sur les calomnies publiées contre luy es Protestations de ceux de la Ligue qui se sont eslevez en ce Royaume*, Ortes, 1585, p. 46–48. The theme of the duel is used again two months later in the *Declaration et protestation du Roy de Navarre, de Monsieur le Prince de Condé et de monsieur le Duc de Montmorenci: sur la paix faicte avec ceux de la maison de Lorraine, chefs et principaux auteurs de la Ligue, au prejudice de la maison de France*, Bergerac, 1585. In this work, the king of Navarre sets himself up as the champion of Henri III, threatened by the ambition of the Guise: the House of France is 'attacked' by the House of Lorraine (B4) and France is martyrised by the 'violence and conspiracies of her enemies'. The discourse against the Guise is a discourse against 'the passions'.

[38] F. Billacois, *Le Duel dans la Société française des XVIe–XVIIe siècles. Essai de psychologie historique*, Paris, 1986, p. 91.

[39] *Ibid.*, p. 110.

prove to all that the victor is no ordinary mortal. The groundwork is thus prepared for a step towards personal divinity which will strengthen over successive years as a result of a constant duel with death and the passions. The king in some ways becomes Christ, and thus conquers France in the desire to 'bring down on myself all the perils of France, to save her from suffering, making myself, by my own accord, equal to those whom nature made inferior to me'. The Béarnais is proposing to take onto himself the immense sufferings and anxieties of the people of France, his intentions and his wishes being of a purity that contrasts strongly with the passions that move the Guise brothers, and which prevent them from accepting the duel, because they acquiesce with the 'public confusion' and a war that is 'unnecessary and therefore unjust'[40].

What we find here is an expression of an essential element in the history of the religious troubles. A man is claiming to take upon himself in his earthly life all the problems of this world that his fellow-man has encountered and crystallising them in one super-human action which will be for the benefit of all because detached from what characterises humanity, namely human passions. The combat of Henri of Navarre is, in symbolic terms, a redemptive combat, a gesture detached from its physical perpetrator by which all the sins of France will be redeemed little by little through this sacrificial act.

Henri of Navarre's conquest of the kingdom of France is brought about in the context of a Stoic representation of time and of man's action in time. A few years later, after the death of Henri III, the picture of the history of League and of the conflict between Henri of Navarre and its members which is offered to contemporaries, in fact interprets the uprising of the League in the light of the Stoic theme of a great conflagration which gives way to regeneration. Far from suggesting anxiety, the present represents hope. The League's violence is said to have embroiled France in a 'great chaos', a great confusion, a 'general madness' desired by God. Through the League, France became the very inversion of divine order, an inversion which is 'personified' by Paris, which the *Panegyric Au tres chrestien Henri IIII* claims to be a town full of unspeakable and filthy things. The capital is a microcosm of the chaos created by the League in that it is in the hands of the 'rabble, the pernicious citizens' of society, the base elements which have taken the place of the superior elements[41]. But as C. Vivanti has shown, the object

---

[40] *Lettres du Roy de Navarre premier Prince du sang et premier Pair de France, à Messieurs de la ville de Paris*, 1586, BII–C.

[41] *Panegyric Au tres chrestien Henry IIII. Roy de France et de Navarre. Par*

in describing the present chaos is to heighten awareness of the inevitable renaissance[42]. Pamphlets glorifying Henri of Navarre predict that he is the king who will bring about the long-awaited Golden Age, after a series of purifying conflicts. The pamphlet entitled *Le Labyrinthe de la Ligue* transposes the Stoic idea of the 'ekpurosis' onto current happenings[43]: the French are invited to understand and foresee that 'it is under this King that we can expect the return of the Golden Age to our century, after we have been sufficiently purified by fire, by the sword and by the troubles that we have brought upon ourselves'. A new order emerges thanks to Henri of Navarre, by which virtue takes the place of vice and the force of law replaces anarchy. It is significant that at this point this vision falls into place with the cyclical vision of time characteristic of astrology. Thus for Jean Aymé of Chavigny, Henri of Navarre has been happily designated the king of the renewal of the centuries, of earthly happiness[44]. The reconquest of the kingdom is conceptualised within the limited sphere of a cyclical interpretation of history, an idea inspired by the Stoic philosophy, and which is represented in celebrations, where the end of the chaos caused by the League is often depicted by throwing a dummy or the arms of the League, symbols of violence and passion, into the purifying flames.

The new order is also said to be a corollary of the identification of Henri of Navarre with fate, thus enabling it to be said that his monarchy is predetermined, and because it is predetermined, it is in agreement with the order of Reason which has governed the universe since the beginning of all time. This identification is made via two different channels. The king of Navarre is defined as 'the king of the ancient prophesies'. The prophesying that gives emphasis to the different phases of the conquest of the kingdom, is inseparable from the cyclic vision of time, which leads the Béarnais to be identified with Alexander the Great, conqueror of the world. In the *Panegyric Au tres-chrestien Henry IIII* of 1590, the end of a period of troubles is seen through the expected reign of the Béarnais[45] through whom France destroyed by the violence of the League will be resuscitated if she returns to the path of obedience: '... we have survived the dangerous year, the climacteric year, ordinarily accompanied by troubles and illnesses

le S. D. I. E. S. L., Tours, Jamet Mettayer, n. p.

[42] C. Vivanti, *Lotta politica e pace religiosa in Francia fra cinque Seicento*, Turin, 1963.

[43] *Le Labyrinthe de la Ligue et les moyens...*, *op. cit.*, p. 143.

[44] J. -A. de Chavigny, *La premiere face du Janus François...*, Lyon, 1594, epistle to the king.

[45] *Panegyric Au tres-Chrestien...*, *op. cit.*, p. 88.

of the body and mind, we will now be healthy, refreshed and happy if we do that which we must do'. The period which is just beginning will see the king, having brought the whole kingdom under his rule, bringing to his subjects 'all the happiness of the heavens'. The chronicle of the reign that is just beginning is integrated into the mystico-prophetical legend of the French monarchy. Thus in his work of 1595, *Les trois visions de Childeric quatriesme roy de France*, Pierre Boton makes Basine predict that after a period of intense chaos:[46]

> La France revivra sous son Henry quatriesme;
> Tant ce nombre de quatre est en force supresme:
> C'est un nombre sur tous bien-heureux et fatal
> Qui sacré à la vie est appelé vital.

The identification of Henri of Navarre with the king of a golden age announced by the prophesies leads to the necessity of all laying down their arms. In *l'Oracle ou le chant de Protée*[47], 'a Henri will be born who will never find a king his equal in war or in peace'.

One of the primary foundations of this second absolutism can be found in this deterministic vision of history, in this inevitable succession of events which will lead France from a period of chaos into a time of order and of happiness, and the events favourable to Henri of Navarre begin gradually to persuade people of the implacable logic of this vision.

But the justification of the marvellous reign of Henri of Navarre goes beyond an argument whose only end would be to persuade the French that they should view politics as the realisation of destiny through an individual. It goes beyond this and becomes bound up with a Stoic or neo-Stoic ideal. The submission required of the people of France is explicitly legitimized by the perception of a cosmic force acting through the royal figure. Henri of Navarre, in the apologies that emphasise his work of pacifying the kingdom, appears all the more to be a historical necessity dictated by the order of the universe, since he is perceived as destiny, as the order of Time fixed

---

[46] P. Boton, *Les trois visions de Childeric Quatriesme Roy de France, pronostic des guerres civiles de ce Royaume: et la Prophetie de Basine sa femme, sur les victoires et conquestes de Henri de Bourbon Roy de France et de Navarre, et sur la rencontre fait à Fontaine Françoise*, Paris, Federic Morel, 1595, p. 14.

[47] [Jean Godard], *l'Oracle ou le chant de Protée. Contenant la Prediction des vaillances et victoires de Henry IIIIe tres Chrestien et tres Victorieux Roy de France et de Navarre. Avec les Trophées du mesme Seigneur. Dediez à sa Majesté par I. G. P.*, Paris, Jamet Mettayer and Pierre l'Huilier, 1595, p. 2.

by all eternity and the incarnation of the super-human. Already in the reports of the victories of Arques and Ivry, he is said to be a divine force, a king whose rule has been predestined since all eternity, because he is France's destiny, the very Reason which is behind the balance of the future of the kingdom: he is the force that decides the right of all to live or die, and through whom the people of France will gain access to a positive phase of their history, rediscovering life in a period of peace predetermined since time began. All the French people must realise that their individual destinies depend entirely on the achievement of the destiny embodied by the king of Navarre. To recognize him as their king is to stop resisting the inevitable, to stop fighting fate and Reason which, according to the Stoic philosophy, governs the universe. A collective detachment from history, and thereby from the events of the present and the anxiety they generate, is thus essential as a direct result of the assertion that 'man cannot foresee the evils of the future, nor turn from them when they happen, and it is often the case that the more he seeks to hold back from them, the more he tries to escape his destiny, the more quickly he rushes into its clutches'.[48]

As a result of the portrayal of the actions of Henri of Navarre, the French are called upon to put on the mantle of wise Stoics. The aim of the prevailing polemic is to persuade them of the validity of the theory of a royalty of Reason: they must obey God whose revealed will is destiny or providence, by identifying their own desires with destiny or with providence. To be free under the monarchy that is developing in the decade from 1590 is to obey God by following the king, who since time immortal has been destined to rule France. This precept is bolstered up even more by the assimilation of the king into the Herculean legend: Stoic royalty takes on the aspects of a legend through the person of the king who is none other than the reincarnation of the mythical hero of the renewal of the world. A major discovery of the political utopia accompanies the birth of the new authority, which will bring about a society at last reformed and purified: the new Hercules, through his labours will 'clean up France' and will at last honour those who merit it 'by a harmonious and rightful distribution of rewards and recompenses'[49]. The monsters will be cut down, and the Golden Age will be a reality for all. The Herculean action of the king distances the horror of eschatalogical imminence, and over-shadows the resulting anxiety as it can only be achieved through the elimination of Evil and by the coming of an earthly world purified and content. This action

---

[48] [G. Joly], *Le Panegyrique ou discours des Louanges du Roy Henry IIII. Par M. G. I.*, Chaalons, Claude Guyot, 1592, p. 80.

[49] *Panegyric Au tres-chrestien Henry IIII...*, *op. cit.*, p. 70.

points towards benign regeneration, absolute in its purity[50].

Perhaps one of the keys to Henri's conversion to Catholicism can be found in this heroico-Stoic representation of the king of Navarre. Henri of Navarre, by being identified as 'the Hercules of our troubles', no longer the *Hercule gaulois* of the first Renaissance but the Hercules who suffers and acts for all[51], is a king in the Stoic mould: he is destiny, the reason of the world. His fate is to follow his destiny which is to be king in the face of everything, to put an end to the troubles that are undermining the kingdom, even if this means sacrificing his own religious convictions. Suffering and renunciation must be accepted because they are implicit in the progression of time.

The images are not only images. They reflect a psychological turning point. The assimilation of the legend gives rise to a relationship between the king and his authority which is different to that which derived from his divine election, or which, rather, superimposes on that election an active rationality. The bible-monarch mystery becomes secondary when compared with the evidence of an heroic epic which is returning France, or rather leading it on, towards a Golden Age. The power is the power of a man because that is inevitable, because fate gave it to man. It is an absolute power because its close identification with destiny, with a need of the history of the world, effectively eliminates all possibility of political opposition. When Henri IV makes his entry into Abbeville, the king encounters his own picture painted on a huge oval, which signifies to him that he is above the ordinary order of men because of his destiny: he is Hercules, the victor over violence and war, who has reached the top of a steep mountain, Oeta. He has climbed a path covered with thorns. Beneath him lie the trophies of his victories, the body of a lion, of a wild boar, of the hydra...[52].

---

[50] *Continuation de ce qui est advenu en l'armée du roy depuis la prinse des faux bourgs de Paris, jusques à celle de la ville de Fallaiz*, Tours, Jamet Mettayer, 1590, p. 58.

[51] *Discours veritable de la victoire obtenue par le Roy en la Bataille donnée près le village d'Evry, le Mercredy quatorziesme jour de Mars, mil cinq cens nonante*, Tours, Jamet Mettayer, 1590, p. 58. On the significance of the Heruclean myth, see M. R. Jung, *Hercule dans la littérature française du XVIe siècle. De l'Hercule courtois à l'Hercule baroque*, Geneva, 1966, and G. Monsarrat, *Les thèmes stoïciens dans la littérature de la Renaissance anglaise*, Université Lille III, 1975, and M. Simon, *Hercule et le Christianisme*, Paris, n.d.

[52] E. Prarond, *La Ligue à Abbeville, 1576–1594*, Paris, 1868–1873, t. III, p. 233.

Thus in the years between 1589 and 1594, the conflict between the League and the royalists saw the confrontation of two different visions. In opposition to the spiritual messianism of the Reign of the Cross towards which the League tried to draw the faithful, a new temporal messianism was developed. The temporal world is envisaged as the site of a rational action, which strives above all to eliminate anything that might give rise to 'abuses and disorder'[53]. The idea of a reign founded on eternal Reason does not prevent the men who surround and advise Henri IV, and who know that one should always forestall destructive tendencies, from conceiving the political world as a mobile order. The immobility of the order of Reason can only be preserved by dynamic action which should be aimed at 'the comfort, the enhancement and the enrichment of your kingdom and your people' as Sully puts it[54]. The Calvinist disenchantment with the world is not unfamiliar to this conceptualisation, the elaborators of which are for the most part Huguenots, from Barthélemy de Laffemas to Olivier de Serres[55]. The agricultural renewal that the monarch encourages, and the 'social mercantilism'[56] which accompanies it, only make sense if they are viewed within this ideological context. The primary aim is to 'get rid of the poverty which is increasing daily' and which risks becoming a serious problem to the reign of Reason. The reinstitution of the lines of communication, the improvement of the navigability of the rivers and the projects for canals, the creation of new industries, the diffusion of new agricultural methods and urban intervention should certainly not be overestimated as far as their economic impact is concerned which in fact remained essentially limited and which left France still fragile in 1610; but they are indicative of a political will to lead the world gradually towards earthly happiness and which aims at defeating Time, and thus its power of anxiety over men, by the creation of a secular utopia. The Golden Age will be the age of 'happiness' of men, governed by an Eternal king.

---

[53] 'Edit sur les monnaies' September 1602, quoted in P. Deyon, *Le mercantilisme*, Paris, 1969, pp. 92–93.

[54] Sully, *Mémoires (sages et royales Economies d'Etat)*, L. R. Lefèvre ed., Paris 1942, p. 285, on the culture of the mulberry tree. On the general politics of Sully, D. J. Buisseret, *Sully and the Growth of Centralized Government in France, 1598–1610*, London, 1968.

[55] Various references in J. Bieler, *La pensée économique de Calvin*, Geneva, 1961, F. Lequesne, *La vie d'Olivier de Serres*, Paris, 1942, and C. W. Cole, *French Mercantilist Doctrines before Colbert*, New York, 1931.

[56] The expression is that of H. Hauser, *La modernité au XVIe siècle*, Paris, 1963, pp. 168–169.

The identification of the king with Hercules implies that the king is immortal, and the obsession of royalist propaganda is henceforth to convince the nation that Henri IV will never die because he is the incarnation of the Reason of the world and Reason is eternal. Stoicism was the basic element in this sacralisation of the king. The king embodies life and the principle of life, Reason. God, or half God, he cannot die. Any questioning of the immortality of the king would signify the sweeping return of human passion and the forces of destruction.

It is in 1600, however, when the Wars of Religion are over but still present in the collective consciousness, that the heroic nature of the king's life is dramatised most effectively, at the time of the entry of the queen Marie de Medici into Avignon. The town centre is transformed into a journey along the paths of fate by the construction of a 'septenary' labyrinth built around seven triumphal arches built 'according to the hypothesis of seven of the most important labours of Hercules'[57].

There is first of all the arch commemorating the victory over the Hydra, dedicated to Mars, god of bravery, meant to portray, contrary to the impious calculations of the astrologers and disciples of Machiavelli, that only the providence of God governs the world, and that any intervention on the part of man is hopeless[58]. Then there follows the arch of Apollo, where Hercules is depicted relieving Atlas of his burden, a clear indication that it is Henri IV that is to bear the weight of the world henceforth[59]. The arch of Jupiter depicts the garden of the Hesperides, celebrating the return to civil life and to the peaceful reign of the law which the king has restored[60]. Royal clemency, a willingness to forget the destruction of the past is exalted in the arch of Minerva, goddess of humanity and leniency. Hercules — Henri IV throws himself into the flames at the summit of Mount Oeta: 'this generous heart found within himself a far more difficult victory than all the others, for, by throwing himself into the flames, he defeated him who had

---

[57] *Labyrinthe royal de l'Hercule gaulois triomphant sur le subject des Fortunes, batailles, victoires, Trophées, Triomphes, Mariages et autres faits heroïques, et memorables du Tres-Auguste et tres-Chrestien Prince Henry IIII. Roy de France et de Navarre, Representé à l'Entrée triomphante de la Royne en la cité d'Avignon. Le 19 Novembre l'An M. D. C. Ou sont contenuës les Magnificences et Triomphes dressez à cet effect par la dite ville*, Jacques Bramereau, Avignon, [1601], p. 1.

[58] *Ibid.*, p. 55.

[59] *Ibid.*, p. 67.

[60] *Ibid.*, p. 123

subjugated all the universe — himself'[61]. Reason recreates the mystery of the monarchy, Reason becomes the truth which compels everyone to submit to their king and to understand that he is pre-destined, a Stoic king who by his very person shows the path to follow, the renunciation of passion. The new royalty is an objectively divine monarchy through the rational impersonality of the king, whose destiny has consecrated him entirely to France.

This objectivisation of the divine nature of power, and thus the personalisation of divinity in the person of the monarch is equally apparent in the permanent authentication of the virtues through which Henri IV becomes personified as the king of Reason, forming a part of the divine order, of this 'harmony which is in all things that the great Creator has moulded according to the perfect idea of his eternal power'[62]. A distinction by which he is accorded the cardinal virtues of the sages of Antiquity.

In 1591, having appealed to the 'wise' Catholics to leave 'quarrels of State to those who want to get involved through propriety, reversion through conquest or other causes', Pierre Ayrault lauds the 'paternal' forgiveness of the king. His soul is haunted by a single fear which is 'to ruin us and to cause our downfall', and which finds expression in his insistence on making peace the new fundamental law of his kingdom. He is the king of Reason, and Reason must lead his subjects to have an absolute confidence in his clemency. Because he is the natural monarch of France, unlike the tyrant who rules through usurpation and who must always be a prey to

---

[61] *Ibid.*, p. 136. For an analysis of this text, see M. R. Jung *op. cit.*, pp. 175–185. The arch of Mercury shows the defeat of Geryon, and thus the peace with Spain. The sixth arch is that of Diana, a 'simple' image of the church, illustrating the royal Catholicisation through the theme of the liberation of Prometheus bound. The final arch, dedicated to Venus, shows the capture of the hind of Ceryneia, solemnising the fruitful union between the king and Marie de Medici.

[62] A. Perigaud, *Notes et documents pour servir à l'histoire de Lyon — règne de Henri IV*, Lyon, 1842, p. 68. Before 1589–1590, the apologists insist above all on the innocence and selflessness of the king of Navarre, on his great availability and his spontaneity of action for example; [Michel Hurault, sieur du Fay], *Excellent et libre discours sur l'Etat present de la France Avec la coppie des lettres patentes du Roy depuis qu'il s'est retiré de Paris. Ensemble la coppie de deux lettres du Duc de Guyse. Par un docte personnage, bien versé aux affaires d'estat de la France*, 1588, p. 48: 'a very good man, frank, open, and so busy dealing with pressing current concerns that he pays less attention to the past and to the future: can scarcely conceive of convoluted plots, content with hope alone'.

doubt and mistrust as far as the loyalty of his subjects is concerned, Henri
of Navarre only has to love his subjects unceasingly and forgive them everything: 'his assurance is reason'. A true prince, then, he is by nature
clement, and if the rebels will only submit to him, 'he could pass a single edict that would erase all past confusions without forcing anyone away
or dispossessing anyone'.[63]. The celebrations highlight the willingness to
forget. Clemency abolishes history, it allows the setting up of an eternal
Golden Age, purified of all passion.

Prudence is another of the king's characteristics. Before governing
others, the king must rule himself. The picture is one of a monarch who lives
his life completely according to the saying of Marcus Aurelius, 'commune
with yourself'. Henri IV is also presented by his apologists as the opposite of
an autocrat, concerned above all, both 'docilely and gladly' to take counsel
from his subjects. Thus prudence is 'the mother of all his actions and the
root of all his other perfections'[64]. Prudence signifies the mastery of Time,
a royalty in many ways outside time, an eternal force, divine perfection.

The third cardinal virtue is sometimes called 'piety' sometimes 'justice', and sometimes 'charity'. The king had gone so far as to want to shed
his own blood for his people. From Hercules to Christ, a fusion already
suggested becomes apparent in the system of representation. Henri IV is
said to 'approach divinity'. He is perfect. In all his acts not only does he
follow God by making his life conform to nature and to reason, but he also
makes himself like God, for the virtue by which he is possessed is Reason
which governs the whole universe; he is a god, and after the restoration of
peace or the 'law of nature'[65], he will be the unifier of the world.

His courage, the fourth of his virtues, elevates him to the level of the
divine heroes who have tried to bring together human and universal order.
Henri IV is compared to Alexander the Stoic's hero through whom, according to Plutarch, Zeno's dream of unification under one order of humanity
was made possible[66]. The king's courage is natural. The fact that he is

---

[63] [Pierre Ayrault], *Consideration sur les troubles, et le juste moyen de les
appaiser: Aux villes de Paris, Rouen, Tholoze, Orleans, Lyon, et autres*, 1591,
C*II*–C*IIII*.

[64] [G. Joly], *Le Panegyrique ou discours...' op. cit.*, p. 11.

[65] *Poeme en forme de Dialogisme sur l'arrivée de la Paix*, Lyon, Loys Clo-
quemin, 1598, p. 6.

[66] Quotation from Plutarch's 'de la fortune d'Alexandre', chap. VI, in E. Bre-
hier, *Histoire de la philosophie, I, Antiquité et Moyen Age*, Paris, 1981, pp. 292–

super-human is seen through the 'innumerable exploits of this new Hannibal or Caesar'. For the apologists nothing is impossible for this purifying hero, all the more so as the exhilaration of virtue is communicated from him to his soldiers; it permits them to enter the order of the accomplishment of reason, for 'their hearts become larger than their bodies and fly without fear towards each new blow, as if they had been transformed by him into dragons and lions eager to set upon the enemy prey'[67].

Thus a new royalty was created, or rather a renewed and amplified royalty as the traditional sacred elements of power remained, and in this new form of royalty the king is less an image of God, as he had been before, but rather God made man through the divine reason or fate that he represents and which mark him out as the providential accomplishment of a human order called upon to conform to universal order.

The reign of Reason could begin as soon as this authentication of the divine future in the person of the king had taken place, and thus as soon as a relationship involving the rational submission of the subjects to authority had been established, a relationship of acceptance if not of resignation. A king in the Stoic mould shatters eschatalogical anxiety, or rather succeeds where the Reformation failed, in diverting the collective consciousness by the affirmation of divine monarchy. This is where the great break occurs. The absolute monarchy sets itself up on the foundations laid by the cultural revolution of the Reformation. And I am far from agreeing with J. Garrisson-Estèbe when she suggests that one can only interpret the apologetic discourse of the saviour king in terms of a Machiavellian strategy[68]. I believe that through the praise that assures his authority of a divine necessity and which highlights its rationality, the never-ending quest for human appeasement is prolonged. Against anxiety is set up the humanist utopia of a Golden Age in a world open to action. After a great many trials, Reason triumphs over panic through the exaltatation of an absolute monarchy. The political rationality of modern France has been born out of the struggle against an extraordinary surge of eschatalogical anxiety and of tension concerning the spiritual accomplishment of humanity, an anxiety destroyed or diverted by a king who sacrifices himself completely to the happiness of his people. It was in this first period of the reduction of eschatalogical

---

293. On the relationship between Plutarch and Stoicism, D. Babut, *Plutarque et le stoïcisme*, Paris, 1969. For a comparison between Henri IV and Alexander, see *Le Panegyrique adressé au Roy...*, *op. cit.*, p. 11.

[67] *Le Panegyrique adressé au Roy...*, *op. cit.*, Lb^{35} 306, p. 15.

[68] J. Garrisson-Estèbe, *Henry IV*, Paris, 1894, p. 338.

anxiety and thus of collective violence that the second absolutism could have a certain historical logicality.

One must however put the solidity of the stabilisation of the monarchy in the years that follow the end of the religious troubles into perspective. When the king was murdered by Ravaillac, the League was still a living reality in the minds of the French people. Proof of this is the decapitation of a *gentilhomme* in the Place de Grève on the third of May 1608 for having used 'charms and sorcery and the sticking of pins into a wax model with the aim of harming the king's person'[69], and 'bad rumours' continue to be spread until 1610[70]. There has still as yet been no real chronological break in the struggle for mystical union with Christ.

For although it is greatly reduced and overshadowed by the triumphant ideology of the Golden Age and by the age of Reason, eschatalogical anxiety is nevertheless at times very real. The constant anticipation of divine punishment subsists in the perception of signs giving forewarning of God's violence, which allow one to imagine a strong resistance to the political vision of the conquest of the kingdom by Henri, a collective resistance which demonstrates the continuing obsession with the prophesy of eschatalogical punishment. On 17 November 1605, many thousands of people are reported as having seen in the skies of Paris a sign 'in the form of red staffs'[71]. In March 1606 there is the sighting of a new star which 'filled the people with new terrors'[72]. On Thursday 29 June, the rumour once again went around that the town was destined for destruction that night. The revela-

---

[69] L'Estoile, *Journal pour le règne de Henri IV et le début du règne de Louis XIII — 1589-1611, Œuvres diverses*, L. R. Lefèvre, A. Martin eds., Paris, 1948–1960, t II, p. 334: 'there was also talk of some people having procured poisons, which are far more frightening than all these prickings and charms... A surgeon, very expert in his art, but a great sorcerer, was hanged.

[70] *Ibid.*, t. II, p. 175. On the subject of the assassination attempt of 19 December 1605, according to the story, the king while returning from hunting, encountered on the Pont-neuf 'a madman who having a bare blade beneath his cloak, tried to harm His Majesty (...) and said that he wanted to kill the king, because he held his goods and the best part of the kingdom unjustly; then, laughing, he said that at least he had given the king a good fright. This madman was called Jacques des Iles, native of Senlis, practitioner and prosecutor in that town, and had been completely deranged for a long time'. The king pardoned him.

[71] *Ibid.*, t. II, p. 174.

[72] *Ibid.*, t. II, p. 186.

tion of the catastrophe is attributed to the Pope, and it unleashes a wave of anxiety such that 'many of the more simple and credulous folk left the town and the suburbs'[73]. Predictions of misfortunes to come were again circulating in July, and the prophesy of the destruction of the capital resurfaces once more on the twenty seventh of that month[74]. Throughout the months of September and October 1607, after the astrologers, in March, had once again entreated the masses to leave Paris, a town cursed by God[75], it is a comet that foretells the future misfortunes and punishments[76]. The pressure of eschatalogical anxiety becomes increasingly potent and l'Estoile cannot resist out of curiosity sending his 'man' out on 23 June 1609 to buy 'a warning to all Christians on the great and horrible arrival of the Antichrist and the End of the world in the year 1666'[77]. In August 1609 'the whole of Paris' is filled with the rumour of the birth in Babylon of a child who is none other than the Antichrist, depicted in terms most likely to strike the imagination[78].

Cannot these short and often repeated waves of eschatalogical fever be interpreted as so many manifestations of resistance to the political system of Reason, to the dream of Eternity which underpinned the ideological construction that had assured the triumph of Henri IV? Are they not symptomatic of a disjuncture between the reduction of anxiety which results from the imagined reign of Eternity under the royal peace, and minds which continue to live in the emotion of collective guilt and the fever caused by the thought of the violence of God? In addition, the decade from 1600, despite

---

[73] *Ibid.*, t. II, p. 193.

[74] *Ibid.*, t. II, p. 198.

[75] *Ibid.*, t. II, p. 302.

[76] *Ibid.*, t. II, p. 274. See *Discours prodigieux de la terrible et espouventable Comete aparue le 26, Juillet, 1607, au pays de Frise avec le combat des nuees et vents furieux qui coururent le lendemain 27, dudict moys qui ont fait un grand degat des personnes, bestail et ruyne de bastiment. Traduict (...) par Sebastien Vemberg*, Lyon, 'sur la Coppie imprimée à Zurich', n.d., Arsenal 8° S. 1506 (5) and *La comete qui est aparuë le 25 de Septembre 1607. Par G. L'Apostre*, Saint-Omer, F. Bellet, n.d., B. N. V. 21086.

[77] *Ibid.*, t. II, p. 464.

[78] *Ibid.*, t. II, p. 500. This work was found by J. P. Séguin, *L'information en France avant le périodique, 517 canards imprimés entre 1529 et 1631*, Paris, 1964, p. 106: *Coppie de la lettre du grand maistre de Malthe envoyée au Roy, en laquelle on luy donne advertissement de la naissance de l'Antéchrist né en Babylone. Laquelle lettre a esté traduicte d'Italien en François. Le 15. du mois de Juillet, 1609.* Paris, G. du Puis, [1609]. B. N. Res. G. 2854.

economical improvement resulting logically from the return of peace, is far from being a Golden Age.

The important thing is that in 1610, despite the relative distancing between different attempts at regicide, there are clear indications of a logical malfunction in the ideological system founded on Reason. In my opinion, a disruption of the equilibrium is at work which leads to the legitimisation of both an exaltation and a revision of the royal legend. This can be seen through a close examination of the *Description et explication* of the motifs and the emblems that decorated the route to be taken after the coronation on 13 May by the cortège of Marie de Medici. The town becomes the site of a 'mystic' route, in the sense that 'a whole series of triumphal arches, artificial boulders, archways, stages, mottoes, inscriptions, figurines and emblems' with either biblical or mythological significance according to L'Estoile, transfigure the capital into a place of exaltation of the monarchy of Reason.

The first argument is that of the king as restorer of the State and of universal peace of France and who 'quite rightly merited the title of the greatest, most perfect and most august monarch who has ever reigned'. The capital celebrates a most virtuous royalty by uniting with it through dramatisation. But it is the perception of an imperfection in the perfection which is said to have given rise to the transformation of the capital and thus of the kingdom into a 'mystic' world, into a world of the language of signs: 'until then nothing could add to our desires if not that the virtue of this great prince could make him immortal to us'. Because Reason has told him that everything in the world is finite, the king wanted to make the peace everlasting and ensure the 'continued tranquillity' by providing a line of descent, through his marriage to Marie de Medici. This marriage makes him the king for Eternity: 'We may say that God having blessed them with his holy graces and benedictions, particularly in the matter of the happy fruitfulness of their sacred marriage, that from that day France saw itself to be the possessor of true peace and tranquillity, all subject of division and faction banished forever, all the evil plans that could be hatched against this state...'.

The ultimate effect of the royal entry is, through a veritable apotheosis of the living king, to put France definitively into a period that abolishes time, the inauguration of an earthly reign that can know no more disruptions or crises. The earthly sphere affirms its autonomy as the place of the bringing about of Divine Reason, embodied by the king-God and accepted by all the subjects as a rule of life: 'France, so superb and triumphant joins its wishes to the virtues of its prince, whom all the world proclaims to be most great and victorious, and God who never leaves such actions without recognition or reward, promises to their Majesties longevity and eternity to their rule... and that their actions and gestures, raised up to the Heavens, will live on amongst men for century after century of glorious posterity'[79]. Through the image of Fortune, no longer portrayed attached to a wheel, but 'standing, fixed' on a pedestal, her folded wings signifying that she has ceased to be fickle and that she has chosen France as 'the place of her repose and eternal resting place' for all times, there appears a desire to transmit the idea of the suspension of time, to prolong infinitely the divine destiny of the king who has initiated the Golden Age of the kingdom; a desire to link to the restored state, not only the divinity of the king, but also that of the dauphin in whom this divinity is naturally reborn according to the divine order of nature. Henri IV has given the kingdom 'fortune as a possession'. Without the force of life that is in the dauphin and which has come from the king and from whom there come 'all sorts of good fortune', there is only chaos, tyranny, violence and ruin.

Two niches contain two enormous statues: in the first, *Jupiter Stator* holds a lance in one hand and a thunderbolt in the other. There is an eagle at his feet, a symbol of the fact that it is the king who has returned life to all through his valour and his virtue. The second statue, also a Jupiter, is crowned with olive branches, the preserver of the world, the 'father of all, without whom nothing can survive, who produces, nourishes and protects all species'; a king who is said to be 'the soul of the world' and the 'author of life', a Stoic image, the cosmic fire which gives life to the world, the fundamental flame that is the breath of the divine. An inscription describes the monument, reminding the observer that the king has returned France to 'Reason', France that was previously the prey of the devil, and that through his reign he assures a peaceful France of Eternity.

There are other reminders of Stoicism: an inscription claims that, by his clemency, the king has above all won a victory over himself, that he has been a Hercules defeating monsters. His life is a fine example of the domination of the passions. A picture also portrays him on horseback, 'stretching out a bare hand, just as one sees in the statue of Marcus Aurelius in the Capitol...'[80]. Further on, the fourth triumphal arch is in a different

---

[79] *Registres de délibérations du bureau de la ville de Paris. 1499–1624*, F. Bonnardot ed., t. 14, 1908, p. 473.

[80] *Ibid.*, pp. 474–479.

style, showing the glory of the king around the theme of 'great fertility'. A first huge statue has Henri IV as the sun, 'which is the life-giving force of all natural things'. A second statue represents the queen in the person of Cybele, thus evoking another element, the earth. The main aim of these representations is to connect the union between Henri IV and Marie de Medici with a system of life in which the primary movement is from the sun to the earth, before a second movement goes from the earth to the sun. The king gives life to the earth 'works on the earth through the force and the virtue of his gaze, and as the earth receives its influence, so it produces in abundance all varieties of plants, of flowers and other forms of life through the heat of the sun that has been communicated to it'.

But the symbolic portrayal of the royal fertility and happiness is extended to royal births, which will continue forever the current marvellous prosperity, and which represent perhaps the finality of this mystic route[81]. That is to say that in the microcosm of the royal family, life, which is also the life of the kingdom according to the principles of Stoic physics, is called upon to be born, die and to be reborn unceasingly, and that life has already been reproduced in the descendants of the saviour king. At the end of the route through the town there is a temple dedicated to the two elements of the earthly life, the king and the queen, an important key to the fantastical dramatisation. Square on the outside, the interior of the temple is conceived as a cave, 'in accordance with the idea of those who claim that eternity lived with Demogorgon'. It is overhung by a huge picture depicting Eternity, her head veiled, holding in her left hand a snake biting its own tail 'to show that Eternity is without end and contains within her all the ages and the centuries that turn and circle within themselves'. This immutability is seen to be transmitted to the royal couple and their children by Eternity who is presenting them with a sceptre.

Here we see a necessary mutation from the period of the conquest of the kingdom and the stabilisation of the years of peace. It is no longer the king alone who assures the kingdom of being enclosed in a secular zone divorced from time, and who provides his people with a strategy of anxiety-reduction in a period where time is suspended in a Golden Age. It is no longer to his person alone that the negation of time is attached, but to a 'fertile race' from which only a constant renewal of happiness can emerge, a race to which Eternity has given the kingdom which 'flourishing forever will have no end'.

---

[81] *Ibid.*, pp. 485–487 and 499–500.

From this we can see that the stage-setting of the *Entrée* is designed to palliate a deficiency in the construction of the legend that took place in the 1590s. It is the construction of a huge spectacle aimed at exalting for the Parisians the life-giving and life-preserving nature of the royal blood. Without it ever being explicitly stated, the statues and the inscriptions are speaking of the death of the king. The celebration underlines an obsession with death through the insistence on Eternity. The statues immortalise the king by making him a God who has preserved and benefited the kingdom, but they already portray him, through the fixedness of the images, at the moment of his death, signifying that he is like the phoenix who is reborn through his children, the repositories of his *'genus immortale'*, because 'goods rightly acquired are maintained for a long time in families and the graces and benedictions of the heavens cover not only the great Kings, but also their kingdoms and their descendants. Never was France more flourishing nor ever by such just means, never governed by more august Majesties, never more magnanimous, more religious, more prudent, more just, more good-natured. The heavens also seem to promise them a length and an eternity in their rule, of which we see sure signs in the form of the young princes their children, who we can see already taking on the virtues of their parents, of whom they are the living and breathing picture'.

The objective of the conceit is therefore to show the people the divinity of the royal *genus*, and to convince them that the continuation of happiness on earth and the accompanying civilization is inseparable from the perpetuation of the dynasty. The king will never die because his power to be in conformity with the god-created universe will continue in those of his race; Reason which is naturally in him and his descendants is the only mystery of the monarchy. It is the culmination of a revolution of the political culture which can be seen in these images to which Paris plays host. Paradoxically, the apotheosis of the king has the effect of demystifying the political system, by basing it on its rationality alone, which is to provide those governed with earthly happiness. The king is to the State what Jupiter, God of Reason who determines universal movement, is to the universe. Without him everything stops, and disintegrates in a terrifying cataclysm. Man's reason must recognise this. One cannot help noticing in this insistence on the question of Eternity, an awareness of fragility.

The *Entrée* of 1610 takes on its true significance in the light of this obsession with the death of the king, both desired and dreaded at the same time, through the central affirmation of the immortality of the royal 'genus', and the representation of a time of Eternity and peace. But it goes beyond the representation of the ideology of perpetual renewal, through the blood of Henri IV, the royalty and the order that royalty has re-established. It does not merely reproduce the truth of an absolute State which must maintain its position as such, even after the disappearance of the person who has been its divine structurer, it provokes it, it brings it to life: it is action. It must not be forgotten that in Antiquity, ritual had a creative as well as a conservatory function. Since it authenticated destiny as the only principle in the life of men, did it not seek to manifest it in its fullest realisation, seen as a victory of Reason over the passions?

On reflection, it seems evident that Ravaillac's intervention occurs against a backcloth of triumphant Reason and the deifying of the monarchy, in a city where utopia is portrayed, and that this is like a radical and knowing challenge directed at the state of mind prevailing in the post-League period. It is a kind of provocation which seems to me to be as much aimed at preserving the monarchy from all further questioning, as to force the king to accomplish his destiny, to submit to God's will and thus to show once and for all that he incarnated the order of Time.

A number of indications, widely-known but rarely analysed in relation to the Stoic mythology at the root of the new power, prove that Henri IV foresaw the fatal occurrence, but that he adopted towards it a Stoic attitude of passivity and acceptance. It is Sully who once again recounts the resigned words of the king when faced with the violence that he felt to be mounting in Paris, a violence which he knew had never left Paris...'By God, I will die in this city and will never leave it, they will kill me for I see that there is no other solution to their fears but my death'[82]. Does the term 'fears' not refer to eschatalogical anxiety and its capacity for violence? It is Bassompierre more than any other who, in his *Mémoires* describes the royal fatalism, the king's submission to that fate that made him a saviour and a restorer of France and which he has to let run its course in order for it to be perfected: 'On several occasions he said to me and to many others too; "I think I will die soon"'. Whilst Henri IV never fails to show his basic scepticism at all the predictions that for the last thirty years have been announcing his imminent death, he does say that he has been overcome by an internal certitude that he is at the end of his earthly path, as if he were letting death approach him, a death which he does not fear in the least: 'You do not believe me now, you others, but I will die one of these days'.

Beloved of his subjects, and in response to Bassompierre who tells him

---

[82] Sully, *op. cit.*, p. 392.

that he must still reign many long years and enjoy 'in all tranquillity the most flourishing kingdom in the world', he replies with a sigh: 'My friend, I must leave all that'[83]. Words that sum up all the Stoic vision of Henri IV: in the same way that he has built up his power on the assumption that he was led divinely by fate and that the French people should prudently ratify the divine nature of his action by not rebelling against him, so, in the period before his death, he shows his concern to continue to be led by fate, to remain in the superior order of Reason to the end and not to attempt to resist this irresistibility which he ordered his subjects to recognize and which is at the basis of all peace.

Does it not seem clear that from the moment that the politico-cultural system of monarchy had been founded on the Stoic heroism embodied by Hercules, it was only logical that the legend should reach its logical end, and that a sacrificial apotheosis should definitively consolidate the victory of Reason over Chaos? Consciously or unconsciously, perhaps drawn by the very force of the mythology structuring his reign, did not the king embrace his destiny, the destiny that he realised very early on would be his? Had he not prepared himself to make this sacrifice which he already contemplated in 1585, when he challenged Guise and when he said that he was ready to let his blood flow in order that the kingdom could at last live in peace?

It is particularly striking to note that on Friday 14 May when, at 4 o'clock the king was making his way towards the Arsenal in his carriage, at a time that was almost suicidal given its provocative nature for the post-League mentality, that he 'paid no attention to his surroundings[84]. Is his premonition of destiny not making him in some way tempt fate and death, rationally to tease death and the violence of human emotions in order that Reason should be rendered eternal by his death; this death that is his fate, the order of Time that he has imposed on his kingdom and which can only last if he accepts it and all its implications including that of sacrifice? Henri IV knows, perhaps through the subjectivisation of an ideology elaborated as the objective basis of power, that his fate is to die one day, and that his must be a good death and one in conformity with the order of Reason, a tragic death which like that of Hercules, consumed by the fire at the top of Mount Oeta, is the very condition of the durability of the reign of Reason.

---

[83] Maréchal de Bassompierre, *Journal de ma vie. Mémoires...*, Chanterac ed., Paris, 1870, t. I, pp. 270–273.

[84] *Ibid.*, t. III, p. 75. For an analysis of the context of 1610 see the impressive work of R. Mousnier, *L'Assassinat d'Henri IV. 14 mai 1610. Le problème du tyrannicide et l'affermissement de la monarchie absolue*, Paris 1964.

It is for this reason, and we should not overlook the fact, that L'Estoile talks of 'the work of God' when he hears about the assassination. It is the recognition of a governing rationality which has trapped irrationality and which is taking advantage of it to put itself in an even more dominant position than previously[85]. Death immediately becomes life, the dead hero becomes divine, he lives again in the person of his son. The people, needless to say, feel very strongly the death of the king who has restored the State: great sorrow, weeping and collective shock follow. There has been a judgment by God, the king has achieved what he set out to achieve in 1585. The fatal encounter has taken place, he has sacrificed himself for the good of all. But the important thing is that the allegories of the *Entrée* are no longer fiction. They become collective discourse, they take hold of the collective consciousness. The spectacle has become reality, the baroque illusion triumphs and ceases to be an illusion, drawing all the town into the ideological fiction that it signified. Time is dominated by the adherence of all the people to the ideology of the eternal monarchy, the collective determination to live only for the person that is of his blood and who has inherited all his virtues: at the Louvre, all, without exception, soldiers, courtesans, valets, come sorrowfully to greet Sully 'with the most piteous gestures you could have seen , crying out : "Alas! sir, we are all lost having lost our good master. We all beg of you, having served the father so well, to consent to serve the children in the same way, and not to abandon them"'[86].

Contrary to the fears of the supporters of the assassinated king, Reason wins definitively and collectively over the passions of the League that seemed ready to rise up once again. Which leads L'Estoile to say: 'Thus, the union of good people that God had blessed found itself to be stronger that the League of bad people, of which there are quite a few in Paris: which is why God had to intervene as he did'[87].

---

[85] L'Estoile, ... *Henri IV, op. cit.*, t. III, p. 81.

[86] Sully, *op. cit.*, p. 399.

[87] L'Estoile, ... *Henri IV, op. cit.*, t. III, p. 82.

6. The Public Context
of the
Abjuration of Henri IV

MARK GREENGRASS

By sixteenth century public relations standards, Henri IV should have been well pleased with the stage-managed events of Sunday 25 July 1593[1]. It was an elaborately planned royal occasion for which the grounds had been strenuously and systematically laid out in the two months since the announcement of his intentions on 17 May. Those most involved — clergy like Renaud de Beaune, Jacques Davy Du Perron and Claude d'Angennes as well as the king's negotiators in the conference at Suresnes — cultivated

---

[1] Older general surveys of the abjuration include Y. de la Brière, *La conversion de Henri IV. St Denis et Rome*, Paris, 1905; P. de Vaissière, 'La conversion de Henri IV', *Revue de l'Histoire de l'Eglise de France* xiv, 1928; Adair G. Williams, 'The Abjuration of Henry of Navarre', *Journal of Modern History*, ii, 1933, pp. 143–171. J. Lestocquoy, 'Du Perron et l'absolution d'Henri IV', *Notices, Mémoires et documents publiés par la société d'arch. et d'hist... du département de la Manche*, lxiii, 1955, pp. 75–83. The research for this conference paper was conducted in ignorance of the recent doctoral thesis of Martin W. Wolfe, *The Conversion of Henri IV, King of France (1584–1595)* (Johns Hopkins University, 1985). This is a fundamental reappraisal of the king's conversion. I have drawn on its conclusions at some points with acknowledgement but it is to be hoped that the work will soon be published.

a political climate in which powerful but undirected desires for peace and reconciliation in France might be channelled to the king's benefit through the royal act of volition at the centre of the abjuration ritual. Invitations to attend were issued en bloc to certain groups such as the clergy[2]. There were also a variety of personal letters despatched to catholic aristocrats and magistrates of proven loyalty to the king of Navarre for it was vital to its political purpose that the ceremony be manifestly public, engaging representatives from a wide spectrum of corporate France. League *acharnés* were, of course, to be excluded yet there was everything to be gained by securing the collaboration of wavering Parisian *curés* such as René Benoist, Claude Morenne, Jean Chavagnac, Jean Lincestre or Louis Séguier, dean of the cathedral of Notre Dame and the most senior cleric in Paris in the absence of the bishop; thereby would be demonstrated the disunity within the Parisian League[3]. The letters addressed by the king to René Benoist, for example, appealed in a direct and personal way to the preacher's reputation and sense of fidelity[4].

> Dès l'heure que j'ai eu la volonté de penser à ma conversion, j'ai jeté sur vous pour l'un de ceux desquels j'aurais l'assistance fort agréable à cette occasion. La réputation de votre doctrine laquelle est suivie d'une vie non moins louable, me fait espérer de recevoir beaucoup de service et de contentement de vous.

It reads almost like a personal invitation to a private function and mentions nothing of what would have been taken by most catholics as its principal public purpose, namely, to demonstrate the king's penance before the Almighty. At the heart of the abjuration of Henri IV lay a fundamental and intentional ambiguity as to the degree of accountability he was to render,

---

[2] B[ibliothèque] N[ationale] Ms Dupuy 770 fos 225–6, a pro-forma invitation drafted on the 18th May 1593.

[3] For invitations to aristocrats, see e.g. that to Nevers in B. N. Ms fr. 3625 fol. 12. For that to Louis Séguier, see B. N. Ms fr. 17533 fol. 78 and [Pierre de] l'Estoile, *Journal pour le règne de Henri IV*, 3 vols; ed. L-R. Lefèvre, Gallimard, 1948–60, i, pp. 288–93.

[4] Cited in [Abbé] E. Pasquier, *Un curé de Paris pendant les guerres de religion: René Benoist, le pape des Halles*, Angers, 1913, p. 223. The original letter was published as the *Lettre missive du Roy, escritte à Monsieur Benoist, Docteur en Theologie...*, Tours, 1593; copy in the *Bibliothèque de l'Hôtel de Ville de Paris* — Réserve 550348.

both to the Almighty and to catholic France.

Of the events of Sunday 25 July, little needs to be left to the imagination, so closely are we informed of what happened[5]. Before Renaud de Beaune, archbishop of Bourges, unofficial primate of France, and over 60 senior clerics (more than in attendance at the League Estates General) the penitent king arrived at the door of the abbey of St Denis[6]. Dressed in white doublet and hose, only a sword of majesty might indicate to the casual observer that here was the king of France, always supposing that he had overlooked the presence of the archers of the royal guard, the 800 gentlemen of the body in full accoutrement, the royal trumpeteers, and the Vivats from a crowd variously estimated at 10,000, 50,000 and 70,000. It was more like a royal entry (albeit prior to the coronation) and the brief ceremony of penitence before the king entered the nave was both symbolic and also perfunctory. The king knelt in supplication but was not ceremonially struck by the bishop's mitre. A brief summary of the king's act of submission was handed by the king to Renaud de Beaune, who had largely composed it, but it said nothing of any acts of penance or even of contrition. And so the king was led towards the High Altar, the archbishop of Bourges to his right and the abbot of St Denis to his left, there to attend Mass. The Seventh Sunday after Pentecost had probably not been chosen

---

[5] The royalist accounts of the abjuration ceremony were widely disseminated in print — e.g. *Bref Discours de ce qui s'est passe à Sainct Denis en France: sur la conversion du Roy à l'Eglise Catholique Apostolique et Romaine*, Angers, Hernault, 1593, and *Cérémonies observées en la conversion du Roy*, Melun, 1593; copy in *Bib. de l'Hôtel de Ville de Paris* Réserve 048,22. Manuscript versions of the abjuration ceremony are to be found in B. N. Ms fr. 3430 fos 28–39, 'Procès-verbal de l'absolution du roy Henry 4', reproduced in an edited version in Cimber and Danjou, *Archives curieuses de l'histoire de France*, 1st Series, vol ix, pp. 343–51. B. N. Ms fr. 7774 fos 258–64; more briefly in the *Procès verbal de ce quy s'est passé à Sainct-Denis à l'instruction et absolution du Roy Henry iiii 1593*, by Claude Gouyn, dean of the cathedral chapter of Beauvais; I have used the copy in B[ritish] L[ibrary], Add Mss 30.606 fos 4–12. Cf B. N. Ms fr. 3997 fos 66–141, 'Journal des événements qui ont précédé et suivi la conversion du roi' — 17 May-November 1593. Additional processional detail is to be found in [Dom] M. Félibien, *Histoire de l'abbaie royale de St-Denys en France*, Paris, 1706, pp. 421–3. There is a spirited brief modern account in J-P. Babelon, *Henri IV*, Fayard, 1982, pp. 560–66.

[6] B. N. Ms fr. 3430 fos 28–39 for mention of most of the clergy who attended although it is by no means complete. M. W. Wolfe, *op. cit.*, p. 467 estimates that around 100 clergymen were in attendance during the abjuration ceremony.

completely at random. The Proper lessons for that Sunday have as their theme God's renewal of the church through the servants of Christ. The Epistle from St Paul to the Romans told believers not to yield to sin but to deliver themselves unto righteousness, whilst the Gospel from St Matthew warned of the dangers of false prophets, of hypocrisy. This had clearly been preferred to the parable of the Lost Sheep which was set for earlier in the season of Pentecost and regarded by at least one League preacher as 'un évangile de Politiques'[7]. It certainly provided the occasion for a tactful sermon from René Benoist on God's boundless mercies which the king reportedly had approved of. Henri IV then vowed obedience to the catholic church (in under 200 words) and took Mass in both kinds, the Host being left on display for a month afterwards which attracted substantial crowds. At that moment, a flock of doves flew from the church roof, the cue for an inevitable claim of a miraculous sign from God of his blessing upon the king and the imminence of peace[8]. But, to the League *curé* of St André des Arts, Jean Boucher, this was mere superstition 'joinct que ce n'estoit rien de nouveau, & qu'on se voye tous les jours. Estant l'ordinaire des pigeons & au lieu mesme, d'y voltiger de la sorte'[9]. These, and many other details were retained to furnish proofs to the Roman Curia that the conversion had been *bona fide* and to ensure that the pregnant propaganda value of the abjuration continued to reap rewards throughout the summer and autumn of 1593.

But, for all that, the abjuration raised awkward questions. The likelihood of a false conversion and the dangers which sprang from it were eagerly pointed out by the League preachers in Paris and the invective which had already been marshalled against Navarre at the time of the siege of Paris in 1590, was diligently reorchestrated to fit the new circumstances. There, Requiem Masses were held on the same Sunday to highlight the extreme danger in which the catholic church found itself and, reinforcing orders not to leave the city given by the city authorities, League preachers threatened immediate excommunication for all who attended[10]. There was also the matter of Papal involvement and approval. The consistent statements of the papal legate in Paris, Filippo della Sega, cardinal of Piacenza, were to the effect that no papal absolution had been pronounced; that none was

---

[7] Pierre de l'Estoile, *op. cit.*, p. 279.

[8] In the pamphlet by Gabriel de Lurbe, *Discours sur l'apparition des columbes blanches au haut de l'Eglise sainct Denis lors de la conversion du Roy* in *Chronique Bourdelaise*, Bordeaux, 1595.

[9] J. Boucher, *Sermons de la simulacrée conversion*, Paris, 1594, p. 78.

[10] Pierre de l'Estoile, *op. cit.*, pp. 297–8.

likely to be forthcoming in the immediate future; that it was a matter for censure that individual catholics had chosen to attend the bogus ceremony but that this censure should not be allowed to provoke popular outrage which he rightly (as a number of incidents recorded by l'Estoile suggest) feared might occur[11]. This was to be a Gallican absolution at a moment when slumbering Gallican sentiments in many parts of the French polity had already been sensitised and reactivated. All sorts of questions as to the powers and privileges of Gallican clergymen were thus raised of the kind which might keep Gallican lawyers and catholic theologians preoccupied for years[12]. Yet whilst loyalist clergy might have chosen to stand upon their Gallican privileges in July 1593, in fact they relied on more traditional grounds, ones which had already been recently rehearsed at the time of the assassination of Henri III. The last Valois had been excommunicate at the time of his wounding and he was absolved and administered the last rites upon the cautionary faculties issued *ad cautelam* to catholic priests, and confirmed at the Council of Trent[13]. Royalist catholics accepted that this ceremony was a kind of 'preliminary affair', one which would require fuller confirmation from the papacy at some future date. In which case, replied Jean Boucher in his *Sermons sur la Simulacrée Conversion*, preached during the first nine days of August 1593, it was no ceremony at all. Boucher, as de Thou said, 'après avoir si souvent déchiré le feu roi par des discours furieux et outrageux, n'épargna pas son successeur' and proceeded to publish the sermons in March 1594 which had asked some uncomfortable questions about the underlying nature of the ceremony itself[14]. It was not in order

---

[11] *Ibid.*, p. 296. Cf his *Exhortation de monseigneur l'illme cardinal de Plaisance, legat de n. s. p. le Pape, Clement VIII & du siege apostolique...*, Paris; R. Nivelle, R. Thierry, 1593, gives his reactions at the time of Henri IV's announcements of his intentions whilst his 'belle et longue lettre' of July 1593, the *Lettre de monseigneur l'illme et rev^{me} cardinal de Plaisance... Touchant la convocation de quelques ecclésiastiques faicte par Henry de Bourbon...*, Paris, R. Thierry, 1593, reiterated his position on the eve of the abjuration.

[12] The arguments were assembled in treatises like B. N. Ms fr. 3449 fos 78–82, 'Episcopos in Francia jure potuisse absolvere Henricum Borbonicum ab excommunicatione, in casu sedi apostolicae reservato', and, most renowned, P. Pithou, *Traicté de la iuste et canonique absolution de Henry IIII, tres chrestien roy de France et de Navarre*, Paris, 1595, published in Latin the previous year.

[13] J. Benedicti, *La Somme des Pechez, et le remède d'iceux*, Paris, 1595, p. 644. B. N. Ms fr. 3475, 'Raisons et moyens pour monstrer que le feu roy n'est mort excommunié comme l'on pretend à Rome...'.

[14] [Jacques Auguste] de Thou, *Histoire Universelle*, 16 vols. London, 1734, xii, pp. 34–5.

because there was, he argued, no proof that the king had changed his mind. It involved an oath of obedience without any sign of the king's intention to uphold it. There was, he argued, no public catechism of the king, no public penance demanded, and no evidence to support the king's change of heart adduced before the world at large[15]. Why, the king had not even agreed to a general truce with the catholics in his kingdom. Instead, the royalist capture of Dreux in the interim between 17 May and 25 July represented the most significant royal military victories for almost a year (resulting in one of Henri IV's better witticisms: 'Vous voyez un roi poudreux mais non pas cendreux')[16]. The resulting truce in the Paris region (7 July) was merely the lull in the fighting provoked by the fall of Dreux. Boucher, Rose, Cueilly, Feuardent and others knew precisely what kind of stage-managed event they were confronting, a public ceremony which emphasised that the king's conscience was a personal, and not a public, matter, an *arcanum imperii* which subjects questioned at their peril. The king owed no duty to account for his conscience to any, save to God. Attempting to attribute the king's conversion to divine inspiration was, said Boucher, a screen behind which to hide Navarre's 'feinte conversion', his lack of contrition and the fraudulence of the episcopal absolution which he had been given, devices which carried no conviction at all[17]. 'Quels signes ne faites vous, afin que nous nous croyons?... Car d'alléguer la simple ceremonie, cela ne pût estre suffisant. Estant tout constant qu'assez d'autres Huguenots en ont autant faict qui pourtant ne sont Catholiques'[18]. The clergy attended, said Boucher, by royal summons and therefore were in no position to demand a proper penitential submission. And what sort of absolution was it, in any case, when the catholic capital of France, most of the catholic provinces and cities of France refused to have anything to do with it?

Nor did it take very long for the League to learn that not all had gone as smoothly behind the scenes as appearances had suggested. Among the clergy assembled, first at Mantes and then, a week before the absolution transformed to St Denis, there had been considerable and prolonged debate amongst senior churchmen. We have the official *procès-verbal* of their deliberations, kept for us by their elected secretary, Claude Gouyn, dean of the cathedral canons of Beauvais, although the debates would have been

---

[15] J. Boucher, *Sermons... passim.*

[16] After two weeks of siege, Dreux capitulated on 6 July: l'Estoile, *op. cit.*, p. 286.

[17] J. Boucher, *op. cit.*, pp. 47ff.

[18] *Ibid*, p. 74.

more pointed than it suggests[19]. Representing the king were those whom he invited 'secretly' to his *cabinet* on the Friday morning, 23 July, to undertake his instruction — Philippe du Bec, bishop of Nantes, Jacques Davy Du Perron, bishop elect of Evreux (he had received no papal letters of nomination), Renaud de Beaune, archbishop of Bourges, primate of Aquitaine, and Claude d'Angennes, bishop of Le Mans[20]. Beaune was a clerical politician in the Renaissance mould, who, or so it was widely believed, wanted to elevate his primacy over that of the other provinces of France[21]. But there were also other churchmen in the assembly who expected the king to make formal, public statements, both as to the heresy he was renouncing and of the need to repress it in his dominions. If he did not, what sort of coronation would they see? Would the church really be safe in his hands? And how was the Vatican to be satisfied with what had been carried out? Amongst these latter was certainly Charles III de Bourbon, archbishop of Rouen and cardinal de Vendôme[22]. Vendôme was abbot of St Denis and primate of Normandy so that there was more than a touch of personal rivalry with Beaune behind his stance. He claimed primacy over Beaune in the absolution ceremony itself and might have been in a strong position except that, although a cardinal, he had neglected that small matter of taking clerical orders. Technically Vendôme was not (and Gouyn, for example, was careful never to ascribe to him the title of) 'Révérend Père en Dieu' which was why Beaune undertook the honours on 25 July in Vendôme's abbey, doubtless to the cardinal's distress. Henri IV's 'instruction' took place, therefore, in a 'secret' meeting on Friday morning, 23 July in order to avoid the inevitable obligation upon the king of calling upon the advice of a tiresome cousin whose ignorance he overtly despised[23].

The meeting lasted over five hours — hardly long in terms of its enormous significance for the future shape of Bourbon rule in France over the next two centuries. The surviving account of the king's instruction presents the king as examining closely the controversial arguments used to persuade

---

[19] B. L. Add Ms 30.606 fol. 4ff.

[20] *Ibid.*, de Thou, *op. cit.*, xii, p. 30 also includes Nicolas de Thou, bishop of Chartres.

[21] F. Baumgartner, 'Renaud de Beaune, politique prelate', *Sixteenth Century Journal*, ix, 1978, pp. 99–114.

[22] Basic biographical details in [Père Pierre de Guibourgs] Anselme, *Histoire généalogique* ..., 9 vols Paris, 1726–33, i, p. 334; vi, p. 519. Cf J. P. Masson, *Clarissimi viri J. P. Massonis*, Paris, 1638.

[23] de Thou, *op. cit.*, xii, p. 24.

him to abjure his errors[24]. But many of the areas covered were already clas-
sics in Reformation apologetic literature — the eucharist, saints' worship,
purgatory, auricular confession and the spiritual authority of the pope over
the Church. Henri IV was apparently sufficiently well apprised of all the
arguments on the eucharist, for example, for him to require no prolonged
debate. And, given the bulk of catholic apologetic literature specifically
directed towards him in the years between 1589 and 1593, it is hardly surprising that he should have felt that many of the issues had been already
well rehearsed, and in public[25]. To what extent we should accept this, or
indeed other later carefully pre-packaged versions of the meeting, as the reality of what had happened must remain an open question. The instructors
apparently pressed the king to accept binding and comprehensive oaths relating to all the major doctrines of the catholic church, rather than just a
renunciation (without detailing them) of his former Calvinist errors and a
short declaration of faith[26]. But they were forced to return to the assembly
with a heavily abbreviated draft of the king's renunciation of his former
errors and no promise that he would accept anything more specific by way
of profession of catholic belief. The texts failed to secure the unanimous
assent of the clergy present[27]. Later that same afternoon, and doubtless
in some embarrassment, the deputies returned to the king to ask him to
accept their less than total unanimity. On the following day, Saturday 24
July, the king hastily summoned a council of notables, the great officers of
the crown and the senior magistrates from the parlements. The king complained about the machinations of Vendôme and, by way of reply, Achille
de Harlay offered to act as mediator. He doubtless utilised legal arguments
along Gallican lines to the cardinal and they were seemingly to good effect since, despite the last minute alarums, the royalist clergy were broadly
united behind the abjuration on the following day.

This still left the less than convenient public reactions amongst the
Protestant community. Boucher must have had remarkably good infor-

---

[24]   B. L. Add Ms 30.606 fos 5–7. For a later, carefully tailored account, see B.
N. Ms fr. 3706 fos 26–35; 'Les sept preuves et tesmoignages rendus par ledict
Seigneur Roy à la veue de tout le monde de la candeur et probité de sa foy et de
sa conversion'. Wolfe, *op. cit.*, p. 427, argues convincingly for the dating of this
document to between 1595 and 1598.

[25]   M. Wolfe, *op. cit.*, pp. 169ff., explores a number of themes in this substantial
body of literature, the majority of which was produced by catholic laymen.

[26]   Pierre de l'Estoile, *op. cit.*, p. 293.

[27]   Claude Groulart, *Mémoires*, eds. Michaud and Poujoulat, 1880, vol xi, pp.
560–1.

mants at St Denis because he knew that the king's Protestant preacher, La Faye, had been spotted scuttling out of the back door of the *Hôtel de Ville* at St Denis where the king had stayed overnight, on early Sunday morning after a tearful farewell at the morning *levée*, having been assured by the king that he meant the Protestants no harm[28]. To many in the Protestant political elite, the conversion was not an unexpected event, even if it was unpalatable. Their attitudes indicate, however, manifest internal tensions. Some, like Jean de Serres, argued on pragmatic grounds that the king should stick with his loyal co-religionists rather than trust to the more feckless fidelities of new catholic bed-fellows[29]. François de La Noue had also warned of the dangers of hypocrisy amongst former League adherents in a famous letter of 1591[30]. Others reminded the king of the dishonour of betrayal and the inevitable disaster which might follow. Sully, on the other hand, went as far as it was possible, or so it appears from the *Economies royales*, to lay out the considerable pragmatic advantages which the king would achieve through a conversion whilst stressing that the Protestant movement would remain stoically loyal to him[31]. But Du Plessis Mornay, influential amongst Protestant *gens de consistoire* for the moral authority he commanded, confidently expected Protestants to be involved in the conversion process, perhaps by means of the general council for the instruction of the king and, naively, he hoped that Protestant replies to catholic advocacy would at the least dissipate the king's desire to convert. As Navarre's advisor before 1589, Mornay had drafted his statements on confessional matters and consistently said that he was always open to being instructed, if in error, by means of a national council[32]. Indeed, Mornay may have anticipated that the announced intention to convert in May 1593 was connected with the permission to call a Protestant political assembly to Mantes which had already been agreed by the king — the first to be summoned since that held in La Rochelle in late 1588. At the time, the king may have imagined that such an assembly would be a useful counter-weight to the League Estates General (just as La Rochelle had been to that at Blois).

---

[28] J. Boucher, *op. cit.*, p. 224.

[29] J. de Serres, *Advertissement au Roy où sont deduictes les raison d'Estat, pour lesquelles il ne luy est pas bien seant de changer de Religion*, n. p. (La Rochelle?), 1589. I was alerted to the existence of this pamphlet by M. Wolfe, *op. cit.*, p. 160.

[30] H. Hauser, 'François de la Noue et la conversion du Roi', *Revue Historique*, ii, 1888, pp. 313–23, which includes a transcript of the letter.

[31] [Maximilien de Béthune, duc de] Sully, *Oeconomies royales*, eds B. Barbiche and D. Buisseret, 1970, i, pp. 335–9.

[32] R. Patry, *Philippe Du Plessis Mornay*, Paris, 1933, chs iii-v.

Letters had been despatched by Du Plessis Mornay to leading congrega-
tions and he privately hoped that the consistories would choose delegates
who would not be unduly influenced by those grandees of the Protestant
movement (especially Turenne) who wanted the election of an alternative
protector to the king[33]. But as the plans for the abjuration became clearer,
those for the assembling of Protestant deputies became less so. In a memorandum circulated round the colloquies of the reformed churches, probably
prepared by Du Plessis in May 1593, the case for and against assembling at
Mantes on 20 July 1593 as planned, was aired[34]. If the Protestant ministers were going to be given no opportunity to dispute before the king, and
the dangers inherent in their journeying to Mantes, would it not be wasted
time? On the other hand, might not His Majesty give them assurances as
to their future well-being, and might not the fact of their presence engender
'des mouvementz en l'Ame de sa Majeste synon pour le Retirer du change-
ment de la Relligion, au moings pour leur accorder plus libéralement ce qui
sera pour leur bien. . . '. It may have been as late as 22 July when the hand-
ful of Protestants who had braved the journey to Mantes finally accepted
that there was nothing to be gained from remaining at court and, having
submitted a bitter memorandum, withdrew[35]. Poor Du Plessis Mornay
had, however, already realised the inevitable, writing from Saumur to the
Protestant minister Morlas in Nérac in early July; 'Et toutesfois je veux
encore esperer en nos larmes; je veulx croire, s'il peult oublier Dieu, Dieu
ne l'oubliera pas'[36]. Du Plessis Mornay once more saw his vision of an
end to sectarian divisions in a great royal colloquy collapse before his eyes
and he must have realised that the abjuration would inevitably increase
the internal pressures within the Protestant movement for the election of
a separate protector, even though some thoughtful Protestant opinion still
clung to the hope that he would be catholic in name alone[37].

   To understand the abjuration properly, however, it needs to be put into

---

   [33] [Philippe] Du Plessis Mornay, *Mémoires et correspondance de Du Plessis
Mornay*, 12 vols, eds A. D. de la Fontenelle and P. R. Angius, Paris, 1824, v, pp.
421ff.

   [34] Public Record Office [PRO] SP78/31 fol. 163 'Mémoire envoyé aulx Eglises
Reformées de France', despatched to Burghley on the 20th June 1593.

   [35] Wolfe, *op. cit.*, p. 473. The memorandum which they submitted is in B.
N. Ms Dupuy 753 fos 240–8, 'Copie de certains Mémoires dresses par ceulx de la
Religion reformée lors que le Roy Henry le Grand allant à la Messe Embrassa la
Religion papistique', n. d.

   [36] Du Plessis Mornay, *Mém. et corr.*, v, p. 424.

   [37] E. g. the treatise, perhaps a translation, in PRO SP78/32 fos 439–48.

a broader context. The *cursus honorum* of the French monarchy from Valois to Bourbon was dominated by the issue of the king's conversion. It was one of the utmost delicacy and it touched the heart of matters of intense political debate, the nature of French kingship, the relationship between clergy and kingship in the French polity, the importance of a public trust, of mutual, binding and accountable loyalties in the maintenance of that polity. And yet the historical commentary upon the abjuration has tended to be limited to the rather narrow debates over the precise moment at which Henri IV decided to convert and whether he was sincere[38]. Neither of these are answerable questions. In the case of the former, the evidence is fragmentary and for good reason; the king intended to keep people guessing. In the case of the latter, it begs the key question since the whole point about confessional changes in the sixteenth century is that nobody could know whether they were sincere or not. In a period when confessional identities were solidifying, each against the other, the more important questions to address are: how did people, especially the all-important catholic loyalists, expect to be able to measure sincerity? And how did the very public debate about the king's conversion between 1589 and 1593 affect the nature and chronology of the final decision to convert?

The literature about religious conversion was of great antiquity but the religious reformation of the sixteenth century, as well as the discoveries of the New World, rendered it — whether Pauline or Augustinian, sudden and dramatic, or slow and tortuous — central. Catholic scholastic theologians had very clear ideas on the matter which have to be understood when considering League attitudes to the abjuration and they had been reinforced by the important canons in the fourteenth session of the Council of Trent in 1551[39]. These were developed in the context of penitential advice in the great Spanish manual for confessors composed by Martin Azpilcueta (Navarro)[40]. Beginning with the essential concepts of contrition, confession and satisfaction, Navarro laid out the psychology of conversion as conceived within the sacrament of penance. Contrition was the vital change of heart, stimulated by perfect humility. Then came confession, the change of mind in which the confessor could play a major role, leading to the final penance or satisfaction. Navarro's treatment of the subject was well-known in France, not least through the respected French penitential

---

[38] Still the emphasis in, e.g. J. Garrisson, *Henri IV*, Paris, 1986.

[39] J. Waterworth (trans), *The Canons and Decrees of the Sacred and Oecumenical Council of Trent*, London, 1848, pp. 92–104.

[40] M. Azpilcueta (Navarro), *Enchiridion sive Manuale Confessariorum...* (I have consulted the Louvain edition of 1592).

manual of Jean Benedicti (Benedetti)[41]. The area of greatest psychological difficulty remained, however, in precisely the area of the extent to which true humility was possible in this world, and, therefore, the extent to which other emotions such as fear were legitimate in the process. Navarro followed scholastic theologians in distinguishing between contrition and attrition, the latter being, as Benedicti said, 'une douleur imparfaicte, ou pour bien dire une demie contrition', based upon human fear of the consequences of not being humble, a second-best but often the beginnings of true contrition. They all agreed that contrition, and even more, penance, were not valid sacraments when based upon purely pragmatic grounds — knowledge of the world or fear of the consequences in this world, rather than knowledge of the world to come, or fear of the hereafter. Louis d'Orléans' *Le Banquet et Apresdisnee du Conte d'Arete...*, a sustained critique of Henri IV's sincerity, made precisely this distinction between prudence as knowledge of God and prudence as knowledge of the affairs of the world, the latter breeding *Politique*, or forced, conversions, which were universally agreed to be a private tragedy and a public disaster[42]. Jean Boucher's fourth sermon against Henri IV's conversion concentrated upon it as an act forced upon him by political circumstances — the Estates General of the League and their threat to elect a king to the French crown. Royalist pamphlets in 1591, answering the challenge laid down by the League that he should fulfil his promises and undertake instruction in the faith, had argued that the more they attempted to convert the king by force, the more likely was the consequence that he would become merely a 'Catholique d'Estat'[43]. Similar arguments had been deployed by royalist catholics in the wake of the edict of Union in 1585 so they were not at all new. Pomponne de Bellièvre would utilise them again in his artful efforts at encouraging diplomatic negotiations in the course of 1592. Not that knowledge of the world ruled out every mundane consideration entirely. In his statement before the bishops on Thursday 23 July, Henri specifically said that he had been moved to consider his faith 'touché de compassion de la misère et calamité de son peuple'[44]. Royalist catholic commentators argued that this was not the acceptance of a worldly prudence but a king recognising his responsibilites

---

[41] J. Benedicti, *la Somme des Pechez, et le remède d'iceux*, Paris, 1595, Book v, ch. iii. The marginal annotations to Benedicti make clear his indebtedness to Navarro.

[42] Louis d'Orléans, *Le Banquet et Apresdisnee du Conte d'Arete, ou il se traicte de la dissimulation du Roy de Navarre, & des moeurs de ses partisans*, Paris, 1594, *passim*.

[43] Wolfe, *op. cit.*, pp. 175–95.

[44] B. L. Add Ms 30.606 fol. 5ᵛ.

before God.

Then came penance and satisfaction. Contrition, for the most part, was a private psychological transmutation but, to catholic League commentators, penance and satisfaction were the public face to that transmutation, the proclamation of that change before society as well as a public recognition of fault. There are some interesting group acts of devotion to pray for the king's conversion before 1593 and there would be others (for example in Béziers) in the 12 months following the conversion[45]. There is an important subject still awaiting exploration in rigorist catholic attitudes to oath-taking, and the particular public context which was required to their enjoying respect and validity. There was something distinctive, for example, about those formal occasions during the Estates General of 1576 or 1588 when binding oaths were mutually sworn to uphold the catholicity of France before the assembled corporate body of the kingdom. Surviving registers of catholicity containing signatures of those who recanted heresy, or those who put their signatures to the League in 1576, give us little hint as to the context and atmosphere in which these acts took place. But on occasions there were spectacular conversions of individuals whose notoriety could be exploited to good propaganda effect[46]. Take, for example, the well-documented case of the conversion of the former Protestant pastor and leading figure in the Protestant politics of the Midi, Geoffroy de Vaux, in the cathedral church of St Etienne in Toulouse, on 19 January 1597[47]. According to the pamphlet on the event, the ceremony began on the steps

---

[45] [Père] Appollinaire, *Les Prières pour le roi en 1593*, Nîmes, 1892. Monks in Béziers and elsewhere persisted in praying for the king's conversion after the abjuration had taken place.

[46] For an example within the Protestant tradition, see the *Conversion Du Sieur Melchior Roman, Espagnol, Iadis Procureur de l'Ordre des Iacobins à Rome...*, A Pontorson, 1600 — copy in Trinity College Library, Cambridge W. 1. 11. 10 — the account of a conversion of a noted Toulousain Dominican preacher at Bergerac, 27th August 1600.

[47] *Célèbre conversion de la personne et famille de M. Geoffroy de Vaux après avoir esté Ministre de la doctrine Calvinienne ès pays de Dauphine*, Paris, 1597; copy in the B. N. Réserve, also cited in Wolfe, *op. cit.*, pp. 45–7. De Vaux had been pastor in Millau from 1561, had been sent on mission to Germany from the Protestant political assembly at Millau in 1573, a signatory for the Protestants to the peace of Bergerac in 1577, the peace of Nérac in 1579 and was present at the assembly of La Rochelle in 1588. His conversion was, according to d'Aubigné, stimulated by Du Perron, and he died shortly after his conversion, regretting that he had 'sold himself' to the court.

outside the cathedral with the statement of the letter written by the convert outlining his change of mind. Then came a lavish ceremony in which several bishops, the cardinal de Joyeuse at their head, received the individual before a crowd numbering, it claimed, 10,000. The penitent appeared dressed in a penitential habit and barefoot, kneeling and in tears, was ceremonially struck by the archepiscopal mitre before declaring his penitence and accepting penance and being led into the nave of St Etienne to receive the Mass. There are reasons for thinking that the atmosphere in Toulouse was, at that date, highly charged, but the procedures, for all that, were not exceptional in their fundamentals. Contrition, like faith, in the sixteenth century, inevitably had its public dimension. Oaths were the basis for social discipline and part of the accountability of the individual to society at large. Conscience was not an individual privilege, a private function. For confirmation of the fact, we need only turn to the famous confessions of Hugues Sureau in 1572 and again in 1574, or Jean de Sponde's controversial *Confession de Foy*, roughly contemporaneous to the king's, and the ripples of commentary which they generated[48]. It was the sense that the conversion formed something of a 'private deal' between God and the king which so outraged Boucher and other League preachers. This was the beginnings of the 'maquignonnage' of those who swear to catholicity but 'préfèrent leurs affaires particulières aux publiques, et qui veulent seulement conserver leurs maisons', of the treacherous waters of those 'officiers politiques' who 'vont à la messe... font la Pasque... vont les premiers aux Processions... ont les premières places et les premiers rangs. Mais o bon dieu ce n'est qu'en corps. L'esprit est à composer comment ils pourront ourdir les tromperies pour retenir leurs bons amis les hérétiques'[49].

Behind their concerns, however, also lay the king of Navarre's first conversion, well publicised by catholic preachers and much discussed[50]. It took place with Navarre technically in the plenitude of power and yet the circumstances had been undeniably unusual. The king would later claim that it was one of those despised 'forced conversions' i. e. that he had been pressurised into converting to the faith by the fact of his close confinement

[48] Hugues Sureau du Rosier, *Confession de Foy faicte par H. S. du Rosier*, 1572; copy in B. L. 9200 bb 29); and his *Confession et recognoissance de Hugues Sureau, dict du Rosier...*, Basel, 1574; Jean de Sponde, *Confession de foy*, La Rochelle, 1593; cf A. Boase, *Vie de Jean de Sponde*, Geneva; Droz, 1977.

[49] *La vie et innocence des deux frères...*, Paris, 1589, p. 18.

[50] P. Hurtubise, 'Mariage mixte au XVIe siècle; les circonstances de la première abjuration d'Henri IV à l'automne de 1572', *Archivum Historicum Pontificae*, xiv, 1976, pp. 103–34.

at court, his recent marriage to a catholic, the demands of his mother-in-law, and the inevitable fears for his safety in the wake of the massacre. Whilst the particular circumstances were understood, it ill became royalist commentators to dwell too much upon forced conversions in the delicate circumstances of 1593. There was, however, a second argument which ran that, since the king of Navarre had only converted privately in 1572, there had never been a public ceremony, no demonstration of a change of heart, and that therefore the whole affair had been mishandled and was, thus, of no effect. Acceptance of that argument did, of course, mean that royalists had to make sure that procedures at St Denis at least outwardly could be said to conform to the requirements of orthodoxy in these matters whilst, at the same time, not offending elevated senses of royal dignity. The whole issue of the first conversion was important because there was an argument for saying that one relapse into mortal sin was a dangerous accident whilst two looked like conscientious carelessness. The case had been put plainly enough as it related to Henri IV's recidivism in the Papal Bull *Brutum Fulmen* of 9 September 1585[51]. According to this Bull, the prospect of future reconversion did not arise since the king was a recidivist, a notoriously relapsed catholic, and therefore outside the realm of civil society and the grace of the church. This was still formally the position of the Roman Curia in July 1593.

Other shadows from the recent past were the declarations which Henri IV had made at St Cloud, immediately after his accession to power, and the letters patent at Mantes of July 1591. The declaration at St Cloud was delivered orally to the catholic grandees assembled at the court of Henri III, a court that was still in a state of shock at his assassination[52]. As Du Plessis Mornay, probably principally responsible for its eventual shape, recorded laconically: 'Les Catholiques sont en alarme de leur religion. Il fault une déclaration pour les en asseurer'[53]. They included some of the leading figures in the royal army as well as vital figures in the council and court such as the chancellor, keeper of the seals and superintendent of finances. In practical terms, these were all vital to the developing credibility of Navarre's candidature to the French throne. The declaration promised 'par la foy et parole de Roy' to maintain the catholic church, pledged to fill offices vacated by Huguenots with catholics and promised that the king would seek

---

[51] A French translation in Cimber and Danjou (ed.), *Mémoires curieuses de l'histoire de France*, xi, pp. 59–60.

[52] *Le serment et promesse du Roy à son advenement*, n. p. , (Tours?), 1589. J. P. Babelon, *op. cit.*, pp. 452–8.

[53] Du Plessis Mornay, *Mém. et corr.* ii, p. 394.

religious instruction the moment a national council of the church could be convened, within six months at the latest. These declarations came to be regarded by some as almost the equivalent of the king's coronation oaths. The king invited reciprocal and provisional oaths from the great offices of state swearing a contingent loyalty to him. Not all the catholic officials at court were prepared to give such oaths and perhaps up to a third of the court and army dissolved into prudent neutrality. The declaration at St Cloud carries all the hall-marks of Du Plessis Mornay, with its twin notions of a national council and also the reciprocal obligations between king and people, a rare, perhaps unique moment when a servant of the French absolute monarchy under the Bourbons until 1789 issued a declaration under royal warrant based upon a political theory very different from that of the traditional monarchy. It was a dangerous hostage to fortune and when the senior clergy came together in general assemblies, as in Tours in May 1590 or again in 1592, they reminded the king forcibly of his promise. The king was aware of it too for, on the eve of the conversion of St Denis, he blamed the delay upon the 'continuelles Guerres, empeschemens et traversés'. It was the kind of hostage to fortune which the king seemed determined to avoid repeating in July 1593.

But how much did the issue matter in practice in these years, beyond the Parisian clergy or the senior ecclesiastics in the French polity? Were there not military and political imperatives which determined what happened more than a matter which lay outside the power of individuals to command? To catholic loyalist nobility it appears to have been more important than one might imagine. These individuals had consciences to salve, some, like the duke de Nevers, decidedly *pointilleux*. The same might not be so decidedly the case with an Epernon or Biron but Henri IV's army was in part volunteer and religiously heterogeneous, even at the level of the king's *conseil de guerre*, and there are occasional suggestions that it acted as the forum for debate. When it did not, we may still envisage the exchange of correspondence amongst some of these neutralist and prudent aristocrats, waiting and watching, wooed by both sides, growing more numerous and restive as the war gradually went the king's way. Catholic loyalism inevitably had a forum at the Navarre court. It was bound to do so if Henri IV fulfilled his promise at St Cloud to appoint only catholics to court offices. In 1590, he appointed Cheverny as his chancellor, in order to put an end to a rather unseemly wrangle over the keepership of the seals. Cheverny was someone of experience, well-respected, and he was given the task of reorganising what was left of the royal court[54]. He did so, reinstitut-

---

[54] Cheverny, *Mémoires*, eds Michaud and Poujoulat, 1880, x, pp. 503–6.

ing the royal chapel with catholic services, the post of king's almoner going to Renaud de Beaune. But Navarre's largely Protestant entourage from the wandering years in south-west France was still in place, a reminder, if it were needed, that Henri IV stood at the head of an uneasy coalition which might easily fragment and collapse.

If collapse was ever likely, it would have occurred with the growth of what contemporaries almost universally christened the *tiers parti*. Agrippa d'Aubigné referred to them in 1597, in another *récit* of a messy conversion, as akin to Purgatory: 'Par occasion, j'ai comparé le tiers parti au Purgatoire, lequel a esté seulement *in potentia*. L'autre ne fût jamais *in actu* et de faict la question n'est pas de petite importance'[55]. The last phrase carries a sense of nervous relief that he could afford to dismiss the *tiers parti* as more shadow than substance. But this had emphatically not been the case in 1591–2. It would remain a persistent, albeit sometimes nebulous, influence upon Henri IV and his advisors, exercising more of an effect upon their actions than the reality perhaps warranted. The period of its greatest effectiveness came after the death of Charles, cardinal de Bourbon in May 1590. The failure of the king to live up to his promises at St Cloud was shortly to be reinforced by his revocation of the edict of union, which had been solemnly sworn to in public as a fundamental law of the kingdom before the Estates General of 1588, which took place in letters patent issued at Mantes in July 1591.

If the *tiers parti* failed, it was partly a matter of incompetent leadership. Some had perhaps initially looked to the young Charles d'Angoulême, illegitimate son of Charles IX who could claim a closer blood relationship to the Valois than the Bourbon and who could have been legitimised. He was married to a daughter of the duke of Montmorency who, more than anyone else, could claim to have given Navarre the necessary strength in the Midi to claim the kingdom of France. But Auvergne was young, wayward, feckless and people had their doubts, even as they voiced the possibility. Henri IV would later dismiss him as the 'Prodigal Son', the real lost sheep of the family. There were also Navarre's uncles, Henri de Montpensier and cardinal Charles de Bourbon-Vendôme. Montpensier always remained staunchly loyal to Henri IV and was well-rewarded for his pains. Vendôme's position was more interesting and J-P. Babelon's biography of Henri IV is the first to have given us something of the measure of the potential importance of

---

[55] Agrippa d'Aubigné, *La Confession du sieur de Sancy*, in *Recueil de diverses pièces servans à l'histoire de Henry III . . .*, Cologne, 1662

Vendôme's role[56]. He referred to the engraving of Vendôme by Thomas de Leu which carried the device; 'Ce cardinal parait l'autre espoir des Bourbons'[57]. He was politically ambitious (refusing to surrender the keepership of the seals in 1589 until forced to) and, since he had not taken full clerical vows, he was marriageable, close to the blood royal and certainly no Navarre sympathiser. Nearly every one of the rumours behind a conspiracy by the *tiers parti* in 1591–2 had Vendôme located close to its epicentre.

There are many reasons why the *tiers parti* remained closet conspirators[58]. So long as Spain's influence in the League seemed in the ascendant especially after Parma's intervention in August 1590, they had, on the whole, no wish to weaken any resistance to it. Nor did they want to force Navarre into a conversion of political necessity which would defeat their purpose. For similar reasons, as well as the aristocratic bias of their support, they had no desire to act the demagogue, even supposing that they would have gained a following. And so long as there was hope of a negotiated settlement between Navarre and the League, and so long as the door was never closed upon his abjuration, they were always liable to be wrong-footed, never clear as to their objectives.

As a conspirator, Vendôme left a great deal to be desired. The king kept reliable informants in the cardinal's entourage who kept him abreast of all that was going on. As early as January 1590, Henri IV's suspicions led him to instruct Jacques-Auguste de Thou to go to Tours 'expressément de ne point quitter le cardinal, ni le comte de Soissons son frère'[59]. Politically, it was perhaps his most sensitive and important political role and, thanks to his *History*, we know more about Vendôme's machinations than otherwise we would. Claude Groulart also obediently reported loose talk back to the king from Vendôme[60]. Jacques Davy Du Perron, the close confident of the cardinal and the most active thinking head among the potential *tiers parti*, was also quickly incorporated into Navarre own service so that the influence of the 'grand convertisseur' (as d'Aubigné christened him) would thereafter be directly upon the king rather than indirectly mediated through Vendôme. Others in Vendôme's entourage, such as the abbé de Bellozane, were also less than completely loyal. How many others there

---

[56] J-P. Babelon, *op. cit.*, pp. 523–9.

[57] *Ibid*, p. 526.

[58] Wolfe, *op. cit.*, p. 346ff. explores these points and I follow his argument closely here.

[59] de Thou, *Mémoires*, Amsterdam, 1713, p. 351.

[60] Groulart, *op. cit.*, p. 556.

ever were who contemplated joining him in closet rebellion we shall never know. The English ambassador Henry Unton kept a very close eye on all that was afoot in 1591 and his despatches mention, among others, François d'O, Biron, Epernon, Longueville, La Guiche and others — most of them in one way or another plausible adherents if the conspiracy had shown any signs of making headway[61].

That it never did. Just as the lineaments of a political agenda for the *tiers parti* were set in place during the early months of 1591, they were destroyed by lack of secrecy. Superficially, the moment was well chosen. The siege of Chartres was going badly for Henri IV, negotiations with the League had reached deadlock, and there was a new and possibly more receptive pope in the Vatican. In early March 1591, Vendôme despatched a memorandum to Rome which outlined his plans, including ones which begun with the premiss that he should be considered the natural successor to the cardinal de Bourbon by all French catholics. Probably at the same time, an anonymous pamphlet, often known as the echo written by the cardinal's secretary Touchart and Du Perron, threatening that, unless the king promptly converted, catholics would find a prince more worthy of their cause to support[62]. Unfortunately the document sent to Rome was captured by the League and Mayenne authorised its wide circulation in order to embarrass Navarre. Rome distanced itself from the memorandum and, within two or three months, Gregory reissued the bull *Brutum Fulmen* against Navarre whilst Parma led a new expeditionary force to assist the League. Henri IV's reactions to Vendôme were measured and shrewd. In early June, he requested the cardinal's presence at a council meeting at Mantes, ostensibly to consider the papal action. Vendôme prevaricated, but finally arrived, to find Henri IV effusive in greeting him. But when it came to council discussion, it was to consider the proposed letters-patent in favour of the Protestants and a heated debate occurred with the cardinal threatening catholic loyalist reactions and his departure from council. The king imperiously called him back, according to de Thou (who was also present) 'd'un ton de mespris' and humiliating him.

This was not the end of the *tiers parti* and fears of their politicking, as well as their stockpiling of arms in the provinces persisted intermittently throughout the shadow boxing and complex negotiations with the League

---

[61] PRO SP78/24-6 — various reports from Henry Unton, Otywell Smith and other agents. I hope to explore the precise importance and chronology of *tiers parti* politics in greater detail in due course.

[62] J. Lestocquoy, *op. cit.*, p. 94. De Thou, *op. cit.*, p. 348–50.

which occupied so much of people's energies in 1592 and early 1593. This is not the place to analyse those in detail, although they resolved themselves into a fairly basic set of issues. Would the king agree to convert before the League submitted to his authority? Or would the League renounce its Spanish pay-masters and accept Navarre's right to the succession before he converted? At one stage, in Bellièvre's country house at Grignon in June 1592, the negotiators very nearly arrived at an agreed timetable mutually acceptable to both parties. But then Navarre pulled back, concerned, perhaps, at Mayenne's Spanish support, worried perhaps too that catholic royalists might make common cause against him and to his disadvantage. Yet the more the king delayed his abjuration, the more it would look as though force of circumstances rather than conscience had made him change his mind. And what circumstances could one imagine stronger than an empty treasury, a catholic Estates General on the verge of electing an alternative king of France with active Spanish participation and negotiations between the two sides stalled because neither could agree on a timetable for submission and conversion?

This has been an exercise in context. The context for discussing Henri IV's conversion, it is suggested, was not the king's supposed cynicism or sincerity but how contemporaries went about judging such matters. In the process, we have seen how delicate it was to apply the criteria commonly accepted amongst sixteenth century catholic opinion to circumstances where it was important to preserve some sense of the divinity which hedged a king, even when it palpably could not. For at the core of the problem lay notions of oaths publicly arrived at, coupled with senses of public accountability as against notions of the privacy of conscience and senses of a private domain of accountability to God alone. The very public debate over the nature of conversion was not one in which Protestants by and large participated; one of the more striking things is how muted their role was, how stoical their reaction to what was taking place. By contrast, the shadow of the *tiers parti* was much more important than its eventual impotence would suggest. It was as close as the soft middle of catholic opinion in France came to political activity. But it was that opinion which Henri IV had to take very seriously if he, and his direct descendants, was to enjoy the Lily throne.

7. Henri IV

and the problem of

the French episcopate

JOSEPH BERGIN

One of Henri IV's many skills was that of being his own best propagandist; it was a skill that was nowhere more manifest than when critics or petitioners were trying to corner him. His responses, and his *bons mots* generally, are an integral part of his personal myth. Only a few of them seem to relate to the French church. But we can point to two major occasions on which he deployed his skills. Both followed general assemblies of the clergy, which traditionally ended with a formal address to the king by one of its leading members. In 1598, when the archbishop of Tours gave this, he ventured a criticism of ecclesiastical appointments, underlining the need to end the scandals of entrusting major offices to men who merely held them on behalf of others, even of women and military men. Henri replied by referring to the difficulties he had until recently had with his realm, and rejected all responsibility by claiming that these scandals pre-dated his reign. In December 1605, the archbishop of Vienne made substantially the same charge and the same recommendation, repeating earlier demands that French bishops be elected by cathedral chapters. This time, the king was more assertive, putting the clergy on the defensive. He answered, referring to the alleged abuses, 'pour ce qui est des simonies et confidences, commencés à vous guérir vous-mesmes et exciter les autres par vos bons exemples à bien faire. Quant aux élections, vous voyés comme j'y procède. Je suis glorieux de voir ceux que j'ay establis estre bien differens de ceux du passé; le récit que vous avés faict me redouble le courage de mieux faire à l'advenir'[1].

There is no record of anyone present trying to gainsay the king on either occasion, and it is fair to say that the king's own verdict on his policy towards the episcopate has been widely accepted by historians. In 1598 he distanced himself from the practices of past régimes; by 1605, he was effectively asserting that he had reshaped the French episcopate. Up to a point, and for diplomatic reasons at least, the clergy in 1605 agreed with him: although they complimented him upon the good choices he had made of bishops, that did not prevent them from repeating the complaint of 1598. It would be made again, and in more detail, at the Estates General of 1614 and the Assembly of Clergy of 1615. Moreover, neither the habitual reserve nor the guarded language of papal diplomacy could hide the fact that Rome consistently worried throughout Henri's reign about his decisions, and about the poor quality of royal nominations to the French episcopate taken as a whole.

Ritual complaints by occasional assemblies, as well as pressure from Popes on rulers holding ecclesiastical prerogatives, are perhaps only to be expected. But they should serve to remind us that not everyone took the same positive view of matters as Henri himself did, and to suggest that there were problems with the episcopate which ensured continuing concern and criticism of his handling of this royal prerogative. Raising the question of what he did rather than what he said is not a matter of awarding the king good or bad marks for his success or failure in meeting an arbitrary or impossible set of criteria. The kings of France may well have secured one of their most valued royal prerogatives by virtue of the Concordat of Bologna, but for a long time, that agreement made the business of choosing French bishops perhaps even more complex than it already was; it certainly did not provide any simple solution to the conflicts of interest that episcopal appointments gave rise to.

More directly, and as Baumgartner's work has recently shown, Henri of Navarre might have had a far more intractable task in obtaining recognition as France's rightful king had he not won the support of a group of French bishops from the moment of Henri III's assassination, and which

---

[1] *Lettres missives de Henri IV*, eds X. Berger de Xivry and J. Guadet, Paris, 1843–76, vi, p. 565, 'réponse du roy Henri IV à M Pierre de Villars'.

grew thereafter in numbers, especially after his conversion in 1593. That support was precious, as the bishops concerned were — and in the circumstances had to be — vocal advocates of his rights. In particular, their stance served to weaken to the Catholic League's claim that his succession was incompatible with the interests of Catholicism. As for the mass of the episcopate, who were either Leaguer, neutral, or at least not actively hostile to him, Henri hardly needed to be told how important they were to the power structure of the provinces and localities whose loyalty and allegiance it proved so difficult for him to secure between 1589 and 1595[2].

An examination of the character and evolution of the French episcopate under Henri IV may therefore help to shed some light, however oblique, on the transition from Valois to Bourbon. As Henri's own attitudes remain elusive, this examination cannot be confined to a study of his 'policy' in the narrow sense. Instead, it will attempt to approach the issues from a series of angles, in the hope that this will result in a more complete view of the character and evolution of the French episcopate in that transition.

Any consideration of how Henri tried to handle the episcopate must begin with a brief evocation of the situation at the end of his predecessor's reign. In general, it is difficult to avoid the impression that the French episcopate of the latter sixteenth century was more demoralized and fragmented than at perhaps any other period of the Ancien Régime — on most levels, its response to the religious and political crisis of the Reformation and Wars of Religion had been slow, uncoordinated, and largely defensive. Besides, several dioceses were effectively occupied by the Huguenots, and their bishops were simply unable to reside. There, and in many other areas, extensive, and still unrepaired, damage to cathedrals and episcopal residences since the early 1560s made residence either impossible or unattractive to bishops. But not everything could be attributed to the wars or the Huguenots. Pluralism, simony, and a high level of horse-trading in benefices among prelates and great families also reached a peak by the second half of the century.

The condition of the episcopate persuaded the Assembly of Clergy of 1579 to sound the alarm. As is well known, it complained bitterly about abuses of appointment to the episcopate, and to make its point perfectly clear, it presented Henri III with a list of dioceses vacant or held under irregular conditions of one kind or another. The problems were particularly

---

[2] Frederic J. Baumgartner, *Change and Continuity in the French Episcopate. The Bishops and the Wars of Religion 1547–1610*, Durham, N.C., 1986, ch. ix.

acute in the south of France, especially in Languedoc, for which the evidence was most damning, and where the clergy claimed that Montmorency, Joyeuse and a few other individuals dominated the bishoprics, keeping them vacant or drawing their revenues through compliant *économes* or *confidentiaires*. In all, the assembly alleged that twenty-six dioceses — or nearly a quarter of the total for France — were either vacant, held by *confidentiaires*, governed through *lettres d'économat*, or had simply been usurped. And this list did not include the provinces of Aix, Arles and Embrun. Only the northern provinces of Sens and Reims were declared exempt from the abuses they cited[3]. Vacancies were not the only, and certainly not the major problem, but rather the 'simonies et confidences' to which Henri IV would later refer. Of the twenty-six dioceses the clergy cited, only eight were clearly vacant; the rest were held or administered in ways which demonstrated that the normal structure of episcopal succession had broken down quite extensively. If such a state of affairs, which would endure under Henri IV, angered the assembled clergy, it raises serious problems for historians attempting to reconstruct the history of the episcopate in this period. How, to put it more directly, does one classify 'bishops' who are variously referred to as commendators, administrators or simply *intrus*?

There is every sign that during the decade after 1579, the condition of the French episcopate worsened further, as an increasingly desperate Henri III continued to abandon his royal prerogative to choose bishops to individuals or families. The Richelieus were only one of a number of families to benefit from such largesse. By late 1588, perhaps up to one-third of all sees were subject to one or another of the conditions described by the 1579 assembly.

In terms of disruption and confusion, the worst was still to come. After the Guise murders, the papacy refused, among other things, to consider any new episcopal nominations made by Henri III, a refusal which it naturally extended to Henri of Navarre after August 1589. Then in 1591 the Parlement of Paris imposed a formal ban on royal nominees seeking papal provisions to benefices, a ban which remained in force until lifted by Henri IV in 1596. Meanwhile, bishops continued to die from causes natural and unnatural, and their sees were left, formally at least, vacant. Estimates of the total number of sees actually vacant by the time of Henri's absolution by Clement VIII in September 1595 vary. When Cardinal Medici, the papal legate arrived in France the following year, he calculated that between

---

[3] L.Serbat, *Les assemblées du clergé: origines, organisation, développement 1561–1615*, Paris, 1906, appendix xvii.

thirty-three and forty-three dioceses were without a bishop. The real total was probably nearer to thirty, but the crucial point is that even Medici had considerable difficulty in establishing the true state of the episcopate.

But the first five or six years of Henri IV's reign were characterized by more than just a rising episcopal death toll. The legal and political confusion of these years was unique, one which it subsequently took years to clear up, because it generated a welter of claims and counter-claims from competitors for benefices of all kinds. First of all, Mayenne, as the Catholic League's lieutenant-general of the kingdom from early 1589, claimed that he was entitled to exercise the royal prerogative to nominate bishops — indeed that he had a duty to preserve it against usurpation by, for example, cathedral chapters anxious to take advantage of the political vacuum and to reclaim their ancient rights of electing bishops — and in 1591 Gregory XIV accepted his argument[4]. His cousin, the duc de Mercoeur, governor of Brittany for the League, also claimed in 1594 that Clement VIII had made a similar concession to him for the province[5]. But Gregory XIV's reign was short, and his successor, Clement, adopted a more cautious attitude, as he groped towards some form of reconciliation with Henri IV. Quite how many nominations Mayenne attempted to make between 1589 and 1594, it is impossible to say. No more than three or four successfully sought papal approval during this period, as it was probably independently of him that the papacy itself appointed directly to three vacant sees in Provence, as well as to Vannes in Brittany and Coutances in Normandy. But Mayenne undoubtedly made more nominations than the papacy approved of: four of his nominees, all appointed to northern French sees, actually settled their *régale* payments with the Sainte Chapelle during 1593 alone, but none was successful in securing his see in subsequent years[6]. He did manage to transfer the Guise see of Reims to a family client, Nicolas Pellevé, after December 1588, but failed to repeat that success on Pellevé's death in 1594; equally, he failed to pass on Pellevé's previous archiepiscopal see of Sens

---

[4] *Correspondance de Mayenne*, ed. E. Henry and C. Loriquet, Travaux de l'académie impériale de Reims, Reims, 1860–63, i, p. 410–11, Mayenne to Jacques de Diou, agent in Rome, 23 Jan 1591; *ibid.*, iii, pp. 33–4, Mayenne to de Diou, 11 May 1591; *ibid.*, iii, p. 76, Mayenne to Pope, 22 May 1591.

[5] A(rchivio) S(egreto) V(aticano), *Fondo Borghese*, I, 636, fol. 210, letter to Pope, 8 Oct 1594.

[6] A(rchives) N(ationales), *Minutier Central des Notaires, étude* VIII, vol. 408, 20 March, 10 April, 1 Sept and 25 Nov 1593. The sees involved were Beauvais, Evreux, Noyon and Troyes.

to his own uncle, Claude de Guise, abbot of Cluny[7]. Other attempts at placing well-intentioned men in dioceses even within the traditional spheres of Guise influence were no more successful after 1593. Mayenne's nominee for Troyes, Bishop Péricard of Evreux, a well-known Guise client, failed to maintain his position though he took up residence in Troyes as 'évêque élu' from late 1593 onwards[8]. Perhaps the most surprising of all Mayenne's decisions involved an attempt by Pierre d'Epinac to exchange his archdiocese of Lyon for the see of Beauvais in 1593. Epinac was ecclesiastical leader of the League, but by then Beauvais may have seemed safer than Lyon — and it did come with a peerage which would compensate for the diminution of his ecclesiastical status. Mayenne almost certainly made other nominations *before* and during 1593, thus creating a large number of episcopal pretenders. But Epinac's failure, and that of others, showed that Mayenne nominees could no longer hope to secure bishoprics in the face of political changes that were already strengthening the hand of Henri IV.

While Mayenne, the papacy, and the few cathedral chapters which tried to profit from the political vacuum of these years by reasserting their ancient rights to elect bishops, between them contributed to the confusion that would prevail in the French episcopate during the early 1590s, there were other factors also at work. A number of bishops were effectively exiled from their dioceses because they fell foul of royalist or Leaguer opponents who were dominant within them. In addition, the wars saw the re-opening of older disputes between bishops and their cathedral towns, with each side attempting to defend its privileges or extend its political powers at the expense of the other. Particularly acrimonious disputes are recorded for towns like Marseille, Aix, Rodez, and there were no doubt others. While most bishops were able to recover their dioceses with the ending of the wars, a small number either failed to, or judged it better not to try. Some of these, like the bishops of Lisieux, St Malo, Nantes, Lodève, found themselves looking for new sees.

Finally, Henri IV himself was not inactive during the years before 1595. Although still a Huguenot until 1593, and then a contested Catholic until 1595, he was as keen as Mayenne to exercise royal powers to nominate bishops. Equally, of course, he was not in control of events. Following the details of his episcopal appointments, before and even after 1595, and therefore piecing together something like a coherent policy, is extremely

---

[7] A. S. V. *Fondo Borghese*, I, 636, fol. 150, duc de Guise to Pope, 15 Oct 1593.

[8] See A. E. Prevost, *Le Diocèse de Troyes*, vol. ii, Dijon, 1924, pp. 403–4.

difficult. For one thing, it is clear that he made far more actual nominations to bishoprics than the record of papal provisions would indicate: some of his first nominees to vacant sees subsequently withdrew, some resigned to other parties in return for pensions, while others still were obliged to abandon their ambitions because they stood little or no chance of gaining effective possession of their designated see. A roll-call, admittedly partial, of those who *failed* to become bishops at this time seems more impressive than that of those who did; it includes a son of the duc de Bouillon, Alexandre de La Marck (Meaux), Louis Séguier (Laon), Achille de Harlay (Lavaur), the future marquis de Coeuvres (Noyon), René Benoist, the *pape des Halles* (Troyes), and the poet Philippe Desportes (Rouen). In many cases of vacant bishoprics, Henri was merely responding to demands and circumstances rather than making free choices of his own. Above all, he was ready to regard bishoprics and church benefices generally as a natural part of any political package, and it is not surprising that a king who negotiated and purchased the obedience of his subjects rather than conquered his realm, should have made concessions to the noble families who had their eyes closely fixed on local bishoprics.

Even before his conversion, Henri was providing evidence of this attitude. As early as July 1590, he promised to allow Orazio Rucellai to dispose of the benefices of his brother, Annibale, who was bishop of Carcassonne, should Annibale die before Orazio himself[9]. Sometime later he bestowed the archbishopric of Tours on Gilles de Souvré, a close ally, something he reminded Souvré of in late 1593, when he asked him to give it to the royalist bishop of Nantes, Philippe du Bec, 'avec honneste et raisonable récompense dont ledict sr de Nantes conviendra avec vous'[10]. Other individual concessions of a similar kind may date from the early 1590s. But it was when the political momentum gathered in Henri's favour in 1593–4, that negotiated settlements with political leaders and families began to increase. A few examples of this will suffice to illustrate the king's approach. In 1594, Sully was authorized to deal with the marquis de Villars in Normandy, and Villars drove a hard bargain before he would recognize Henri IV. All concerned had their eyes on the rich benefices of Cardinal Vendôme, archbishop of Rouen, and a complex solution, involving the cross-pensioning of the interested parties, was worked out. It was clearly as a confidant of Villars, that Philippe Desportes was offered the see of Rouen, but when he proved unwill-

---

[9] *Lettres missives*, iii, p. 213–14, letter of 12 July 1590.

[10] *Lettres missives*, iv, p. 73, letter to Souvré, 24 Dec 1593, reminding him of this earlier gift, but with no indication of its date.

ing to serve, the see reverted to the Bourbons[11]. But the most celebrated and far-reaching settlement concerned the bishoprics of Languedoc, where the Joyeuse-Montmorency rivalry had always involved competition for, and control of, bishoprics. During the 1580s and early 1590s, the main disputes had been over the sees of Nîmes, Uzès, Carcassonne, Alet, Lodève, and Albi. The 1596 settlement with Joyeuse created two *lieutenances-générales* in the Languedoc *gouvernement*, one for Joyeuse based on Toulouse and covering twelve dioceses in all, including Narbonne, Alet, Lodève, Albi, Carcassonne; and another, for Montmorency's son-in-law, Ventadour, included Nîmes, Uzès, Monpellier, Agde and Le Puy. Henceforth, Cardinal Joyeuse would be able to protect his episcopal clients, demand substantial pensions, and in some cases, like Narbonne, nominate his own *confidentiaires* in these sees. This deal not prevent continued sniping and competition for sees like Nîmes and Uzès. Other leading political figures pressed for similar concessions: Mayenne demanded the right to appoint to all bishoprics in his govenorship of Burgundy, as would the duc de Mercoeur when his turn came to treat for the province of Brittany, but neither secured anything like the concessions made to Joyeuse and Montmorency[12].

But below the great nobles and provincial leaders lurked lesser families with direct family interests in specific bishoprics. These interests might or might not coincide with those of the principal political figures, and the families would normally attempt to approach the king directly when sees became vacant. In general, the king appears to have responded as quickly as he could, if only to prevent the initiative from passing to Mayenne, the pope or a local cathedral chapter. Successful candidates were usually given royal *brevets* if clerics, and *lettres d'économat* if seculars. While the ban on seeking papal provisions remained in force (until 1596), such titles were anything but universally accepted. To give them greater force, holders sought to obtain decrees from the *grand conseil* which were intended to have the same force as papal provisions, enabling those concerned to exercise full spiritual and temporal control of their diocese[13]. This practice would be one of the papacy's principal complaints against the crown and its episcopal

---

[11] *Lettres missives*, iv, pp. 205–6, king to Sully, August 1594.

[12] See Mark Greengrass, 'Aristocracy and Episcopacy at the end of the Wars of Religion in France: the Duke of Montmorency and the Bishoprics of Languedoc', in *L'Institution et les pouvoirs dans les églises de l'antiquité à nos jours, Miscellanea Historiae Ecclesiasticae*, viii, Brussels-Louvain, 1987, pp. 356–63. I would like to thank Dr Greengrass for valuable information and advice about the Languedoc bishoprics.

[13] A.N., V^5 153, decree of *grand conseil*, 5 Sept 1590.

nominees down to 1600 and beyond. Even when not hastily made, many of Henri's nominations in the 1590s involved men whose identities remain obscure; most of the *économes* whose names are actually known, were either front-men for others, or clerics who later failed or refused to proceed any further towards the episcopate.

Inevitably, many of Henri's decisions took the form, not of actually nominating a bishop to a vacant see, but of granting to someone else — a follower or an important family — the privilege of presenting a candidate for his approval. Well-known instances of this include the grant of Auch in Gascony to Biron in 1590 and then Nemours in 1593, Luçon to the Richelieu family in 1592, Fréjus to Crillon, and Périgueux to the Bourdeille family in 1594[14]. Henri de Noailles, comte d'Ayen, received powers to nominate his choices for the dioceses of St Flour and Dax in 1597, and promptly obliged in both cases[15]. The duc d'Epernon was allowed to dispose of the see of Aire-sur-l'Adour after the death of his relative, François de Foix-Candalle, in 1594, but preferred to keep it vacant for one of his younger sons for over twelve years[16]. When constable Montmorency wrote in 1597 to request the see of Meaux for his brother-in-law, the king replied he had already given it to the marquis de Vitry for one of his sons; he could not, he wrote, back out of his promise to Vitry, 'm'estant si utile serviteur qu'il est'[17]. No doubt, a full record, if it could be made, of such grants would be considerably longer.

Cases like these illustrate the context in which episcopal nominations were made in Henri's early years as king. The high number of commoners and members of religious orders — the latter often amounting to an extension of the former — appointed bishops under him has been noted by several historians, and given rise to contradictory interpretations. Direct evidence, where it is available, suggests that very few of these men were, or would later become, independent agents, and that they were bound, either formally or informally, to powerful local families; the idea that the king either could, or wished to, promote social harmony and reconciliation by

---

[14] F. Caneto, 'Souvenirs relatifs au siège d'Auch', *Revue de Gascogne*, xv, 1874, 346 (Auch); *Gallia Christiana Novissima*, ed J.H.Albanès, Montbeliard, 1899, i, col. 403 (Fréjus); *Lettres missives*, iv, p. 1036, permission to Bourdeille for Périgueux, 10 Nov 1594.

[15] B(ibliothèque) N(ationale) Ms Lat. 17021, fol. 17, 10 August 1597.

[16] Chantilly, Archives du Musée Condé, series L, vol. XXVI, fol. 17, brevet of 28 Feb 1594. I wish to thank Dr Joan Davies for this and other references to material in the Montmorency papers at Chantilly.

[17] *Lettres missives*, iv, p. 809, letter to Montmorency, 10 July 1597.

choosing bishops from all social classes seems to fly in the face of political and social realities after a generation of civil and military turbulence[18]. Henri de Noailles's bishop of St Flour was no more than a domestic, as were the bishops of Périgueux, Luçon, Agde and many other places, and their masters treated them as such. The duc d'Epernon took all the credit for promoting the celebrated Sorbonnist Philippe Cospéau to Aire in 1606, paying for his papal provisions, his *équipage* and even a carriage to get him to Aire, but not before he had ensured that virtually all the revenues remained in his own hands[19]. The Cardinal de Joyeuse did exactly the same with the Dominican friar he elevated to the archiepiscopal see of Narbonne. And when Léonard de Trappes, archbishop of Auch, was slow to pay the hefty pension he owed the duc de Nemours, the *conseil privé* gave him the option of resigning Auch altogether to someone of Nemours' own choosing[20].

Thus, the problem of the episcopate in 1595 when Henri was absolved was not simply that nearly a third of all French sees were vacant. Reality was far more complex than that. Had they been simply vacant, the problem would have been far easier to settle thereafter through systematic royal nominations, and Henri would indeed have had a rare, perhaps unique, opportunity to begin reshaping the episcopate according to his own specifications. But Henri, Mayenne and the pope had all in varying degrees appointed their own men to bishoprics, and it would take several years to resolve the ensuing disputes. For obvious reasons, Henri's own candidates were particularly suspect in Rome — a heretical king could hardly be relied on to appoint reliable bishops. One of the clauses in his absolution was that he would not in future appoint heretics, their sons, or men suspected of heresy to bishoprics and major benefices, and this remained one of Rome's main concerns about his nominees in later years[21]. But the absolution did not mean that Rome dropped its objections to those he had nominated to bishoprics in preceding years — they continued to be subject to delay, suspicion and scrutiny. In fact, it was those clerics who were most closely

---

[18] J. Michael Hayden, 'The Social Origins of the French Episcopacy at the Beginning of the Seventeenth Century', *French Historical Studies* 10, 1977, pp. 27–38; Michel Péronnet, *Les Evêques de l'ancienne France*, 2 vols, Lille, 1978, i, pp. 496ff.

[19] B. N. Ms Lat 17021, fol. 81, 'extraict de la vie de Mre Philippe Cospéau'.

[20] A.N. V[6] 7, no 263, decree of 7 Jan 1604.

[21] See the successive instructions to nuncios in Klaus Jaitner, ed., *Die Hauptinstruktionen Clemens' VIII für die Nuntien und Legaten an die europäischen Fürstenhofen 1592–1605*, 2 vols, Tübingen, 1984.

associated with him and his policies up to his conversion in 1593 who often had to wait longest after 1595 for their papal provisions. Renaud de Beaune, archbishop of Bourges, *the* moving spirit among Henri's ecclesiastical support, had to wait eight years before Clement VIII authorized his transfer from Bourges to Sens; his alleged ambition to become patriarch of France in 1591 was not readily forgiven[22]. As for René Benoist, the king's personal confessor, not even eleven years' patient pressure for his bulls for the see of Troyes produced the desired result, and the king suffered the indignity of having eventually to drop his cause altogether in 1604. If several sees remained vacant well after 1595, it was not merely because of a failure to nominate, but because Rome was in no hurry to oblige him and several of his candidates[23].

While the king's handling of the episcopate for much of the 1590s suggests a man who had more serious matters to worry about, the papacy for its part was genuinely anxious to effect a reconstruction, and took most of the significant initiatives. The most notable and best documented of these was the legation of Cardinal Alessandro de Medici, arguably the most important and certainly the longest (June 1596 to September 1598) of the Ancien Régime. It covered two of the most interesting and eventful years of Henri's reign — coinciding with efforts at governmental reform, an assembly of notables meeting at Rouen, war with Spain and, towards the end, the preparation of the Edict of Nantes. Despatching Medici to France in order to restore ties with the king, and to obtain his ratification of the articles of his absolution (which included a promise to apply the Concordat of Bologna to the letter), Clement VIII took the opportunity of giving him unusual and wide-ranging powers to deal with ecclesiastical problems, and especially to regularize the position of clergy[24]. During his legation, Medici performed episcopal functions in many vacant dioceses, appointed to thousands of ordinary benefices, granted dispensations, and absolved those, whether clergy or laymen, who were guilty of simony and other offences in

---

[22] A. S. V., *Fondo Borghese*, I, 80, fol. 86, Cardinal Aldobrandini, papal secretary of state, to Medici, 18 May 1598, giving quite blunt reasons for Rome's dislike of him.

[23] The Benoist claim, first to Angers and then to Troyes occurs repeatedly in papal and royal diplomatic papers down to 1604, when Benoist himself finally abandoned his claims. See E. Pasquier, *Un curé de Paris pendant les guerres de religion. René Benoist, le pape des Halles 1521–1608*, Angers, 1913,.

[24] Jaitner, *Hauptinstruktionen Clemens' VIII*, vol. 1, no 54, instructions of 10 May 1596. See also A. S. V., *Fondo Borghese*, I, 80, fos. 41ᵛ–42, Aldobrandini to Medici, 18 Sept 1596.

respect of ecclesiastical offices[25].

Medici was not formally empowered to settle problems relating to the upper clergy, because they involved consistorial benefices, which were reserved for pope and curia. But there is no doubt that he was expected to negotiate with those holding nominations to, or claims on, episcopal office and other major benefices, to persuade them to seek provisions in Rome, and to exhort laymen to surrender their hold on major benefices. Already on his journey through Dauphiné and the Lyonnais, he began collecting and transmitting information to Rome about the state of the French church, initially forming a rather negative impression of some of its bishops. But the more he saw for himself and met French clerics, the less despondent he became about the state of the church and the episcopate; soon he was warning Rome that its assumptions about the French church as a nest of irredeemable heretics needed serious modification[26]. The dozen or so royal nominees who presented themselves to him after he reached Paris appeared to him worthy, qualified men, but he quickly realized that the real problems would be with those less willing to show their faces. Once installed in Paris, he began, in his own words, to work on the consciences of the leading figures among those holding benefices without proper title or provisions; he set about finding *tempéraments* and arrangements for disputed sees and, with Rome's approval, promised to treat individual cases in accordance with the 'quality of the families and persons concerned'[27].

Medici's mission began while the Assembly of the Clergy was meeting in Paris in 1596. It had been pushing hard to get the most blatant *économats* and *confidences* withdrawn, but it found the king and his ministers reluctant to offer help. All the latter would say was that this would not be repeated in future, recommending the bishops and the papacy to simply forgive and forget the mistakes of the past. This unhelpful stance, which promised little assistance in resolving current difficulties, was reported to

---

[25] The enormous archives of his legation are in B. N. Ms Lat. 11805–12, and have never been properly investigated in any study of the French church at the end of the wars of religion. M. Bernard Barbiche has recently begun work on them, and I am happy to thank him for keeping me informed of his research.

[26] A. S. V. *Fondo Borghese*, I, 646, fos. 11–12v, Medici to Cardinal Aldobrandini, 25 June 1596; *ibid.*, fol. 121, to same 26 Jan 1597; *Fondo Borghese*, III, 73, Bishop of Torcello to Aldobrandini, 13 July 1596.

[27] A. S. V., *Fondo Borghese*, I, 646, fol. 179, Medici to same 23 April 1597; *ibid.*, I, 80, fos. 49ᵛ–50, Aldobrandini to Medici, 18 Nov 1596; *ibid.*, fol. 75, to same, 18 March 1597.

Rome by no less a figure than Cardinal Pierre de Gondi of Paris, one of the king's closest advisers around 1596[28]. But the king himself evidently welcomed Medici's mediation, aware that his own previous concessions or decisions had created awkward problems which he could not so readily resolve without breaking promises[29].

Medici's task was thus a major and hazardous one; finding solutions depended on the ability to reconcile highly divergent interests. Cardinal Givry had been forced out of his see of Lisieux during the wars, but in 1596 he finally abandoned his futile efforts to recover it in return for a pension and two abbeys, followed somewhat later by the coadjutorship of Langres. Medici welcomed such commonsense, and was upset by the refusal of others, such as the papally-appointed Leaguer archbishop of Aix, Génebrard, to behave equally reasonably. In general, he showed less sympathy than Rome did for ex-Leaguer bishops who were unable to negotiate their own way back to their dioceses, and he encouraged them not to prolong old confrontations[30].

Medici was also convinced that nothing would be achieved by imposing the strict letter of canon law on those involved in *confidences* and *économats*, and therefore proposed that in return for surrendering direct lay control of major benefices, they be given pensions off the revenues. This approach was first tried — or at least became public knowledge — in respect of the wealthiest diocese in France, that of Auch, which had been in the hands of a succession of major Italian prelates for much of the sixteenth century. When Cardinal d'Este died in 1586, Henri III had given Auch to his Savoie-Nemours relatives, a gift confirmed in 1593 by Henri IV. But the intended beneficiary, the marquis de St Sorlin, actually became duc de Nemours in 1595, and was thus unlikely to want to be an archbishop. However, he and his mother, Anna d'Este, were unwilling to relinquish Auch, and despatched a household intendant, Léonard de Trappes, to administer the diocese[31]. Cardinal Medici quickly sought out the duchess in mid-1596

---

[28] A. S. V. *Fondo Borghese*, I, 462–8, fos. 242–3, letter to Aldobrandini, 2 April 1596; *ibid.*, fos. 246–7, same to same, 20 April; *ibid.*, fos. 252–4, same to same 6 May 1596.

[29] A. S. V., *Fondo Borghese*, I, 646, fos. 215–16, Medici to Aldobrandini, 21 June 1597.

[30] *ibid.*, fol. 72, same to same 24 Nov. 1596; *ibid.*, fol. 100, to same 28 Dec 1596.

[31] Caneto, 'Souvenirs relatifs au siège d'Auch', *Revue de Gascogne*, xv, 1874, pp. 346–50.

and remonstrated with her about the bad example a leading Catholic family like hers was giving in respect of Auch. Within a short time, a deal was struck whereby de Trappes would become archbishop, while the duc de Nemours would collect an enormous pension of 8,000 *écus* off Auch, one he could retain even were he to marry. Around the same time, a similar arrangement was made for the see of Beauvais, where Schomberg's son, although a *militaire*, was awarded a pension of 2,000 *écus*[32]. Others had either already been agreed to by Henri IV or were still being discussed in 1596–7, but several bishops expressed their alarm at the granting of pensions to married laymen: this was, they claimed, unheard of, it was against all the provisions of canon law, and it seemed to give the royal and papal sanction to the strong-arm tactics being employed by powerful families. A meeting of bishops, held in Paris at Cardinal Gondi's residence, protested against this partial secularization of church property. The discussions seem to have been animated, with Medici and his advisers having to argue the case for choosing the lesser of two evils which at least freed major church offices from secular control: that was what really mattered, and pensions could be regarded as mere 'cose profane' which the pope would take care to circumscribe[33]. Medici, who complained that these unhelpful 'impertinences' would make a difficult task even more difficult, stuck to his chosen course, asserting that he was not applying general principles, but merely 'particular graces'[34]. The bishops' protest was ignored, and new pensions would continue to be demanded from incoming bishops. The Nemours pension was the largest of all, but for a time the *grand prieur de France*, and later Cardinal Joyeuse, held one for 20,000 *livres* off Albi, the Monluc family one for 10,000 *livres* off Condom, the Lansac family 10,000 *livres* off Comminges, and Henri's own *brave* Crillon 4,000 off Fréjus[35]. Some of the heaviest pensions of either the sixteenth or seventeenth century were

---

[32] A. S. V., *Fondo Borghese*, I, 646, fol. 226, Medici to Aldobrandini, 13 July 1597.

[33] A. S. V., *Fondo Borghese*, III, 73, fos. 455–6, Alessandro Giusti to Aldobrandini, 9 May 1597, for a detailed report.

[34] A. S. V., *Fondo Borghese*, I, 646, fos. 226–7, Medici to same, 13 July 1597, for a long report on these discussions. The papacy showed little sympathy with the bishops' views: *Fondo Borghese*, I, 80, fol. 72, Aldobrandini to Medici, 25 Aug 1597.

[35] See n. 32 *above* (Auch); A. S. V., Acta Miscellanea 53, fol. 272; A. S. V. Nunziatura di Francia 42, fos. 338–9, Bishop d'Elbène to Clement VIII, 7 July 1599 (Albi); L.Mazéret, *Chroniques de l'Eglise de Condom*, Condom, 1927, p. 295; A.N., V⁶ 1180, fol. 454 (Comminges); A. S. V., *Fondo Borghese*, I, 636C, fol. 32, Henri IV to Paul V, 28 April 1608 (Fréjus).

conceded under Henri IV, and in many instances may be regarded as thinly-disguised, albeit legalized, forms of *confidence*. Pensions would gradually be reduced and transferred to ecclesiastics during the reign of Louis XIII.

However difficult it may be to measure Medici's influence, the factual record of Henrician nominees applying to Rome for papal provisions, and securing them, during the final years of the century is eloquent enough — 1 in 1596, 8 in 1597, 11 in 1598, 18 in 1599, 8 in 1600, 7 in 1601, 9 in 1602. The return of peace, the lifting of the ban on papal provisions, the need to obtain a firm title to disputed bishoprics in the face of competitors — these were some of the other factors which impelled French bishops to look again to Rome mid-way through Henri IV's reign. As an example of this, we may cite the highly apologetic letter written to Clement VIII by Cardinal Sourdis in 1599, apologising for the bad example he had given the French church by occupying the archbishopric of Bordeaux without proper title for several years[36]. By the same token, these figures just cited show that vacancies *were* being filled quite rapidly around the turn of the century, so restoring the episcopate to something near full strength at a time when the religious energies unloosed during the wars, and especially by the League, were being directed increasingly towards the material and spiritual reconstruction of the church.

But it would be premature to end on this note. Henri IV continued, after his absolution, to make episcopal nominations that were unacceptable in Rome, and to support candidates who raised suspicions there. Even after 1597–8, there continued to be prolonged vacancies. The average length of episcopal vacancies in excess of one year during Henri's reign as a whole was in the region of ten years; for those vacancies continuing or arising after 1598, the average fell by half, but five years was still a long gap by any standards. This was mainly because provincial noble families retained the power to keep sees vacant. After 1604, Cardinal Joyeuse either personally held or controlled the three great archbishoprics of Rouen, Toulouse and Narbonne. In at least a few cases, however, vacancies continued because of royal readiness to use French bishoprics in an effort to rebuild French influence in Rome. While this had been common practice under his pre-decessors, and Italian incumbents of French bishoprics were numerous, by Henri's time Roman or Italian prelates seemed to prefer inducements of a safer and more secure kind — pensions off bishoprics and abbeys[37]. From

---

[36] A. S. V. *Fondo Borghese*, I, 462–8, fol. 369, letter to Clement VIII, 15 May 1599.

[37] See Bernard Barbiche, 'L'Influence française à la cour pontificale sous Henri

this point onwards, the French episcopate would be increasingly French.

Instructions given to successive papal nuncios in 1599, 1601, 1604 and 1607 all refer to the difficulties still being encountered over French episcopal appointments, and demand vigilance in debarring the unacceptable. Far more frequent and sustained reference to the problems of the episcopate is to be found in the correspondence of both the papal nuncios and the French ambassadors during the decades stretching from the mid-1590s and the late 1610s than throughout the rest of the seventeenth century. The 'mal français' remained the *confidences*, the suspicion surrounding resignations, the continuing unwillingness of laymen to surrender control of even major benefices, and the rising demands, especially in the 1610s, for coadjutorships which guaranteed succession rights to their holders. It seems fair to say that Rome would have fully shared the criticisms made by the archbishop of Vienne in his address to Henri after the Assemblée Générale of late 1605.

That this is more than just an educated guess is evident from the extended report made shortly after this assembly by the nuncio, Barberini, on the abuse of major benefices during the wars by leading families, some of whom were still reluctant to change their ways. In particular, he singled out the constable Montmorency, who now seem suitably penitent, though protesting that the restitution of 100,000 *écus*'s worth of church revenues that he had usurped, was absolutely impossible for him[38]. This report seems to have been commissioned as a part of negotiations between Rome and the French crown over the continuing predicament of bishoprics and other major benefices; though we know nothing about the course of these talks, it may be that the Montmorency case had the effect of raising unresolved general questions[39]. The outcome was that, over ten years after Henri's absolution and Medici's arrival in France, Paul V offered to concede substantial pensions off benefices to laymen if only they would at least transfer direct control of them to ecclesiastics, and to despatch all the nec-

---

IV', *Mélanges d'Histoire et d'Archéologie de l'Ecole Française de Rome*, 77, 1965, pp. 277–99.

[38] B(ibliotheca) A(postolica) V(aticana), Ms Barb(erini) lat(ini) 8683, fol. 11, Barberini to Borghese, 2 May 1606, referring to an earlier report (possibly that cited in following note); A. S. V., *Fondo Borghese*, II, 248, fol. 213, Barberini to Borghese, 30 May 1606.

[39] A. S. V., *Fondo Borghese*, III, 127E, fol. 27, 'exemplar' of Montmorency's petition (in Latin) to Pope, undated. This may be the document enclosed with Barberini's letter of 4 April 1606: A. S. V., *Fondo Borghese*, II, 248, fol. 129.

essary provisions free of charge[40]. Initially, he was so nervous about this offer that he refused to put the decision in writing, but when he did, in July 1606, he insisted that Henri IV keep it as secret as possible — the curia's fear was that the Spaniards and other Catholic rulers would quickly demand similar concessions for themselves[41]. Three years later, a new French ambassador in Rome confessed he only knew of the brief by hearsay, and no one in Rome either could or would tell him its contents[42].

In view of these enduring problems, it would be somewhat naive to talk in terms of any far-reaching reconstruction of the episcopate under Henri IV. His achievements were strictly limited, and perhaps have little to do with his actual choices of individual bishops. But they are not negligible for all that. By restoring peace and containing the Huguenots, his reign contributed above all to the stabilization of the French episcopate. In this connection, a remarkable feature of his reign was how few transfers there were from see to see — most of them took place early in the reign, involving exchanges or promotions to more important sees. This is in sharp contrast to the sixteenth-century pattern, and to a lesser extent to what would obtain at certain times in the seventeenth century, when a stronger crown would be in a position to use episcopal transfers for its own purposes. Modest though this may sound, such stabilization was important. Henri's power to achieve more than that was limited enough, and he acknowledged this by compromising with local families and demands. However, fears about how far this pragmatism would take him rendered both the French clergy and the papacy less than ecstatic eulogists of his policies. It is surely significant that one of the earliest formal letters from Paul V to Henri's widow shortly after his assassination was a firm exhortation to her to attempt to present better candidates for the mitre than her late husband had done[43].

---

[40] Copy in B. A. V., Barb. lat. 8684, fol. 22.

[41] B. N., Ms fr. 18001, fos. 191^v-2, Halincourt, French Ambassador in Rome, to Villeroy, 27 June 1606. B. A. V., Barb. lat. 9684, fol. 21, Cardinal Borghese to Maffeo Barberini, 9 Jan 1607.

[42] B. N. Ms fr. 18004, fos. 9^v-10, Savary de Brèves to marquis de Puysieux, 8 Jan 1609.

[43] See Joseph Bergin, *Cardinal de La Rochefoucauld. Leadership and Reform in the French Church*, London-New Haven 1987, pp. 126ff.

1. Project for the *Pont-Neuf* [Musée Carnavalet, Paris].

8. Royal Patronage of the Arts in France
1574–1610

R. J. Knecht

In his *Institution du Prince*, written towards the end of 1518, Guillaume Budé gave the young Francis I advice on how to govern his kingdom. Among the qualities which he urged him to cultivate was liberality. He was to make frequent use of it to build up his prestige in the eyes of foreign nations and to promote the ascendancy of men of learning. The Prince, in Budé's judgment, needed to be the supreme Maecenas[1]. It seems that Francis I followed this advice to the letter. The extent and quality of his artistic patronage are beyond dispute. He built some of the finest palaces in western Europe, employed several of the leading artists of his day and collected paintings, statues and other works of art which were eventually to form the nucleus of the collection now at the Louvre — no mean achievement for a monarch who has all too often been dismissed as little more than a playboy[2].

By contrast the artistic patronage of the later Valois kings seems pitifully inadequate. Francis II was too short-lived to do anything. Charles

[1] C. Bontems, L.-P. Raybaud et J.-P. Brancourt, *Le Prince dans la France des XVIᵉ et XVIIᵉ siècles*, Paris, 1965, p. 53.

[2] R. J. Knecht, *Francis I*, Cambridge, 1982, pp. 99–104, 253–73.

IX did at least have one ambitious project in mind. He acquired extensive lands on the banks of the river Andelle and called on Jacques Androuet Du Cerceau to build a palace worthy of Francis I's grandson. It was to be called Charleval, and the plan, which survives in the form of engravings, show the vastness of the scheme envisaged. It would have been possible to fit Chambord in the *basse-cour* of the château[3]. Henri III had many of the intellectual gifts of his grandfather. In 1577 his erstwhile tutor, Jacques Amyot, declared that Henri owed 'la capacité de son entendement' to Francis I. What is more, he had the patience to listen, read and write which his grandfather had lacked[4]. But his artistic enthusiasms were mainly focused, it seems, on the theatre, music and dancing, rather than architecture and painting. He did have a favourite architect in Baptiste Androuet Du Cerceau and was generous to some churches and religious houses in Paris. For example, he gave 2000 *écus* for the completion of the church of St Etienne du Mont. Among the religious orders he was generous especially to the Capuchins and the Feuillants. When the church of the Cordeliers burnt down [1580] he helped pay for the rebuilding of the choir[5].

But Henri III's most important achievement as a patron of building was the Pont Neuf in Paris. The idea of a bridge linking the bourg St Germain with the right bank of the Seine can be traced back to the reign of Charles V, but it was Henri III, who first took a serious interest in it. He appointed a commission in 1577 to draw up a plan, the architects concerned being Baptiste Androuet Du Cerceau and Pierre des Illes. The first stone was laid by the king on 31 May 1578. The funeral of the *mignons*, Quélus and de Maugiron, took place the same day and the rumour circulated that Henri planned to call the bridge the *Pont des Pleurs*[6]. Initially, a bridge without houses was planned. A grand decorative scheme proposed by the commission survives in an oil painting at the Musée Carnavalet. This shows two triumphal arches reminiscent of the Arch of Septimius Severus in Rome, a cluster of obelisks and a central pavilion at the end of the Ile-de-la-Cité, where the two halves of the bridge met. These may not have been purely formal features. As Sauval has suggested, they would have been useful in stopping a rebellious march on the Louvre. But force of habit and perhaps

---

[3] B. Tollon, 'Les châteaux des guerres de Religion' in *Le château en France*, ed. J.-P. Babelon, Paris, 1986, p. 217.

[4] J. Boucher, *La cour de Henri III*, Rennes, 1986, p. 21.

[5] J.-P. Babelon, *Nouvelle histoire de Paris: Paris au XVIe siècle*, Paris, 1986, p. 137.

[6] H. Sauval, *Histoire et Recherches des Antiquités de la Ville de Paris*, Paris, 1724, Book III, p. 231.

the cost of upkeep caused the plan to be abandoned. Instead a bridge with two rows of houses upon it was built. All that remains of it to-day are the round towers above each pile and a row of bearded masks[7].

The Pont Neuf was incomplete when Henri III was assassinated and an incomplete bridge is not much to weigh in the scales of royal patronage alongside the great châteaux of Francis I. Can it be that Henri III would have built more, but for the political upheavals of his reign? This is possible. But we should not assume, as is commonly done, that the Wars of Religion were a time of architectural stagnation. The period has, in fact, been described recently as 'un moment passionnant de l'architecture française'[8]. In the words of Jean-Jacques Gloton: 'en dépit des misères, des violences, des difficultés de toute sorte, les arts n'ont pas été paralysés: il en va de la Provence, (et d'autres provinces sans doute) comme de la région parisienne, la poursuite de la création d'un nouveau cadre de vie reste à l'ordre du jour, et certaines réalisations les plus représentatives datent en fin de compte d'un second XVIᵉ siècle d'où Mars jamais n'a pu ni voulu chasser Apollon'[9]. The main royal impetus, however, was given not by the king, but by his mother, Catherine de' Medici, who seems to have longed to build in France palaces comparable to those she had known in her Florentine childhood. She employed some outstanding architects, notably Philibert de l'Orme and Jean Bullant, but she started far more schemes than she could ever finish.

Following the accidental death of her husband, Henri II, in 1559, Catherine abandoned the old royal palace of the Tournelles, which had become hateful to her. She had it destroyed and sold off the site. In 1563, she decided to build a new residence close to the Louvre, but outside the walls of Paris. This was the Tuileries, named after a tile-factory formerly on the site. As architect, Catherine surprisingly employed Philibert de l'Orme, who had been dismissed as *Surintendant* after the death of Henri II. It is possible that she had been touched by Philibert's *Instruction*, a work written during his disgrace, in which he rebutted the accusations of his enemies and appealed for better treatment[10]. If we are to believe an engraving by Jean Androuet Du Cerceau, the Tuileries was intended to be

---

[7] J.-P. Babelon, *op.cit.*, pp. 138–9; D.Thomson, *Renaissance Paris*, London, 1984, p. 178.

[8] B. Tollon, *op.cit.*, p. 217.

[9] J-J. Gloton, 'Architecture et urbanisme en Provence au temps des guerres de Religion', in *Gazette des Beaux-Arts*, xcvii, 1981, pp. 9–20.

[10] A. Blunt, *Philibert de l'Orme*, London, 1958, pp. 88–9.

a vast palace with three courtyards, the two smaller ones being divided by large oval halls. But as Anthony Blunt has shown, Du Cerceau's plans and views 'are not consistent among themselves, and secondly they do not agree in detail with what was already built'. Some of the features shown, notably the two oval halls, 'have no parallels in the work of de l'Orme, and their peculiar curved forms are contrary to his general principles'[11]. It now seems likely that de l'Orme never intended the scheme shown by Du Cerceau. Instead he probably planned a smaller palace based on a single courtyard with double pavilions on one side and single ones on the other. In fact, little of this scheme was actually built, for de l'Orme died on 8 January 1570 and two years later Catherine stopped the work. Allegedly she abandoned the Tuileries, as she stopped going to St Germain-en-Laye, after a fortune-teller had warned her that she would die in the parish of St Germain. The Tuileries stood in the parish of St Germain l'Auxerrois. But, as Cloulas has pointed out, the story is suspect, for Catherine continued to visit the Tuileries frequently, as, for example in 1573, when she received the Polish ambassadors, who had come to offer the Polish crown to her son. It is possible that Catherine gave up building the Tuileries because of the cost and the slow progress of the construction. She may also have felt that it was too exposed to attack[12]. Whatever the reason, the Tuileries remained unfinished. Much of it was pulled down under Louis XIV and the whole palace was destroyed in 1871 during the Commune. All that remains of Catherine's building are some fragments in the Tuileries gardens, the Ecole des Beaux-Arts and a château near Ajaccio.

According to Du Cerceau, Catherine decided before 1576 to connect the Louvre with the Tuileries. The first part of this connecting link was the *Petite Galerie*, which was designed either by de l'Orme or by Lescot. But only the ground floor was partially or completely built in Catherine's lifetime. At some time after de l'Orme's death in 1570 work also started on a pavilion at the southern end of the incomplete de l'Orme wing of the Tuileries. The architect of this structure was Jean Bullant, who evidently planned to extend the range of the Tuileries to the river Seine, whence a gallery might be run towards the southern extremity of the *Petite Galerie*. The style of Bullant's pavilion is in sharp contrast to de l'Orme's wing, being much less adventurous and experimental[13].

In 1572 Catherine began looking for the site of a new residence within

---

[11] *Ibid.*, pp. 92–3.
[12] I. Cloulas, *Catherine de Médicis*, Paris, 1979, p. 323.
[13] D. Thomson, *op.cit.*, pp. 172–4.

the walls of Paris. But she wanted one big enough to contain gardens, where she might walk about while discussing matters of state. She began by purchasing the Hôtel Guillart, near the church of St Eustache. Then she launched out into what Cloulas describes as 'une opération d'urbanisme sans précédent à Paris'[14]. While houses and shops were replacing some of the large medieval enclosed institutions, Catherine reversed the trend by sweeping away a whole built-up area to make way for her new palace. With the pope's permission she moved the *Filles Repenties*, an order dedicated to reclaiming young ladies from prostitution, to another religious house appropriately situated in the rue St Denis. She then demolished the convent, except for the chapel. She also acquired and demolished the Hôtel d'Albret and other houses in the vicinity. On the site of these various buildings Jean Bullant built a new palace for Catherine, which was called the Hôtel de la Reine and later the Hôtel de Soissons. It has almost entirely disappeared, but we know what it was like thanks to engravings by Israel Sylvestre of c.1650 and a plan of c.1700. These show a *corps de logis* flanked by a courtyard and gardens. The central wing consisted of three pavilions. In the middle was a large arch flanked by two tall projections decorated with pilasters. All that remains of the Hôtel de la Reine is its strangest feature: a tall, fluted Doric column, which now stands in the midst of the Bourse de Commerce. Its decoration again bears witness to Catherine's grief over the loss of her husband, Henri II. But the column is not just a memorial; it had a function. Inside there is a spiral staircase leading to a terrace that was once balustraded on the architrave. It was wide enough to carry three people and was topped by an iron cage covered with lead sheating and with six portholes offering views of the heavens. At the very top was a small dome carrying an armillary sphere. It seems that the column was used as an observatory by Catherine's famous astrologers. It may also have served as a watchtower from which signals might be sent to the Louvre[15].

Outside Paris, Catherine's architectural activity was mainly focused on two châteaux: St Maur-des-Fossés and Chenonceaux. She purchased St Maur from the heirs of Cardinal du Bellay and employed Philibert de l'Orme to complete it. He submitted a plan, which she rejected as inadequate for the needs of her large entourage. Whereupon he added two pavilions at each end of the main *corps de logis*. On the garden side the pavilions were

---

[14] I. Cloulas, *op.cit.*, pp. 323–4.

[15] F.-C. James, 'Jean Bullant. Recherches sur l'architecture française du XVIe siècle' in *Ecole Nationale des Chartes. Positions des thèses*, 1968, pp. 101–9; F. Boudon, A. Chastel, H. Couzy and F. Hamon, *Système de l'architecture urbaine. Le Quartier des Halles à Paris*, Paris, 1977.

joined by a terrace carried by a *cryptoporticus*. St Maur was still unfinished when de l'Orme died. Some time after 1575 another project was produced by an architect who has not been identified. He doubled the pavilions on the garden side, raised them by two stories and crowned them with high-pitched roofs. Two additional arches were built over the *cryptoporticus* and this part of the building was given a colossal, not to say grotesque, pediment. But this too was only carried out in part and the house does not seem to have been habitable till the late seventeenth century[16].

In 1560 Catherine forced Diane de Poitiers to exchange Chenonceaux for Chaumont, but it was not until 1576 that she assigned large revenues to building work at Chenonceaux. This consisted of two galleries on the bridge which Bullant almost certainly designed. A drawing and engraving by Du Cerceau show a vast scheme which Catherine allegedly planned to erect at Chenonceaux. But, as Blunt has argued, it was probably just a fantasy. Du Cerceau 'sometimes inserted in his book designs embodying ideas which he himself would have liked to see carried out rather than those of the actual designer of the building in question'[17].

Catherine de' Medici was not only a great, if capricious, builder; she was also a notable art collector. This is borne out by an inventory of the movables at the Hôtel de la Reine, which was drawn up in August 1589 after her death[18]. By then, she had already given to her granddaughter, Christina of Lorraine, the famous Valois tapestries, now at the Uffizi[19]. But some notable tapestries remained, notably a series of twenty-four, bearing her device and coat of arms, which has been identified with the first weaving of the *Story of Artemisia*. Apart from tapestries, the contents of the Hôtel de la Reine included, on the ground floor, 25 maps 'drawn by hand' of different parts of the world, more than 135 pictures and several works of sculpture. On the first floor there were portraits of all sorts — 341 in all — many of them by Pierre and Come du Monstier and Benjamin Foulon, the queen-mother's official painters. There were 259 pieces of Limoges ware. One room in the palace had walls covered in costly Venetian mirrors. Catherine's study was lined with cupboards decorated with landscapes and

---

[16] A. Blunt, *Philibert de l'Orme*, pp. 89–91.

[17] *Ibid.*, p. 64.

[18] E. Bonnaffé, *Inventaire des meubles de Catherine de Médicis en 1589*, Paris, 1874. Among the books Catherine kept at hand were *Consolation sur la mort du feu roy Henry*, *Abus du Monde*, *Kalendrier grégorien* and *Prophéties des sibylles*, (*ibid.*, p. 16).

[19] F. Yates, *The Valois Tapestries*, London, 1975, p. xxv.

filled with varied objects: leather fans, dolls, caskets, a stuffed chameleon, Chinese lacquer, numerous games and pious objects. Hanging from the ceiling were seven stuffed crocodiles and many stags' heads. Around the room were a collection of minerals, some terra cotta statuettes and four small cannon. In a cupboard between two windows Catherine kept a selection of books she liked to have ready to hand: they included a set of architectural plans. Altogether Catherine had about 4500 books, including 776 manuscripts. Her printed books were at St Maur. Finally the inventory lists many costly fabrics, furniture of ebony inlaid with ivory and 141 pieces of china, probably from Bernard Palissy's workshop. The Hôtel de la Reine, in short, was 'as lavishly equipped and richly furnished as any of the palaces and châteaux belonging to the Crown'[20].

By comparison with architecture, painting stood at a low ebb in France during the late sixteenth century. Only two painters stand out as recognizable personalities: Antoine Caron and Jean Cousin the younger. Exaggerated claims have been made on behalf of Caron's art. He was not a particularly gifted artist, but he is of great historical interest on account of the themes which he chose to paint. These are of three kinds: 1) Allegorical subjects recalling festivities at the court of Henri III. 2) Massacre paintings. 3) Paintings which express the astrological preoccupations of Catherine de' Medici and her circle. Thus in the words of Gustave Lebel: 'Nous pouvons donc considérer Caron comme le traducteur le plus fidèle de cette société tourmentée de la seconde moitié du XVIe siècle, où les plaisirs de l'esprit, les spectacles, les fêtes et les jeux de la Cour formaient un si saisissant contraste avec les passions déchaînées de la politique et de la religion'[21].

Caron was employed by the Crown in various capacities. He worked under Primaticcio on the decoration of Fontainebleau and in the 1570s he was much concerned with the decorations of various public ceremonies and festivities: the entry of the duc d'Anjou into Paris in 1573, the reception of the Polish ambassadors in the same year, and the 'Magnificences' for the marriage of the duc de Joyeuse. The spirit and symbolism of such events are well conveyed by Caron's painting of *Augustus and the Sibyl*, now in the Louvre[22]. This shows a city *en fête*, decorated with temporary structures of the kind erected for entries and festivals. In the middle are

---

[20] D. Thomson, *op.cit.*, p. 20.

[21] G. Lebel, 'Notes sur Antoine Caron et son oeuvre' in *Bulletin de la Société de l'Histoire de Paris et de l'Ile-de-France*, (1940), pp. 7–34.

[22] J. Ehrmann, *Antoine Caron: peintre des fêtes et des massacres*, Paris, 1986, pp. 129–34.

two large twisted columns, which are probably an allusion to the Temple at Jerusalem. They are surmounted by a crown and are linked by a festoon upon which an eagle is perched. From the festoon hangs the motto: *Pietas Augusti*. This, as Frances Yates has argued 'must surely be a version of the imperial device of Charles IX'[23]. He himself, as Augustus, is kneeling before the Tyburtine Sybil, who points to a vision of the Virgin and Child in the sky. In other words, the Most Christian King is being promised a universal empire, based on the Holy Land, as in the prophecies of Guillaume Postel.

Caron was not employed exclusively by the Crown. About 1560 he was commissioned by Nicolas Houel, an apothecary and art patron, to make various designs for a series of tapestries in honour of the Queen-Mother, Catherine de' Medici. They illustrate the story of Artemisia II, who is renowned in history for her grief at the death of her husband, Mausolus, prince of Caria, (352–350 B.C.). To perpetuate his memory she built the Mausoleum of Halicarnassus, one of the seven wonders of the Ancient World. She vanquished his enemies and educated his children, five of whom became kings. For Artemisia we are meant to read Catherine de' Medici. Each of Caron's drawings (there are 44 in all) have a fine border showing the arms of France and of the Medici with the motto: *Ardorem extincta testantur vivere flamma*. Catherine's tears, though abundant, were not enough to put out the flame of her love for Henri II. Also visible in the borders are scythes, broken mirrors, scattered pearls and floods of tears. The tapestries themselves were not woven during Catherine's lifetime. They had to wait until the reign of Henri IV, who set up a tapestry factory in Paris, which later became the Gobelins. The story of Artemisia was then applied to Marie de' Medici, following Henri IV's tragic death[24].

Caron is doubtless best known for his strange massacre paintings. He did not invent the genre. The *Histoire ecclésiastique* informs us that in 1561, five years before Caron painted his *Massacre of the Triumvirs*, now in the Louvre, were brought to the court 'trois grands tableaux excellemment peints, ou étaient représentées les sanglantes et plus qu'inhumaines exécutions jadis faites à Rome entre Octavius, Antoninus et Lepidus. Ces tableaux furent bien chèrement achetés par les grands, l'un desquels était en la chambre du Prince de Condé à la vue d'un chacun de ceux de la religion'. Caron's massacre is mainly notable for its setting. Hautecoeur describes it as 'a veritable anthology of Roman monuments'. But we should

---

[23] F. Yates, *Astraea: the Imperial theme in the Sixteenth Century*, London, 1975, p. 145.

[24] J. Ehrmann, *op.cit.*, pp. 53–6.

not deduce a first-hand acquaintance with Rome on the part of the artist. As Ehrmann has shown, Caron borrowed extensively from the engravings of Antoine Lafréry, a Franche-Comtois, who had settled in Rome in 1540[25]. The purpose behind Caron's massacre paintings is not clear. Were they condemning violence or glorifying it? As a Catholic working for the Crown it is unlikely that Caron was getting at the Triumvirate that ended in 1561. It is possible that he was expressing fear of a possible Protestant triumvirate. What is certain is that Caron became closely connected with the League and that his pictures often carried political messages that would have been clear to contemporaries. Thus his picture of *Abraham and Melchisedech*, which can be dated 1590, is a critical commentary on the defeat suffered by the duc de Mayenne at the battle of Arques. The fly hovering over the castle is the *mouche de Lorraine* and the red corselet among the heap of trophies in the foreground is the famous red corselet of Mayenne. The upturned cup under the left foot of Abraham presages the succession of Henri IV, who was to be Caron's last patron[26].

Painting interested Henri IV less than architecture, yet he was not insensitive to it. His taste, it seems, was essentially down to earth. He liked portraits that were life-like and allegories that were intelligible. The eroticism that had been so favoured by the Valois gave way to a more direct kind of romantic dreaming. In the words of Babelon: 'L'inspiration du gentil Ovide a déserté la cour de France. Les aventures amoureuses y sont plus brutales que jadis, elles sentent le soudard. Vénus n'est plus couverte de voiles de gaze'[27]. Only three artists need to be mentioned: Ambroise Dubois, Toussaint Dubreuil and Martin Fréminet. Collectively they formed the second school of Fontainebleau. Blunt does not rate them very highly: 'these three artists lacked the imaginative invention of the earlier group, and, as far as we can judge their work, its level is one of even mediocrity'[28]. Other scholars are less severe. Sylvie Béguin writes: 'tout ce qu'ils ajoutèrent de personnel aux modèles de la première Ecole invite à ne pas négliger leur rôle'[29]. All that we need note here is that their Mannerism was more Flemish in its derivation than that of their predecessors and that they liked to choose themes from the works of Tasso and Ariosto.

---

[25] J. Ehrmann, 'Massacre and Persecution Pictures in Sixteenth-Century France', in *Journal of the Warburg and Courtauld Institutes*, viii (1945), pp. 195–9.

[26] J. Ehrmann, *Antoine Caron*, pp. 137–41.

[27] J.-P. Babelon, *Henri IV*, Paris, 1982, p.806.

[28] A. Blunt, *Art and Architecture in France 1500–1700*, Harmondsworth, 1957, p. 104.

[29] S. Béguin, *L'Ecole de Fontainebleau*, Paris, 1960, p. 115.

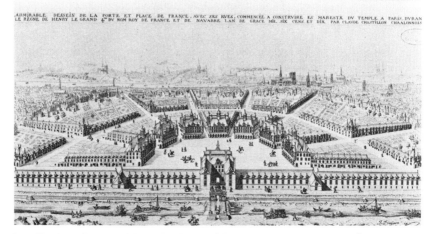

ADMIRABLE DESSEIN DE LA PORTE ET PLACE DE FRANCE, AVEC SES RVES, COMMENCÉ A CONSTRVIRE EN MARESTX DV TEMPLE A PARIS DVRAN LE RÈGNE DE HENRY LE GRAND 4ᵐᵉ DV NOM ROY DE FRANCE ET DE NAVARRE L'AN DE GRACE MIL SIX CENS ET DIX PAR CLAVDE CHASTILLON CHAALONNOIS

2. Project for the *Place de France* [Engraving by J. Poinsart].

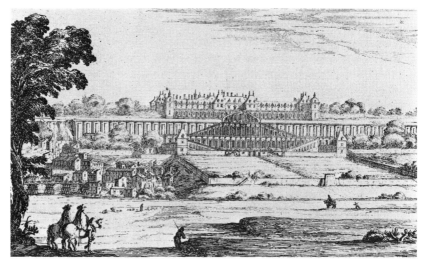

3. A pre-1660 view of Saint Germain-en-Laye.

4. The *Grotte d'Orphée* by Thomas Francini, one of the mechanical marvels of Saint Germain-en-Laye.

Henri IV may not have been a particularly discerning connoisseur of painting, yet he deserves our gratitude for saving Francis I's unique collection of masterpieces from destruction. At his accession they were mouldering away in the humid atmosphere of the baths at Fontainebleau. He removed them to a drier place — too late, alas, to save some of them — and appointed a proper curator, the first of his kind in France, to look after them[30]. Henri also encouraged sculptors and medallists, but it was architecture that really aroused his enthusiasm. He probably built more than Francis I and as much as Louis XIV[31]. Unlike his Valois predecessors, he did not start buildings and leave them unfinished. He did not undertake any new residence. Instead, he took old buildings in hand, completed those that were unfinished and only made additions where necessary. At first, he confined his attention to royal châteaux; later he addressed himself to town-planning, especially in Paris.

Henri's ambitious building programme entailed the reorganisation of the office of works. When the old *surintendant des bâtiments*, Francois d'O, died in October 1594, a commission of three was set up to ensure the king's privacy and comfort in the various royal châteaux. Various funds were collected to pay for the works, notably a tenth of the yield from the sale of timber from the forests. The virtual monopoly of building enjoyed by the Du Cerceau family under the Valois was broken by the appointment of Louis Metezeaux to supervise works at the royal châteaux. Jacques II Androuet Du Cerceau, who had been put in charge of the Louvre by Henri III objected, but Henri managed to reconcile the two men who seem to have worked quite well together. On 12 November 1602, Sully became *surintendant des bâtiments*[32]. He made sure that proper contracts were signed in the presence of notaries and tried to restrain the king's zeal, but, as Barbiche has shown, Henri did spend 4, 786, 275 *livres* on four royal palaces over ten years.

The Louvre was among the first to claim his attention. He toyed with the idea of quadrupling its size, but this original 'grand design' would have entailed too great a destruction of houses in the neighbourhood. It was consequently shelved till the Second Empire. Henri had to be content with lesser modifications. He completed the *Petite Galerie* and carried out

---

[30] J. Cox-Rearick, *La Collection de François 1er*, Paris, 1972, p. 12. The curator was the painter Jean de Hoey.

[31] J.-P. Babelon, *Henri IV*, p. 809.

[32] J.-P. Barbiche, 'Henri IV et la surintendance des bâtiments' in *Bulletin monumental*, Vol. 142 (1984), pp. 19–39.

Catherine de' Medici's idea of linking the Louvre to the Tuileries by a gallery - 450 metres long — which ran alongside the Seine. The ground floor was occupied by artists' lodgings and the upper floor by an immense hall that could serve for festivities or as a playroom for the Dauphin[33]. Henri was especially fond of Fontainebleau, which he treated as a sort of 'capitale-résidence'. This necessitated some major transformations: he completed Primaticcio's work in the Cour de la Fontaine, rebuilt the east side of the Cour Ovale, giving it a central domed gateway, turned the chapel of the Trinity into a handsome royal church with a painted vault by Fréminet, and between 1606 and 1609 added a large Stable court[34]. St Germain-en-Laye was another palace favoured by Henri, but only for short stays of a day or two. The old château was where he brought up his children, legitimate and illegitimate. It was a rather dreary building and he focused his main attention on the *Château Neuf*, which Philibert de l'Orme had built as an annex for Henri II. This was now enlarged by the addition of galleries and pavilions at either end, while the hillside between it and the Seine was elaborately landscaped with five terrasses and as many allegorical fountains. The huge retaining walls contained grottoes adorned with sea-shells, mother-of-pearl etc. and within them were automata: movable figures of bronze or brass operated by water and designed by the Francini, the best Italian water-engineers of the day, whom the king had invited to France in 1598. One was of Orpheus playing upon his lyre as animals issued from caves and passed before him. In another Perseus descended from the vault striking a dragon, which vanished into water, as the chains binding Andromeda to a rock fell apart. There were also water jets intended to catch unwary visitors, especially ladies, by surprise. The most vivid account of the *Château-Neuf* under Henri IV comes from the diary of Louis XIII's childhood physician, Jean Héroard. He describes the little Dauphin amusing himself by turning on the stop-cocks and being frightened by Orpheus. Apparently, there were misgivings about the stability of the new building. On 18 January 1606 Héroard's entry reads: 'I tell him he should go to see his papa in the new building. He replies; "Ho! ho! I don't want to go to the new building, it's all tumbling down; when the frost comes it will all fall down"'. In fact, the great terraces did collapse, but 55 years later[35].

The change of dynasty from the Valois to the Bourbons was marked

---

[33] J.-P. Babelon, *Henri IV*, pp. 814–817.

[34] *Ibid.*, pp. 817–820.

[35] *Ibid.*, pp.821–823; K. Woodbridge, *Princely Gardens: the origins and development of the French formal style*, London, 1986, pp. 129–33.

by an interest in the re-planning of Paris that marked a new departure in French royal patronage. True, Francis I had experimented with urbanism, but only in respect of new towns, like Le Havre and Vitry-le-François. In Paris the Crown had sponsored only bridges: the Pont Notre-Dame under Louis XII and the Pont-Neuf under Henri III. In 1601, Henri IV announced his intention 'de passer les années en cette ville, et y demeurer...rendre cette ville belle et pleine de toutes les commodités et ornements qu'il sera possible...'[36]. His first major project was to develop the site of the Tournelles, which had been laid waste by Catherine de' Medici. She had tried unsuccessfully to develop the land. Now Henri gave part of it to Sully and set up a silk factory close by. Then, in 1605, he decided to build a square which Parisians might use as a *promenoir* or as a setting for public spectacles. As completed, it was closed on all sides except the south and was lined with identical pavilions, each consisting of four bays, two storeys and a high roof. They were of brick with stone quoins. The ground floor consisted of an arcaded cloister. Two of the pavilions were built by the king, the rest by private individuals who were given the land in return for an undertaking to build according to the set plan and for an annual rent to the Crown. The project, which was rapidly completed, proved a great success. The Place Royale became a favourite abode of bankers and rich *officiers*. It survives in a much altered state as the Place des Vosges[37]. Henri IV also completed the Pont Neuf, but he added an embankment round the Ile de la Cité terminating in a triangular square. This too was lined with identical houses of brick and stone. The square, called Place Dauphine, was left open at one end, and Marie commissioned an equestrian statue of her husband to close the vista. She wanted Giovanni da Bologna to do it, but he was too old. So the statue was the work of Pietro Tacca and Pierre de Franqueville. It was Marie's gift to Paris and was put up four years after Henri's death. In 1608 Henri IV learnt that the Grand Prior of the *Temple* was about to sell some land on the north-eastern side of the city, yet within the wall of Charles V. Refusing him a free hand as to how the land would be used, Henri ordered yet another square, this time semi-circular in shape and backing on to the town wall. It was to have pavilions of uniform design separated by roads radiating from a central gateway in the wall. The square was to be called Place de France and each road was to be named after a French province. The scheme, however, never left the drawing board, as Henri was assassinated before it could be carried out.

---

[36] J.-P. Babelon, *Henri IV*, p. 830.

[37] J.-P. Babelon, *Demeures parisiennes sous Henri IV et Louis XIII*, Paris, 1965, pp. 13–25; A. Blunt, *Art and Architecture in France*, pp. 94–6.

In terms of art patronage the reign of Henri IV was more than just a time of national recovery. It was marked by a prudence and a public spirit that had been signally lacking under the later Valois. It also pointed to the future, offering a foretaste of the splendours of the Grand Siècle, even perhaps a glimpse of the Paris of Baron Haussmann.

5. Astrological column of Catherine de' Medici by Jean Bullant. All that survives of the *Hôtel de la Reine*.

9. Was there a Bourbon style of government?

RICHARD BONNEY

A conference devoted to the theme of 'From Valois to Bourbon' must address itself to many fundamental questions, not least of which is did it matter that the dynasty changed, or as Bodin might have put it, was there a consequential change in the 'estate' (*estat*)?[1] This in turn raises the hoary old chestnut of continuity and change. Although the relatively recent study of French institutions by Mousnier[2] takes 1598 as its starting point, very few institutional historians in the past have seen the Bourbon dynasty as a new departure. One needs to think only of Hanotaux's study of the origins of the intendants[3]; while the most recent work by Michel Antoine has sought to reinforce this historiographical tradition by stressing the Valois origins of several institutions which we have sometimes viewed as decidedly

---

[1] J. Bodin, *Les six livres de la république...*, Paris, 1583; repr. Darmstadt, 1977, p. 509. Idem, *The six bookes of a commonweale*, trans. R. Knolles (1606), ed. K. D. McRae, Harvard, Mass., 1962, p. 410.

[2] R. E. Mousnier, *The institutions of France under the absolute monarchy, 1598–1789*, Chicago, 1980, 1984. Original French edn. respectively 1974 and 1980.

[3] G. Hanotaux, *Origines de l'institution des intendants des provinces* (1884).

Bourbon in character[4]. Of course, such an approach must be closely related to the contemporary events — the same institution could be used for quite different purposes in a changed political context.

The transition from a Valois to a Bourbon government, whether it involved a change of style or not, therefore raises some of the most important issues for the historian. Although some may raise a semantic objection to the application of the term 'government' in this period[5], if the historian is to explain political realities, the substance and not just the form of political power, without inhibition, he should not necessarily restrict himself to contemporary terminology. Thus this paper assumes that in this context the use of the term 'Bourbon style of government' is not anachronistic. There is no established methodology for analysing the character of Bourbon government, although there is, of course, Saint-Simon's famous comparison of the first three Bourbon kings[6]. However, a modern assessment of the 'state of the kingdom' at the end of each of these reigns, respectively in 1610, 1643 and 1715 might seem rather trite. An alternative methodology is to leave any long-term changes in the central government out of the reckoning altogether, and to concentrate instead on the state of one particular province at about 1710, a hundred years after Henri IV's assassination. Clearly by that date, if a Bourbon 'style of government' cannot be detected, then there is no purpose in prolonging the discussion. And which province could be better suited to such detailed investigation than the vicomté de Béarn, the Bourbon heartland before the accession of Henri IV in 1589? To what extent had this autonomous province been incorporated into the kingdom by 1710; on what discernible principles, if any, was it governed; and were these different from elsewhere in France? These, then, are the questions that will be addressed in what follows, and in the conclusion we will attempt to establish how far Béarn can be taken as an exemplar, and the differences between the Valois and Bourbon styles of government in France as a whole.

This is not the place to repeat in full the story of the incorporation of Béarn and Navarre into the kingdom of France, but certain crucial steps must be recalled. At the end of 1596, Henri IV had determined that

---

[4] M. Antoine, *Le dur métier du roi. Etudes sur la civilisation politique de France d'ancien régime* (1986).

[5] Cf. M. Antoine, 'La monarchie absolue', *The political culture of the old regime*, ed. K. M. Baker, Oxford-New York, 1987, pp. 11–12.

[6] Louis de Rouvroy, duc de Saint-Simon Vermandois, 'Parallèle des trois premiers rois bourbons' [May 1746], *Ecrits inédits de Saint-Simon*, ed. P. Faugère, 3 vols., 1880, i.

his *domaine ancien,* including these two provinces, would remain separate from *nostre maison de France* 'sans y pouvoir estre aucunement compris ny meslé'[7]. The Edict of Fontainebleau of 15 April 1599 permitted Catholic worship in Béarn[8]; but this measure was criticized elsewhere in France as being insufficiently robust to deal with what was effectively a Protestant state. Moreover, had Henri IV produced a legitimate daughter, she could have inherited Béarn but not France because of the Salic Law debarring female succession. The twin needs to restore Catholic supremacy and to exclude the possibility of a female succession, which could have broken the personal union with France, were powerful factors in leading to the formal incorporation of Béarn and Navarre. Despite a new ruling in July 1607, they retained their independence in Henri IV's lifetime, although the first Bourbon king made some significant progress towards incorporation, not least by appointing Brûlart de Sillery as Chancellor simultaneously of France and Navarre[9].

However, the vital decisions were made during the majority of Louis XIII, at the end of 1616 and in June 1617: first, that Béarn should be incorporated into France, and second that Catholicism should be re-established without restriction there[10]. But it took Louis XIII's invasion in 1620 to implement these decisions, and then only by force, which specifically abrogated the privileges (*fors*) of Béarn 'en tant qu'il seroit besoin pour l'effet de ces présentes'[11]. The estates of Béarn refused to discuss the Edict of Union until a later meeting, when they were no longer under coercion; and when they did so in June 1622 they demanded its abrogation, and resolved to continue to use Béarnais as their language. They never retracted their demand for abrogation or registered the Edict of Union[12]. Meanwhile, on at least four occasions, the estates of Basse Navarre demanded that Louis XIII visit their province and take the oath of loyalty to their constitution; but although the king had promised this in the Edict of Union of 1620,

---

[7] P. Tucoo-Chala, *La vicomté de Béarn et le problème de sa souveraineté des origines à 1620,* Bordeaux, 1961, pp. 126, 194–5.

[8] C. Desplat, 'Edit de Fontainebleau du 15 avril 1599 en faveur des catholiques du Béarn', *Réformes et Révocation en Béarn, XVIIe — XXe siècles,* Pau, 1986, 223–246.

[9] Tucoo-Chala, pp. 127, 195–6. A. D'Estrée, *La Basse Navarre et ses institutions de 1620 à la Révolution,* Paris-Saragossa, 1955, p. 29.

[10] Tucoo-Chala, pp. 130–1, 196–8.

[11] *Ibid.,* pp. 132, 198–9.

[12] *Ibid.,* pp. 133, 199–200.

he did not in fact do so[13]. At the accession of Louis XIV in 1643, they renewed this demand; and despite the fact that apparently neither Henri IV nor Louis XIII had taken such an oath, the Regency government committed the new king to do so at his majority. In 1660, Louis XIV swore the oath before the deputies of the estates at St-Jean-de-Luz, shortly before his marriage to Maria Teresa. However, he resisted subsequent pressure, made on at least five occasions in the later seventeenth century, to repeat the oath in person on the territory of Navarre[14]. The king of France continued to call himself also king of Navarre, thus recognizing that it was not an 'annexe de la France, mais un royaume séparé', while the customs of Basque Navarre were sufficiently different from those of Béarn so that it remained under a separate administration[15].

It is not surprising, given this chequered history of the moves towards incorporation with France, that the privileges of the Pyrenean provinces were always regarded with suspicion by the crown after 1620, and that unsuccessful attempts were made to subvert them[16]. Colbert instructed Faucon de Ris, the intendant of Guyenne, to draw up a secret memorandum on the means to reduce the provinces of Bigorre, Marsan, Tarsan, Gabardan, Labourd and Soule into *pays d'élections* by suppressing their estates; but Béarn was recognized as being too difficult to deal with in this way. The three memoranda sent by Faucon de Ris in 1682 in reply to this instruction provide fascinating insights into the privileges of these *pays francs*[17] and the thinking of governmental officials about regional autonomy in the later seventeenth century. The intendant ruled out *élections* in Labourd, Soule and Marsan because the land was too infertile to produce sufficient tax revenue. There was also the consideration of 'l'humeur volage et impatiente des Basques' which meant that they would not support such an innovation; moreover, in the case of war with Spain 'ce pays seroit à mesnager'. However, the intendant felt that Marsan, Tarsan and Gabardan ('un même pays qui estoit anciennement joint à celuy de Béarn') could be joined to the *élection* of Les Lannes, an area of *taille réelle*[18]. As for Bigorre, an *élection* had been established in 1632, but subsequently revoked

---

[13] Estrée, *op. cit.* p. 38.
[14] *Ibid.*, pp. 38–9.
[15] *Ibid.*, pp. 36, 39.
[16] There are references to various attempts at subversion of provincial privilege in J. R. Major, *Representative government in early modern France*, New Haven and London, 1980, pp. 598, 632–3, 650–1.
[17] For this term used in relation to Labourd: AN G7 131, 5 Nov. 1680.
[18] AN G7 132, 17 Aug. 1682.

the following year[19]. The crown received only 20,000 *livres* per annum from the province, whereas de Ris considered that it could easily pay ten times the amount and the people be less oppressed than at present. The mountain people were 'farouches et indisciplinables' and needed the stamp of justice. Before taxes could be increased, however, the community debts would have to be liquidated — but in the meantime there was no difficulty, in the intendant's view, in suspending the estates[20]. But did it happen? As late as 1691, a subsequent intendant of Guyenne, Bazin de Bezons, hesitated even to extend the rights of the tobacco monopoly to Soule, Labourd and Bayonne while there was a war with Spain, given that these were frontier provinces 'habités par des Basques qui sont gens legers'[21].

Béarn had to be handled even more carefully for two reasons. It had a central place in the falsification of coinage, which was regarded as vital for bringing Spanish gold and silver into the kingdom: any attempt to eliminate this traditional activity would not only be against French interests but would risk the wholesale desertion of the population across the frontier[22]. Secondly, the population was predominantly Protestant. From 1685 the intendant's role was to supervise a population of 8000 'new' Catholics who had taken up their new faith after massive forced abjurations — as late as 1714 there were fears that Béarn could yet revert to its pre-1620 status as a Protestant state[23]. Of course, such possibilities seem in retrospect to have been illusory, but the intendant's difficulties in policing a large Protestant population seem to have been reason enough for not attempting to abolish its estates. In short, the motives of the government in attempting to establish *élections* in this part of France seem to have resulted less from a desire for administrative uniformity, though in principle, no doubt, the ministers would have considered uniformity a worthwhile long-term objective, than from a pragmatic response to perceived local realities. There was no great wish to confront distant provinces on this issue for fear of over-commitment: the crown had many problems to deal with at the same time; the province had only one — to defend its privileges to the death. Those passionate emotions that could bring a *petit pays* such as Labourd close to civil war in 1679[24] would then be directed outside the province and

---

[19] Cf. Estrée, *op. cit.*, p. 156. R. J. Bonney, *Political change in France under Richelieu and Mazarin, 1624–1661*, Oxford, 1978, p. 349, n. 4.

[20] AN G7 132, 13 Aug. 1682.

[21] AN G7 135, 20 Jan. 1691.

[22] AN G7 131, 2 Mar. and 22 July 1680.

[23] '... voir tout le Béarn comme il a esté autrefois': AN G7 120, 14 Apr. 1714.

[24] AN G7 131, 18 Mar. 1679.

exclusively against the government. Faucon de Ris was correct in his belief that Colbert favoured a gradualist policy, a piecemeal process of attrition, with regard to the privileges of Béarn and Navarre.

The result was that instead of converting them into *pays d'élections*, a new intendancy was created for Béarn and Navarre in 1682. It was small, and administrative rearrangement was always on the cards — indeed, it was actively canvassed by the intendant in 1691[25] — prior to the definitive reorganization in 1716 resulting from the establishment of the *généralité* of Auch. The first intendant, du Bois de Baillet, was contemptuous of the estates of Béarn[26]:

> ...c'est plustost une cohue qu'une assemblée réglée. Toutes choses s'y resoluent par caballes et on y consomme le temps en des disputes inutiles et pour des bagatelles qui ne valent pas la peine d'estre agitées.

The intendant told the estates that they must increase the size of their money grant to the crown forthwith; he considered that they could pay four times their present contribution without difficulty. However, when it came to the first financial crisis of Louis XIV's reign, the war of the League of Augsburg, it proved difficult to levy *affaires extraordinaires* in Béarn. Without careful wording of the fiscal edict or decree, the Béarnais considered such measures 'comme faicts pour toute autre province que pour le leur...' Feydeau, a later intendant, commented that the application of French legislation to Béarn was not as straightforward as elsewhere 'à cause de leur for'[27]. The intendants sometimes fell into the trap of referring to Béarn as 'le royaume', alluding to its former status as an independent vicomté linked to the kingdom of Navarre in the person of its prince who happened to have become the king of France in 1589; such comments gave at least some legitimacy to its claims of privileged status. Until 1710 the intendants even tacitly accepted that business at the estates of Béarn should be conducted in Béarnais: it took approximately 170 years for the Valois policy which was enshrined in the ordinance of Villers-Cotterêts of 1539 to be applied strictly to the Bourbon patrimony of Béarn[28].

---

[25] AN G7 113, 7 Aug. 1691.

[26] AN G7 112, 22 Sept. 1682.

[27] AN G7 113, 7 Feb. 1690.

[28] R. J. Knecht, *Francis I*, Cambridge, 1982, p. 359. The deliberations of the estates in 1709 were still in Béarnais, especially in the third estate: A[rchives]

Incontestably, the two most controversial fiscal measures of Louis XIV's reign were the *capitation* of 1695 and the *dixième* of 1710. The first caused little difficulty in Béarn, except that the province sought an *abonnement* on favourable terms such as those obtained by Languedoc and Brittany, while the nobles considered their quarter share of the final assessment excessive. Pinon, the intendant, acted as their mediator with the Controller-General at Paris, and used the argument that it was dangerous to alienate a frontier province at a time of war with Spain. There was little or no sign of social antagonism between the second and third estates over this issue[29]. In contrast, the discussion of the *dixième* provoked a fierce constitutional conflict within the estates of Béarn. The estates offered 50,000 *livres* for an *abonnement* (10,000 more than they had offered for the *capitation* in 1696), but this was rejected by Desmaretz, the Controller-General, as 'modicque... et... peu proportionnée au secours que le Roy a lieu d'attendre...' The crown would accept the offer for the *abonnement des terres* alone. The third estate was prepared to accept the crown's offer, but the second estate, led by the baron d'Arros, refused. The town of Morlàas proposed, and the estates eventually accepted on the casting vote of the president (the vote was 39–39), that the *partage* between the estates should be taken to the ministers for resolution[30]. The demise of the estates of Dauphiné in 1628 had revealed the dangers to a province of social divisions between the second and third estates resulting from fiscal grievances[31]. But the conflict between the estates of Béarn petered out. Why was this? Clearly, the crown held effective disciplinary control: the baron d'Arros was at first debarred from entering the estates for four years as a result of his opposition to the *dixième*; subsequently, the intendant persuaded the ministers that news of his exclusion was sufficient punishment and he could safely be readmitted subject to good conduct. The baron was clearly humiliated and had to thank the estates for helping him convince the king that his conduct had been innocent and in effect misinterpreted[32]. The constitutional crisis in Béarn in 1711 did not

---

D[épartementales des] P[yrénées]-A[tlantiques] (Pau), C 752. St-Macary, the *subdélégué-général* (acting intendant) was himself a Béarnais and spoke to the estates in the local dialect. However, by 1711 there was an intendant from the north (Barillon) and this important session was reported (and presumably conducted) in French.

[29] AD P-A C 744 fos. 354^v-356^r, 426, 447^v-448^r.

[30] AD P-A C 753, fos. 452^r, 457^v, 473, 478, 482, 487.

[31] Bonney, *Political change*, p. 354. D. Hickey, *The coming of French absolutism: the struggle for tax reform in the province of Dauphiné, 1540–1640*, Toronto, 1986.

[32] AD P-A C 2, 29 Aug. 1711, 19 Feb., 9 May 1712. C 754, fos. 126, 184^v.

develop into a sustained campaign between the two orders as had happened in Dauphiné a century earlier; but as in Dauphiné, the crown exploited its opportunity. In this case it did not suspend the estates indefinitely (as in Dauphiné), but it modified its rights.

The first move was made by Barillon, the intendant, who by an ordinance of 1 August 1711 required local communities to have the tax rolls for the *taille*, *taillon* and *capitation* countersigned by his *subdélégués* before the sums could be levied. This was denounced at the estates of 1712 as undermining the privileges of the *pays*. The intendant denied any such purpose; the form in which taxes were levied was not part of the estates' powers, he contended, and in any case his was a reforming measure which placed the communities under a similar regime to that of the estates themselves: as a result of a decree of the council of state of 19 June 1688, the crown required all levies resulting from the deliberations of the estates to be countersigned by the intendant. The communities should not be exempted from a procedure to which the estates were subject (although whether this decree had been enforced was questioned even by the intendant, who blamed the provincial *syndic* for not reading out the 1688 decree at the beginning of each session, as he was required to do). The king had no intention of damaging the estates' privileges, but 'il est de première règle' the intendant contended, 'que le Roy n'accorde point de privilège contre loy même'[33]. This may have been a fair reflection of royal and ministerial attitudes, but it was a tactless statement to make to the provincial estates. The intendant made matters far worse, and ultimately secured his own transfer from Béarn to Roussillon, a less controversial posting, by alleging that the resistance to his ordinance (and indeed, the controversy over the *dixième* the previous year) had been caused by the influence of the Parlement of Pau on members of the estates. At this point, the estates declared that they 'ne peuvent trouver la seureté en la conservation de leurs droits et de leurs privilèges que par un arrêt du conseil'[34]. The estates sought the protection of the king's council against the principal royal agent in the province, the intendant, and the session of 1712 broke up in acrimony.

What was the response of the government to this opportunity to deliver 'province-requested absolutism'? No comfort was given to the estates

---

[33] AD P-A C 754, fos. 68, 145, 177.

[34] AD P-A C 754, fol. 300. The allegation that the Parlement was responsible for resistance to the *dixième* was made in a letter to the Controller-General: AN G 7 119, 31 May 1712: '...c'est le Parlement seul aux Etats derniers dont la brigue avoit emporté au corps de la noblesse...'

of Béarn and Navarre. The sessions of the estates were henceforth reduced from six weeks, the rule that had prevailed since 1670, to four weeks; not surprisingly, this provoked remonstrances from the 1713 estates[35]. Moreover, a decree of the council of state of 13 September 1712 reiterated and strengthened the earlier decree of 19 June 1688 concerning the intendant's powers at the estates of Béarn and Navarre. The estates were no longer allowed to send deputies to Paris or to the court (at Versailles) for any reason without prior written permission of the king, countersigned by a secretary of state. No deliberations of the interim meeting of estates' representatives (the *abrégé*) could take place except in the presence of the intendant on penalty of nullity. The new rules were to be read out at each session of the estates[36]. However much Barillon had foolishly provoked the estates, they had ended up weaker rather than stronger; by 1715 the third estate, led by the town of Morlàas, recognized its almost complete dependence on the good offices of a subsequent intendant, Harlay, for winning fiscal concessions from the government[37].

But the conflict of 1711–12 in Béarn had another protagonist, the Parlement of Pau, as Barillon had indicated. This institution was a creation of the Bourbon dynasty in 1624, and unlike the estates, its business was conducted in French. Originally largely Protestant in composition, the Parlement had been gradually purged of its Huguenot membership so that it sought full implementation of the restrictive religious legislation which culminated with the revocation of the Edict of Nantes in 1685. Indeed, one of its councillors, St-Macary, was given the responsibility of supervising this task as *commissaire pour les contraventions*[38]; he it was who was later entrusted by the crown with the acting intendancy (*subdélégation générale*) during the long absence of Méliand as intendant of Catalonia as well as Béarn after 1704. However, in view of the traditional hostility between the Parlement and the intendant in Béarn[39], the crown made a serious error in 1685 in appointing the first president of the Parlement as caretaker-intendant: he immediately told the Parlement that 'l'execution de lad[ite] commission depend[ai]t naturellement de la juridiction de la cour' and that

---

[35] AD P-A C 755, fol. 4.

[36] AD P-A C 755, fol. 218.

[37] AD P-A C 756, fol. 44ᵛ-45ʳ.

[38] AD P-A B 4539, fol. 14, 16 July 1685.

[39] F. Loirette, 'L'administration royale en Béarn de l'union à l'intendance, 1620–1682. Essai sur le rattachement à la France d'une province frontière au XVIIᵉ siècle', *XVIIᵉ Siècle*, 45, 1964, 77–81. Bonney, *Political change*, p. 404.

he would refer all matters other than secret ones to its judgement[40]. Thus it was that the crown unwittingly assisted the Parlement of Pau in its belief that it, and not the intendant, should be 'seul maître de la province'[41]. Compliments paid by new intendants to the Parlement early on in their period of office could not prevent later structural conflict, which was limited only by the fact that several of the intendants were already members of the Parlement — this was true of St-Macary (the acting intendant) and des Chiens de Launeville; the latter was rewarded with the intendancy because he had acted as the Parlement's agent at Paris and had negotiated the loans to help discharge the successive fiscal demands of the government on the lawcourt[42]. By 1701, the Parlement was becoming restless at these fiscal demands, and it demanded in return an increased jurisdictional area (*ressort*) by the addition of Bigorre[43]; however, the administrative rearrangement of 1716, which created the *généralité* of Auch, specifically rejected any alteration to the respective jurisdictions of the Parlements of Bordeaux, Pau and Toulouse[44].

The Parlement of Pau was thus destined to remain a small and relatively unimportant 'superior court' in the kingdom. This did not make it any the less aggressive in response to the intendant Barillon's ordinance of 1 August 1711, which it claimed overturned the traditional system in the province for the levy of taxation and would result in increased costs and perpetual conflict[45]. Accordingly, it issued a decree on 19 February 1712, which sought to suspend the intendant's ordinance. The constitutional conflict rapidly became acrimonious, and the Parlement drew up a memorandum on the 'entreprises de M[r] de Barillon sur la jurisdiction du Parlement'[46], while the intendant sent his own account of the conflict to the ministers[47]. Matters came to a head when the lawcourt discovered that the intendant had sought to blacken its reputation with the ministers by

---

[40] AD P-A B 4539, fol. 18, 30 Aug. 1685.

[41] Cf. the comment of the intendant Harlay de Cély as late as 1713: '...que cette compagnie souffre impatiam[men]t [*sic*] l'intendance, et que quelque contens qu'ils soient de l'intendant, ils voudroient anéantir absolument ses fonctions et être seuls maîtres de la province...': AN G 7 120, 7 Mar. 1713.

[42] AD P-A B 4542, fol. 80[v]-81[r], 19 Jan. 1693. B 4545, fol. 113[v], 15 Dec. 1702. B 4546, fol. 121[v], 3 June 1707.

[43] AD P-A B 4545, fol. 43[v], 13 Sept. 1701.

[44] A[rchives] D[épartementales du] Gers (Auch) C 430, fol. 1[v].

[45] AD P-A B 4547, fol. 201[v], 15 Feb. 1712.

[46] AD P-A B 4547, fos. 214, 222, 21 and 25 Apr. 1712.

[47] AN G 7 119, 10 Mar., 22 Apr. 1712.

accusing it of interference with the deliberations of the estates of Béarn[48]. The Chancellor attempted to mediate, arguing rather disingenuously that Barillon was a *galant homme* who was incapable of doing such a thing[49]; but the Parlement was not satisfied with this, and took its protest directly to the king, separating this issue from the jurisdictional conflict with Barillon and receiving in the end a special assurance that the king had not gained any unfavourable impression of the Parlement from the intendant's dispatches[50]. The lawcourt undoubtedly had its revenge, since Barillon was unceremoniously moved on to another province; a later intendant, Harlay, recalled the intrigue in 1715 and feared a similar fate because of his own conflict with the Parlement over the administration of the grain supply in time of famine[51].

The constitutional conflict between the Parlement and the intendant was settled by a ruling drawn up by a commission of the council, which was subsequently registered by the Parlement[52]. The essential point was won by the intendant — he alone signed the general levy for the province and the parish tax rolls, the issue which had been at the heart of the conflict; moreover, the council declared it 'd'une conséquence essentielle pour le bien des communautés' that the intendant should advise the crown on any extraordinary levies that might be necessary. However, the *juridiction contentieuse* in these and most other matters rested with the Parlement. It was an administrative fudge, and not surprisingly a later intendant, Harlay, denounced the ruling as an inadequate compromise full of inner contradictions. If the intendant followed the letter of the ruling, he would always find himself in conflict with the Parlement, whose essential aim was to destroy the intendancy and remain in sole charge of the province[53]. Within three years, Louis XIV was dead and the regency government had removed the restrictions on the rights of the superior courts to issue remonstrances[54], thus freeing the hands of the Parlement of Pau to continue its struggle for provincial ascendancy into the reign of Louis XV.

---

[48] AD P-A B 4547, fos. 232ᵛ-234ᵛ, 25 June 1712.

[49] AD P-A B 4547, fol. 240ᵛ, 18 July 1712.

[50] AD P-A B 4547, fos. 241ᵛ, 245ᵛ-246ʳ, 15 Aug. and after 28 Nov. 1712.

[51] AN G7 120, 28 July, 27 Aug. 1715. Harlay made it clear that he feared the hand of the duc de Gramont, the governor, in the attempt to dismiss him.

[52] AN G7 119, Oct. 1712. AD P-A B 4547, fol. 244ᵛ, 15 Nov. 1712. B 4548, fos. 154–156ᵛ, Oct. 1712.

[53] AN G7 120, 7 Mar. 1713.

[54] AD P-A B 4548, fol. 87, 14 Nov. 1715.

At first sight this lengthy digression into the later years of Louis XIV's reign in one of the smallest provinces of France might seem no more than of purely regional interest, and irrelevant to the broader consideration of the consequences of the transition from Valois to Bourbon dynasties. Yet if we ask what significance the provincial conflicts of 1711–12 in Béarn have for the historian, it is surely that they demonstrate that the veneer of Bourbon 'absolutism' was wearing very thin by the last years of Louis XIV's reign. But on one essential point, the Bourbon dynasty had won the argument where the last of the Valois had clearly lost. Everything was now referred to the king's council for arbitration. In its conflict with the intendant, the provincial estates saw the king's council as being neutral — the council alone could guarantee provincial privilege. Similarly, in a more serious and even more acrimonious conflict, the Parlement sought from the king's council a guarantee of its jurisdiction against the alleged encroachment of the intendant. The central government helped safeguard Béarnais privileges; and in the case of the Parlement it doubtless did so in recognition of the considerable financial sacrifice that individual *parlementaires* and the lawcourt as a collective entity had made during the wars of the League of Augsburg and the Spanish Succession.

If, in contrast, we consider the last years of Henri III's reign, clearly his conflicts with provincial institutions such as the governors and the Parlements were serious to a quite different degree: there was no sustained armed rebellion in the later years of Louis XIV's reign comparable to that of the League. But why was there armed rebellion in later sixteenth-century France? It was, in part, because religious conflict and factional rivalry had deprived the king's council of its capacity to act as the neutral arbitrator. There can be no doubt of Henri III's intention, affirmed by Richard Cook in 1584–5, to use his absolute powers 'either by his owne expresse commandment or by his Counsaile of Estate'[55]. What was lacking was any willingness on the part of significant sections of French society to accept the council's decisions. The council was prone to faction, and it was partisan in religious matters; at crucial points in the reigns of Charles IX and Henri III, the Parlements would not accept (and therefore, enforce) the royal Edicts of Pacification. No more, of course, would certain key provincial governors accept either the religious or the patronage policies of the central government. In the great crisis of Henri III's reign, the Parlements themselves fragmented on the question of whether their primary loyalty lay

---

[55] D. Potter and P. R. Roberts, 'An Englishman's view of the court of Henri III, 1584–1585: Richard Cook's "Description of the Court of France"', *French History*, 2, 1988, 328.

with a Catholic king or with the principle of hereditary succession.

Subsequently, the crucial developments were the settlement of Nantes, Henri IV's exclusion of the great nobility from the council, and the systematization of the sale of offices through the introduction of the *droit annuel* in 1604. None of these was inevitable; each formed part of that 'struggle for stability' — Mark Greengrass's phrase — which is so crucial to an understanding of Henri IV's political achievement. The unspoken clause in the settlement of Nantes was that while concessions were granted to the Huguenots in order to ensure peace, the king's council, the institution that ultimately would enforce the peace, would remain a Catholic body. Sully, of course, was the great exception — but one has only to think of the resurgence of the *barbons*, the greybearded former League supporters (Brûlart de Sillery, Villeroy and Jeannin), in the regency of Marie de Médicis to appreciate that his was an isolated role. The collapse of Huguenot support within the upper nobility has rightly been stressed as one reason for the failure of the Protestant cause in the seventeenth century; but the tame acceptance of a Catholic-dominated royal council has perhaps not been emphasised sufficiently. Of course, there was not much that could be done. The significance of the abjuration of Henri IV was that the Bourbon dynasty would remain Catholic; a Catholic king pledged to extirpate heresy by his coronation oath was unlikely to summon many Protestants to serve as his trusted councillors.

But the move towards the establishment of a Catholic-dominated royal council was greatly intensified by the exclusion of the great nobility from the council *before* the wave of abjurations symbolized by Lesdiguières's acceptance of the Constableship in 1622. The Estates General of 1588 had explicitly called for a noble majority in council membership[56]. On 25 November 1594, when the *surintendance des finances* was replaced by a finance commission, the number of great nobles exactly equalled the number of *robins* in the commission, with the Chancellor holding the balance[57]. However, arrangements suitable for a kingdom at war were no longer appropriate in time of peace. By 1598 the baron de Rosny, later known as the duc de Sully, as *grand maître de l'artillerie* and *surintendant des finances*, was almost the sole *noble d'épée* left in the council. After the Chancellor,

---

[56] B[ritish] L[ibrary] Egerton 1668, fol. 132.

[57] Bonney, *The king's debts*, p. 44 n. 6. AN 120 ap 29 fol. 1, 25 Nov. 1594. The *robins* were (besides the Chancellor, Cheverny) Bellièvre, Sancy, Forget de Fresnes and La Grange-le-Roy.

Sully may have enjoyed something close to precedence in the council[58]; but what he made up for in terms of seniority could not hide the numerical weakness of his class — Sully lost the argument over the need to retain *nobles d'épée* in the council even in peacetime[59], and not long after the death of his great mentor, Henri IV, he lost his own place in the council. With the departure from government of Sully in January 1611, the aristocratic presence, too, was gone.

How far this change was a result of latent aristocratic discontent, which came to a head with the Biron conspiracy of 1602[60], and how far it was simply a response to peace and the growing technical complexity of government[61] might at first seem an open question. But at the assembly of notables of 1617, the crown had given its answer[62]. A great number of nobles in attendance at the council meant that 'le secret aux affaires ne pouvoit estre gardé et la multitude des advis apportoit de la longueur aux advis [et] de la confusion.' There were likely to be arguments between the nobles over precedence within the council. In many instances the interests of the great nobility would be discussed within the council, while their offices — especially provincial governorships — required them frequently to be absent from the council: 'pour ces raisons Sa Ma[jes]té a esté jusques à présent contrainte de laisser le maniement secret de ses affaires aux ministres qui en avoient eu charge sous le Roy son père...'

The assembly of notables of 1626–7 considered that 'c'est chose digne de la justice du Roy de donner part aux honneurs, dignités et emplois à ceux de sa noblesse'[63] but it is clear that there were very few nobles employed during the majority of Louis XIII. Schomberg, la Vieuville and d'Effiat were the exceptions — rather surprisingly, an aristocratic background was regarded as a qualification for the *surintendance des finances*. But with the regency of Anne of Austria, the great nobility came back in force: Gaston

---

[58] B. L. Egerton 1680, fos. 57, 63.

[59] If he indeed argued for this systematically: cf. R. E. Mousnier, 'Sully et le conseil d'état et des finances', *Revue historique*, 192, 1941, 82–83. *Idem, La vénalité des offices sous Henri IV et Louis XIII*, 2nd. edn., 1971, pp. 603–5.

[60] Bonney, *The King's debts*, p. 66.

[61] M. Greengrass, *France in the age of Henri IV: the struggle for stability* (1984), p. 111.

[62] C. J. Mayer, *Des Etats Généraux et autres assemblées nationales*, 18 vols., The Hague, 1788–9, XVIII, 54–5. B. L. Egerton 1666, fos. 56ᵛ-57ᵛ. B. L. Add. Mss. 30555, fos. 195ᵛ-196ʳ.

[63] B. L. Egerton 1666, fol. 176ᵛ.

d'Orléans and Condé were named as members of the regency council in the testament of Louis XIII, but were outnumbered by Mazarin and the three *robins*[64]. Once the crisis of 1648 had broken, the council of state varied in number, but the aristocratic presence was certainly proportionately increased[65]. However, this advance was abruptly halted by the defeat of the Fronde, which settled the question of aristocratic participation. Under Louis XIV it appears that only two members of the old nobility were allowed into the *ministériat* (the maréchal de Villeroy in 1661, his childhood guardian, who continued in the position he had held since 1649; and the duc de Beauvillier after 1691). Although the great noble families returned in profusion in the eighteenth century (from 1714 to 1789 there were only three ministers who were *not* titled aristocrats)[66], in the short term, however, the exclusion of the great nobility from the council in the period from the reign of Henri IV to the Regency of Philippe d'Orléans was of profound importance. It was a Bourbon style of government quite different from that of the Valois: although it is clear that the role of the *robins* had been growing under Henri III, their preponderance was not assured. It may be suggested that the exclusion of the great nobility from the council and the ascendancy of the *robins* which filled the resulting vacuum were crucial processes in allowing the king's council to be recognized as the neutral arbitrator.

Paradoxically, the systematization of the sale of offices resulting from the establishment of the *droit annuel* in 1604 undoubtedly facilitated and consolidated the *robin* dominance of the king's council. Paradoxically, because there was a growing distinction between membership of the council and membership of the sovereign courts. The position of king's councillor was not an office, but an appointment by letters patent which was regarded increasingly as incompatible with office in the sovereign courts. On the other hand, in terms of earlier careers, by the seventeenth century king's councillors had almost to a man previously passed through the sovereign

---

[64] Bonney, *The king's debts*, p. 191. The *robins* were Séguier, Bouthillier and Chavigny.

[65] At the council of 4 Oct. 1648, five out of seven, Gaston, Condé, Conty, Longueville and La Meilleraye being balanced only by Mazarin and Séguier: *ibid.*, p. 208. At the council of 15 October, the proportion had reverted to four (Gaston, Condé, Conty, Villeroy) out of ten: Bibliothèque Nationale Clairambault 651, fol. 342[v].

[66] A. Goodwin, 'The social structure and economic and political attitudes of the French nobility in the eighteenth century', *XIIth International Congress of Historical Sciences* Rapports, 1965, I., Vienne, 1966, p. 361.

courts. The ideology of the office-holders was conservative, not revolutionary. It was they, of course, who provided the juristic defence of absolutism, while their legal training, certainly in the seventeenth century, if not in the sixteenth, had imbued them with a profoundly absolutist view of monarchical sovereignty[67]. Thus it was that Louis XIV could rename the sovereign courts superior courts in 1665, and could curtail the Parlements' right of remonstrances in 1673 virtually without a protest. The arbitration of the king's council was accepted under Louis XIV, and it was only the Regency government's disastrous blunder in removing the limitations on the right of remonstrance that reopened the issue once more and paved the way for the constitutional conflicts of the eighteenth century.

The events after 1715, however, should not mislead us about the nature of the Bourbon style of monarchy and the great contrast it made with that of the last Valois kings. There is a degree of continuity in the policies of the first three Bourbon monarchs; but we could not, and should not, expect that in 1610 there would be the full implementation or acceptance of a style of government which reached its apotheosis only in the period between 1673 and 1715[68]. Nor can the historian state with confidence that had the Valois dynasty survived it might not have pursued comparable policies to those of the first Bourbon kings. The historian must content himself with the verdict that, given the assassination of Henri III without a direct male heir in 1589, the assessment of the Valois dynasty must rest on its achievements within a given historical context — the crisis of the League. The style of government pursued by the Bourbon dynasty was shaped and forged by the crisis of the war of succession, the challenge to Henri IV and the political necessity of his abjuration in 1593.

Thereafter, what becomes of crucial importance is the capacity of the Bourbon dynasty for survival. Not only was assassination a real threat in the case of Henri IV; the matrimonial problems of the Bourbons were an important destabilizing factor. The second generation was not entirely secure until the birth of Henri IV's second son Gaston in 1608, the third generation not until the birth of Louis XIII's second son Philippe in 1640. The crisis of the dynasty in the fourth generation is well known, following the decimation of the royal family in 1710–11. The effective period of

---

[67] L. W. B. Brockliss, *French higher education in the seventeenth and eighteenth centuries. A cultural history*, Oxford, 1987, pp. 449–450.

[68] Whether there was any significant development at all would seem to be questioned by R. C. Mettam, *Power and faction in Louis XIV's France*, Oxford, 1988.

royal minority was much longer than the legal minorities of 1610–14 and 1643–51. Twenty-nine years out of the seventy-two years of early Bourbon monarchy were years in which the king did not rule personally[69]. However, personal rule did not necessarily mean strong government, as the reign of Henri III had shown. Developments such as the rise of royal favourites and chief ministers, and other institutional factors, may have papered over the difficulties. But there was little prospect of an end to armed aristocratic faction as long as a king did not rule personally, while the danger abroad was very evident. The Spanish Habsburg enemies of the Bourbon dynasty had not lost sight of their ambition to establish an elective monarchy in France, and to partition the kingdom among hereditary (and preferably subservient) provincial governorships. Unlike the new Bourbon dynasty, which suffered two minorities within two generations, the Spanish Habsburgs had no royal minority between 1516 and 1665. It was therefore not at all inevitable that the new Bourbon dynasty would prevail against its foreign and domestic enemies and that any coherent Bourbon 'style of government' would have the opportunity to emerge. That it did so was due perhaps as much to accident as to design, just as the accidents of Alençon's death in 1584, Henri III's assassination without a direct heir, and the fact that the rival candidate to Henri IV was an ageing Cardinal who was also held in captivity had brought the first Bourbon to the throne in 1589.

---

[69] If we take the early Bourbon monarchy for this purpose to mean the years 1589–1661, the periods in question were the years 1610–21 and 1643–61.

NOTES ON CONTRIBUTORS

Sydney Anglo formerly Professor in the Department of History at University College, Swansea, and a past Chairman of the Society for Renaissance Studies has written extensively on the history of ideas in the Renaissance. His recent publications include *The Damned Art : Essays in the Literature of Witchcraft* (Editor) (Routledge 1985) and *The Courtier's Art: Systematic Immorality in the Renaissance* (University College, Swansea, 1983).

Joseph Bergin is Senior Lecturer in History at the University of Manchester and has specialised in the ecclesiastical history of France in the sixteenth and the seventeenth centuries. His most recent publications include *Cardinal Richelieu: Power and Pursuit of Wealth* (Yale, 1985) and *Cardinal de la Rochefoucauld: Leadership and Reform in the French Church* (Yale, 1987).

Christopher Bettinson, Senior Lecturer in French at University College, Cardiff, has written mainly on French literature but has also researched the history of the *Politiques* and studied the relationship between Catherine de Medici and Henri III. His doctoral thesis was entitled The Intellectual Background and Development of the Toleration Policy of Catherine de Medici (Reading, 1973).

Richard Bonney is Professor of Modern History at the University of Leicester and is a specialist on government and society under the early Bourbons. His publications include *The King's Debts: Finance and Politics in France, 1589-1661* (O.U.P., 1981) and *Society and Government in France under Richelieu and Mazarin, 1624-1661* (St Martin, 1988).

Keith Cameron is Reader in French and Renaissance Studies at the University of Exeter. He has researched widely into the literature of the sixteenth century and its history. His publications include *Henri III. A Maligned or Malignant King?* (University of Exeter, 1978) and *Montaigne and his Age* (Editor) (University of Exeter, 1981).

Richard Cooper, University Lecturer in French and Fellow of Brasenose College, Oxford, has published widely on the literature and history of Italy and Europe during the sixteenth century.

Denis Crouzet is attached to the CNRS in Paris and has been researching the socio-political dimensions of Henri IV's reign. He defended recently his thesis on 'La violence au temps des troubles de religion'.

Mark Greengrass, Senior Lecturer in History at the University of Sheffield, has specialised in the history of the second half of the sixteenth century. His most recent publications include *France in the Age of Henri IV: The Struggle for Stability* (Longman, 1984) and *The French Reformation* (Blackwell, 1987).

R.J. Knecht is Professor of History at the University of Birmingham and the present Chairman of the Society for Renaissance Studies. He has specialised in French sixteenth-century history, especially the first half of the century. His publications include *Francis I* (C.U.P., 1984) and *Francis I and Henry II* (Longman, 1984).

N. M. Sutherland was Professor of Early Modern History at Royal Holloway and Bedford New College, University of London. She has researched extensively in the French history of the sixteenth century and her publications include *The Huguenot Struggle for Recognition* (Yale, 1980) and *Princes, Politics and Religion, 1547–89* (Hambledon Press, 1984).